"With wisdom and wit Ta shares her journey, and that of the Pennsylvania Wilds, as an example and inspiration for all rural communities – beyond a memoir, *PROUDLY MADE* is a new and essential guidebook for every rural economic developer and community organizer."

—Nathan Reigner, PhD, Director,
Pennsylvania Office of Outdoor Recreation

*

"From grand experiment to groundbreaking phenom, *PROUDLY MADE* by pioneering entrepreneur Ta Enos is an inspiring saga that embodies the blood, sweat, and tears of a fearless woman and her thousands of hardworking neighbors who together transformed their largely forgotten expanse of our national tapestry into an American Treasure and iconic recreation destination known as The Pennsylvania Wilds."

— John Schlimm, International Award-Winning Author, Artist,
Advocate, and Harvard-Trained Educator

*

"Ta Enos's *PROUDLY MADE* is a testament to the transformative power of a woman's vision in shaping both Appalachia's future and harnessing its natural beauty."

—Trista Harris, Philanthropic Futurist and
President of FutureGood

ADVANCE PRAISE

"Ta's gripping personal story—in all its struggle, perseverance and redemption—is the story of the Pennsylvania Wilds. This book is a testament not only to the progress of one person, but of a people. Equal parts literary memoir and activist template, it advances the great tradition of American place-based writers like Henry David Thoreau, Zora Neale Hurston, Annie Dillard and Dean MacCannell. This is a compelling and important book, whether you were born and raised in the Pennsylvania Wilds, or dream of building such a place wherever you call home."

—**Sam MacDonald, Author,**
The Urban Hermit **and** *Agony of an American Wilderness*

*

"Ta Enos' new book is a remarkable story about a special person and a special place. Reminiscent of Cheryl Strayed's storytelling in *WILD: From Lost to Found on the Pacific Coast Trail*, *PROUDLY MADE* tells the story of the PA Wilds, a beautiful but neglected region in Pennsylvania's Appalachian Mountains. It is about the hardy people and wild places that make this region unique, but it is also a story of self-discovery and reinvention and a primer on entrepreneurship in rural America. The parallel stories of a region and a person rediscovering themselves is a story anyone can relate to, but especially other rural areas that are trying to make their way in a rapidly changing world. I found myself cheering for Ta and the PA Wilds Initiative. You will too."

—**Ed McMahon, Author,**
Balancing Nature and Commerce in Gateway Communities

*

"As a child of the Pennsylvania Wilds (born and raised there long before it had that name), to me what's most remarkable about Ta's drive and impact isn't just that we come from one of those places where it's uniquely hard to influence change—but that it's still nearly impossible to get people to listen to you if you're a woman. That's a huge part of her triumph with *PROUDLY MADE*. In an era that's testing the strength of women—Mother Nature most of all—this is a story, in a time, that needs to be told."

—**Kristine Gasbarre, #1 New York Times bestselling writer**

*

"Ta Enos' memoir is a gripping story full of grit, creativity, and an unrelenting belief in a place and its people, including herself. It's a story about the myriad gifts that rural PA has to offer its residents and visitors; Ta's gift is in showing what that experience can mean for us all."

—**Tony Pipa, Brookings Institution, founder of the *Reimagining Rural Policy* initiative, and host of the *Reimagine Rural* podcast**

*

"*PROUDLY MADE* is a testament not just to a devoted mother, community advocate, storyteller, and coalition builder, but also to the deep-rooted gumption shared between rural people that has carried the Pennsylvania Wilds through the great unknown and transformed the region into national recognition. When we work to illustrate the benefits of the $1.2 *trillion* outdoor recreation economy to members of Congress and state governments around the country, Ta's work and the Wilds tell the story better than we could ever hope for."

—**Chris Perkins, Vice President Programs, Outdoor Recreation Roundtable**

*

"Ta's can-do spirit and entrepreneurial talents helped revitalize the region known as the Pennsylvania Wilds and champion fellow Appalachians who respect the land, cherish its traditions, and work to improve the lives of current and future residents. This honest account of her challenges and triumphs is a testament to Ta's fortitude, vision, and leadership. *PROUDLY MADE* is a must-read for anyone who values the attributes of home – wherever it may be – and seeks inspiration on how one individual can be a force for positive change and local impact."

—**Cheryl M. Hargrove, Author, *Cultural Heritage Tourism: Five Steps to Success & Sustainability***

A STORY OF REINVENTION IN THE BIG WOODS AND SMALL TOWNS OF THE PENNSYLVANIA WILDS

TATABOLINE ENOS

an imprint of Sunbury Press, Inc.
Mechanicsburg, PA USA

an imprint of Sunbury Press, Inc.
Mechanicsburg, PA USA

Copyright © 2025 by Tataboline Enos.
Cover Copyright © 2025 by Tataboline Enos.

Sunbury Press supports copyright. Copyright fuels creativity, encourages diverse voices, promotes free speech, and creates a vibrant culture. Thank you for buying an authorized edition of this book and for complying with copyright laws. Except for the quotation of short passages for the purpose of criticism and review, no part of this publication may be reproduced, scanned, or distributed in any form without permission. You are supporting writers and allowing Sunbury Press to continue to publish books for every reader. For information contact Sunbury Press, Inc., Subsidiary Rights Dept., PO Box 548, Boiling Springs, PA 17007 USA or legal@sunburypress.com.

For information about special discounts for bulk purchases, please contact Sunbury Press Orders Dept. at (855) 338-8359 or orders@sunburypress.com.

To request one of our authors for speaking engagements or book signings, please contact Sunbury Press Publicity Dept. at publicity@sunburypress.com.

FIRST CATAMOUNT PRESS EDITION: May 2025

Set in Adobe Garamond | Interior design by Crystal Devine | Cover design by Andrea Lanich, Laughing Owl Press Co. / Cover Photo: Piper VanOrd, Allegheny Outfitters | Edited by Gabrielle Kirk.

Publisher's Cataloging-in-Publication Data
Names: Enos, Tataboline, author.
Title: Proudly made : a memoir / Tataboline Enos.
Description: First trade paperback edition. | Mechanicsburg, PA : Catamount Press, 2025.
Summary: The story of an intrepid rural boomeranger getting over her own hangups to go all-in for her distressed region. Told with humor and guts, heart wide open, this memoir takes readers on an unforgettable 20-year journey that heralds the difference one person with a little mettle can make, and the greater good that can come when many of us work together.
Identifiers: ISBN : 979-8-88819-272-6 (hardcover) | ISBN : 979-8-88819-273-3 (softcover).
Subjects: BIOGRAPHY & AUTOBIOGRAPHY / Memoirs | BIOGRAPHY & AUTOBIOGRAPHY / Women | BIOGRAPHY & ECONOMICS / Industries / Hospitality, Travel & Tourism.

Designed in the USA
0 1 1 2 3 5 8 13 21 34 55

For the Love of Books!

*To my boys, my inspiration, may you fill your days
with purpose and adventure, and always try to leave
things better than you found them.*

*To my husband, who knows better than anyone
the sacrifices; thank you.*

*To my mom and sisters, thank you
for believing in me.*

*For anyone who is trying to get over their own
hangups to accomplish a greater good: Don't quit!*

DISCLAIMER

This memoir is a recollection of events in the author's life. Minor details of some individuals or events may have been changed or omitted to respect their privacy, and some events have been compressed. The author relied heavily on public meetings, public records, first-hand accounts and interviews to help tell this story. This book represents the personal views and opinions of the author and does not necessarily reflect the positions or opinions of any organization, institution, or individual with which the author is affiliated.

CONTENTS

CHAPTERS

1	Hearing the Words	1
2	The Road Less Traveled	8
3	Stand-To	17
4	A Calling	23
5	Nature's Pull	29
6	Starting Over	36
7	Building Outdoors	44
8	What Have I Done	50
9	The High Plateau	62
10	A Brand and a Strategy Are Born	70
11	More Seats at the Table	81
12	Investment	90
13	Subsistence Season	94
14	Changing the Narrative	98
15	On the Precipice	110
16	Rediscovering My Roots	113
17	The Way You Live	124
18	A Crucible Moment	128
19	Taking the Leap	134
20	Networking a Region of Rugged Individualists	145
21	Breakthroughs	155
22	Lightbulb	159
23	Shucking Away the Bullshit	166

24	Hitting our Stride	171
25	Building on a Legacy	177
26	Rural Development	189
27	Learning to Lead	196
28	See Us	201
29	COVID	205
30	Doing It On Purpose	215
31	One Hundred Million Dollars	226
32	Putting It All Back	236

Afterword	245
Acknowledgments	248
About the Author	252

CHAPTER 1

HEARING THE WORDS

It's 2002, my second week on the job as a crime beat reporter for the *Anchorage Daily News*. I am riding around Alaska's largest city in a police cruiser with a respected teddy bear of a sergeant, who is retiring after 25 years on the force. While we are out, his officers respond to a rape of a young woman, and then on the opposite side of town, sixteen high school students are arrested after a brawl.

I report both stories, fill my notebook with color for a feature later about the sergeant, and write a third piece about two teens busted for a dine-and-dash in a small town outside the city.

Back at the office, wrapping up for the day, urgent chatter crackles on my desk's police scanner. A chlorine spill at a nearby college campus pool. Dozens of potential victims. Kids. The city is activating the emergency command center.

Two editors walk over to my desk and listen. Within seconds, they start assigning reporters and graphics and recasting the front page.

My heart beats faster as I watch the newsroom swing into action. I've never covered a big breaking news event. Coming from the altweekly *Anchorage Press*, I was used to having hours or days to prepare for and conduct interviews, to write and rewrite my copy. But I'd long been drawn to the seriousness of daily papers, to their watchdog role and responsibility to keep the public informed. I tried for three years to get the *Daily News* to hire me. Finally, it happened. But I still had a lot to prove. At least to myself. Today was my chance.

"Get to the campus," my editor tells me.

I grab my coat, head to my car, and race across town. The leaves are turning, the Canada geese are leaving, and "termination dust"—snow—is creeping down the Chugach Mountains. Fall, my favorite season, feels so short here compared to the months-long show Mother Nature puts on in rural Pennsylvania, where I grew up. A few more days, I knew, and the trees near my house in downtown Anchorage would sit naked, their round yellow leaves scattered across the sidewalks like gold coins.

At the entrance to the campus, a cop stands in the middle of the road directing traffic away. I stop my car in front of him.

"I'm a reporter for the *Daily News*," I say. "Can I go in?"

He waves me away like a gnat.

Annoyed, I go look for a parking spot. Finding one, I turn off the vehicle, quickly pull my hair into a ponytail, grab my keys and notebook, and step into the crisp air. I run my hand across the pocket of my black pea coat and upon sensing a pen there, shut the door and jog toward the flashing lights.

On the way, my cell phone rings. It's my editor. I slow to a speed walk, hit the green button, and put the phone to my ear.

The details come at me in a staccato rhythm: Fifty or sixty swimmers. Mostly kids. Swim club practice after school. A chlorine gas cloud from an auxiliary room. Reports of people choking and gagging. Some rushed to area hospitals. Other reporters are covering the emergency rooms.

"Okay," I tell my editor as I walk toward another barricade. "I'm at the campus. I'll call you back in a few minutes."

I hang up, slide the phone into my coat pocket, and approach the cop standing guard. I identify myself and ask if I can pass. I promise not to get in the way of emergency responders or go near the pool.

"I was told the people who weren't badly hurt were taken to another building on campus," I say. "I just want to go see them."

He tells me he can't let the press in, those are his orders.

Frustrated, I look around. I can't even see the evacuation from the barricade, let alone find someone to talk to about it. My hands are cold, so I walk to a nearby building to warm up and figure out my next move. As I step through the entrance, I realize I've been there before.

I could go out the back door, through the woods, and re-enter the campus inside the police barricade, I realize.

I run. When I emerge from the woods, I walk with purpose across the campus lawn, so no one questions what I'm up to. I have no idea where I am going. I am still catching my breath when my editor calls back.

"No one can get past the police barricade," he says. "If you get on campus, you need to get to the Atwood Center. That's where the victims and families are."

I look up at the building in front of me. "Atwood" it says across the front.

"I'm there," I say, exhilarated, and then confess how I did it. "Am I in trouble?"

My editor chuckles. "We'll talk about that later. Just get inside that building and interview everyone you can."

I do. Later that night, after we put the story to bed, I walk out on the catwalk at the paper's printing press. The industrial machinery below is loud and powerful. I lean over the railing and smile as I watch thousands of copies of the paper roll off the press. My story is on A1, above the fold, the best placement there is. I wasn't the lead writer, but I didn't care.

I'd conquered my first major breaking news event. I was on top of the world.

* * *

Fast forward two years. The dark events I've covered are seeping into my soul like acid from a coal strip mine, altering the pH of my being.

There's the story of the young Black mother whose two boys, eight and five, went missing. Last seen after dinner playing outside. Ground and air searches, and then all eyes turning on mom. Police turn up the heat with 24-hour surveillance and theorize maybe the kids were kidnapped by drug dealers. Some people won't even take the mom's missing children fliers when she or family members try to hand them out. The investigation intensifies for twenty-three days until the sun starts to melt the ice around Anchorage, and a child's shoe floats to the surface of a pond near the boys' home. At first, authorities wouldn't even let the mother into the morgue to see her dead sons.

"This poor woman's been through two weeks of hell," her attorney told our reporting team, radiating anger over the phone. "She's been accused. Her family's been accused. All this time these kids are under a damn ice pack. She's very angry. If they had dredged that water like they should have, they would have found her babies the first day. Everybody said they checked the pond."

I had given up hope that the boys would be found alive, but this news hit like a gut punch. For days after I felt sick. Had the paper's coverage made things worse for this poor mother? If I had asked better questions sooner about when and where and how long they had dredged the pond, it could have pressured more focus in that direction, and maybe investigators would have discovered sooner that the deaths had just been a tragic accident. Nothing could have brought the brothers back, but better reporting might have saved their devastated mother from the public shaming she endured.

Another day, a different part of town, the story is about a single mom with mental health problems who shot and killed her three boys before school one day.

On another, I am flying to Nome, not for the triumphant end of the world-famous Iditarod sled dog race, but to cover the murder of a 19-year-old basketball star fresh out of high school, her promising life cut short by someone the community thought they could trust: a cop.

In my journalism career, I remember people warning me about carpal tunnel from typing, about the importance of proper ergonomics given the many hours spent in front of a computer, about not getting into a Bush plane if you don't trust the pilot. But not about how to deal with repeated exposure to traumatic events. Sometimes, I try to run the grief out of my system, hitting Anchorage's paved trails and rocky peaks. Other times, I try to numb it away with alcohol.

Today, May 3, 2004, marks the end of the year-long search for Bethany. I am the lead writer. Another reporter will be dumping notes to me from the gravel pit outside Talkeetna, where police have just found her remains.

My emotions push at my throat like a branch dammed in a rain-swelled crick. It feels selfish to consider my own feelings when others have lost so much. I swallow hard, sit down at my computer, and start stitching the story together.

I know the outlines by heart.

A small-town girl raised in Talkeetna by a close-knit homesteading family. Young, beautiful, strong, independent. Grew up in a log cabin built by her father in the shadow of Denali, the tallest mountain in North America. Loved the outdoors. Excelled in academics and sports and traveled to do missionary work in Nepal.

In May 2003, at age 21, Bethany moved to Anchorage to attend college. She rented an apartment in Bootleggers Cove, a nice neighborhood that overlooked Cook Inlet, and got a part-time job cleaning her apartment building for her landlord.

A few days after moving in, Bethany's mom came to visit. She found her daughter's door unlocked and her purse, keys, and cell phone inside. Bethany never showed up.

Overnight, the city was plastered with posters of Bethany's smiling face. I identified with her. We both came from small towns. I'd taken side jobs cleaning to help pay for school. My sister lived in an apartment a few doors away from where she went missing. We even looked similar, both in our 20s, roughly the same height and weight with straight brown hair.

I thought of Bethany each time I visited my sister or jogged through the neighborhood on my way to the Tony Knowles Coastal Trail. Each time I saw her smiling back at me from a poster on a telephone pole.

Alaska has many amazing qualities. Beautiful mountains and rivers and glaciers, Native arts and culture, stunning wildlife, and many wonderful quirky, independent people with a can-do spirit. But it also has some of the highest rates of drug and alcohol abuse in the country and one of the highest violent crime rates. I try not to internalize the things I see, but it is hard. Much has been written about the power of writing things down. One can almost double their chances of accomplishing a goal by writing it down in detail. But the flip side of that is if you spend hours covering a tragedy, interviewing the victims or their distraught families, reading arrest and court documents, weaving all those notes together on a page, and then rereading, rewriting, and editing that story multiple times, parts of it stay with you. Forever.

It had been clear for a while that police had a suspect in Bethany's case—the landlord, who had a history of violence against women. They got him and his brother on fraud charges and then got the brother to turn state's witness. It would eventually come out that the landlord shot Bethany and then called his brother to help clean up the mess. The brother arrived to find Bethany dead and naked on the floor of a duplex. The brothers put her body in their Mercedes, drove it to Talkeetna, dumped it, returned to Anchorage, set fire to the duplex, and then went out to meet friends at a local bar.

Police waited for the snow to melt so they could search for the remains and bring murder charges.

As I scan my notes, I think about Bethany's family and Glen Klinkhart, the detective. Everyone on the news desk knew Klink's story, how his own sister had been murdered two decades earlier under spookily similar circumstances involving a deadly assault and then a fire to cover it up. He'd been wrapped around Bethany's case since the day he arrived on scene for the missing person report. A supposedly unrelated duplex fire still smoldering nearby, his instincts told him otherwise. He pursued the case doggedly.[1]

Bethany's family had granted a lot of media interviews since she disappeared, but today they pulled back and asked for privacy. At my desk, I scan Klinkhart's interview. Bethany's family had considered that she may never come home, he told us, but still took the news hard. One of Klinkhart's quotes jumps out at me, and I type it into the narrative, my hands flying across the keys without looking.

```
"To hear the words, you're never quite ready,"
Klinkhart said.
```

I skip the catwalk in the press room that night and drive home in silence. As I walk through the door of my one-bedroom house downtown, my border collie, Lox, walks over to me in the quirky sideways way she does, so happy to see her person.

I give her a half-hearted smile and scratch her head. Purse still over my shoulder, I lower myself into a kitchen chair, lay my head on my forearms, and sob. The dam finally broken, Lox puts her paws on my thighs and lays her head in my lap.

"Just a really hard day at work," I say quietly, sliding my fingers over her silky black-and-white head and soft ears.

After a while, I lift my head and sit in silence, staring blankly at the empty kitchen wall in front of me.

You can't keep doing this, I think, and then try to push it out of my mind.

Journalism was everything to me. Something I believed in. Everything I'd worked for. How I related to the world and viewed my place

---

1. Klinkhart would go on to write and publish a true crime memoir, *Finding Bethany*.

in it. To walk away from that connection, that purpose, that *belonging*, after everything it took to get here, left me reeling. Without it, I'd do—be—*what*?

Scared of the uncertainty, I wipe away my tears and grab a beer from the fridge and a cigarette from my purse.

"Tomorrow, let's go run our favorite mountain," I say to Lox. "OK, girl?"

CHAPTER 2

THE ROAD LESS TRAVELED

Almost two years after Bethany's remains are found, many tragedies later, I'm sitting at my desk at the *Daily News*. Most of my colleagues have gone home for the day. The overhead lights in the large, open newsroom have been turned off. My computer glows in the dimness, surrounded by pods of empty cubicles and dark monitors. It is February. Big windows line the wall. The days are short this time of year. The cumulative darkness penetrates like grief, heavy and inescapable until time changes it. Fifteen years in Alaska and I still struggle with it.

My phone rings. I grab the headset sitting on my desk, slide it over my hair until the speakers cover my ears, and hit the answer button.

"Newsroom, this is Ta."

It's my younger sister, Piper. She is talking fast, trying to convince me or maybe herself that it is a good idea to scrap her career as an air traffic controller and move back to rural Pennsylvania where we grew up. She wants to buy a canoe rental business on the Allegheny River. This conversation has been building for a few weeks. Each day brings a new development.

Piper, who is twenty-six, moved to Alaska after leaving the Navy a few months ago. Our older sister, Sandoz, lives here, and our mom recently moved here too. It is the first time we've all lived near each other since being split up as kids, and I want so much for it to work, to have us all settle down near each other. For once, we can create something stable, normal.

Piper is in a tough marriage. Some days, I don't know how she holds it all together. My life, personally and professionally, feels like it could blast apart at any moment, too, and I'm holding onto this vision of my family being together like a remedy that can save me from difficult decisions I don't want to face.

The universe seems to be on to my bullshit. The Federal Aviation Administration has a hiring freeze, leaving Piper temporarily unemployed, and she is also finding Alaska to be a little too extreme. Mother Nature hasn't helped, bringing in a winter that has been particularly unwelcoming, with weeks of temperatures cold enough to freeze your eyelashes and nose hairs. The other day, when a cold snap finally broke, Piper bundled up her three children, all under age four, and set them loose in her yard to play. A moose stepped over the fence, and she had to chase it off with a snow shovel. Since then, Piper has started reading the *Warren Times Observer* online for opportunities that might give her a way to move back home. The paper serves Warren County, Pennsylvania, the place where we grew up and where our parents, grandparents, and great-grandparents eked out livings in small towns and villages near the Allegheny National Forest.

I stopped by Piper's house shortly after the moose episode.

"There's this thing called the Pennsylvania Wilds," she told me. "It's all these people working together to grow nature tourism. The state is involved. It makes so much sense. I mean it is so freaking beautiful back home. The woods. The river."

It was the first time I'd heard the term "Pennsylvania Wilds." My sister has a way of willing what she wants into existence, so it doesn't surprise me when a few days later, she finds a "business opportunities" ad online for Allegheny Outfitters, where she used to rent canoes in high school.

"Very reasonably priced," it says.

Over the next few days, she researches the Allegheny River, the Pennsylvania Wilds Initiative, and how to buy and operate a business. She finds an article about Pennsylvania's new governor, "Big Ed" Rendell, discussing the "Principles of the Pennsylvania Wilds," and it inspires her to stay up half the night reading a 300-plus page report, "A Recreation Plan for the State Parks and State Forests in the Pennsylvania Wilds." When she can't make a deal with the owners of Allegheny Outfitters, she finds a smaller outfitter downriver that is also on the market.

FOR SALE: Canoe and Kayak Livery with all equipment, paddles, jackets, 3 vans, 3 trailers, also house and all contents. Two car garage, new septic system and 300-foot river frontage. Owner is retiring, serious inquiries only please.

She strikes a deal with the owner. Which brings us to the present moment, and her phone call to me that night at my desk at the *Daily News*.

"I have to sell my house," Piper tells me.

"In February? In Alaska?" I say, panicked, more for me than her. "You just bought it! You don't know anything about selling a house."

The Pennsylvania Wilds sounds promising, but moving home to rural PA to start a business is not something people our age—or *anyone*—did, as far as I could tell. The area has seen decades of population loss. Factories have closed. Small towns, dying on the vine.

Pictures run through my mind of the village near Warren where my mom and grandparents used to live. The Bushel & A Peck country store, the local gas station, the pet shop, and Dad's hardware store, all of them shuttered the last time I was home. A ghost town. If I remembered right, the only establishments still open were the post office, playground, church, and cemetery.

I worry Piper is making a rash decision that will compromise her career and mean taking on a lot of debt. We didn't grow up with much, and she worked for years for little pay in the Navy to create the FAA opportunity. Financially, there is no one to help if she missteps. But she knows this, all three of us sisters do. It has always been this way.

I sit back in my office chair. My bony back relaxes against the cushion. I look out the window at the *Daily News* and listen to my sister as I watch red taillights cut through the night.

"I just got this for-sale-by-owner kit," Piper says. "It's the only way. We have to make enough on the sale to ship our stuff home."

"Are you sure this is a good idea?" I ask.

I can hear Piper smiling over the phone. Change is in our blood. It was our one constant growing up. So many schools, so many apartments. I want to try something new, too, but am afraid to take the leap. I've put down roots in Alaska and have worked hard to build my career. For the first time, I have security: a 401K, health and dental, bad-but-stable pay doing a job I find purposeful, even if covering rapes, murders, suicides, and other devastating events is corroding the hope and optimism that fueled me as a kid and young adult.

Unlike my sister, at thirty-one, I've spent half my life in the Last Frontier. Our parents grew up in rural PA and had kids right out of high school. They got divorced before I was old enough to have any memories of them together. Mom raised us while putting herself through nursing school. She moved us from apartment to apartment, job to job, eternally optimistic that the next place would make life better for her and her girls.

Without access to a truck to help us move, we often left belongings behind. By my teens, we had moved and switched schools so many times my sisters and I made a game of pulling pennies from a jar and reading the year on each one and trying to remember where we were living at the time. The apartment above the Century 21 office? The basement apartment where we played drive-through at the kitchen window? The attic apartment in the old Victorian house with the endless stairs, or the duplex with the weird door that led to our Vietnamese neighbor's hallway? The room upstairs at my grandparents, or the court where Sandoz got the nickname "She-ra" for how she could send a baseball over the tops of the row houses during our neighborhood games? The apartment where the momma rabbit got hit on the road out front and all the neighborhood kids tried to save the babies? Or the one where my teacher lived at the end of the street and glowered at me because she'd caught me stealing change for an ice cream sandwich from a fundraiser box while the class watched *Old Yeller*? The list felt endless. Years later, as an adult, I'd panic the first time I had to do one of those credit verifications where they give you a handful of street names and ask you which one you used to live on. I'd call Sandoz and ask, "Do any of these sound familiar?"

I'd be transfixed when I found author Sarah Smarsh writing about similar experiences in *Heartland: A Memoir of Working Hard and Being Broke in the Richest Country on Earth*.

"Having no money looks and feels different in different places," Smarsh wrote, echoing things my mom had told me. "Are your neighbors helpful? Is the landlord raising the rent? Can you walk to work if the car goes out? . . . Among the poor, the potential risks of starting over are more severe for women, people of color, and other disadvantaged groups. But often, by moving, there is little to lose and at least a chance at finding something better."

We left rural PA for Virginia Beach, a bigger, faster-paced place than we'd ever known, just as Sandoz and I hit our rebellious years. Mom tried to set boundaries, but her work schedule left us with a lot of unsupervised time. I snuck out, skipped school, hung out with teenage drug dealers. By the seventh grade, I was lost. I took a handful of pills from the medicine cabinet, ones I was pretty sure wouldn't kill me, ate them, then went to school and told people I wanted to die. It was a plea for attention more than anything, but it rightly freaked Mom out. She called Dad for help.

Dad, a carpenter, hadn't been in the picture much. We saw him from time to time. He was a fun, likable person. He played in a soccer league, hunted, and played golden oldies while he fixed up camps and houses around Warren. Before long, he remarried and started another family. He liked to say he loved all his kids equally, but his lack of investment in our lives seeded in me a very different message: that I wasn't worthy.

Dad had a trailer with an add-on and some land in the country. I begged Mom not to make me go, that I didn't want to leave all my friends again, but it was done. Sandoz and I moved back to rural PA. At middle school, I tried to get reacquainted with kids I'd gone to kindergarten or first grade with, but I didn't fit in. Sandoz was at the high school, so I didn't have her to lean on. One gaggle of girls stalked and bullied me. At home, I fought with my stepmother.

Like Mom, Dad was a hard worker (so was my stepmother). He grew up in the country with a lot of brothers and sisters and not many resources. I never thought he'd leave rural PA, the way he talked about it. He loved the country, the woods, his land. But as rural PA's economy declined, his hardware business failed, and construction jobs dried up. He had a friend who had recently moved to Alaska and decided we would move there, too.

"Piss on it," he said, a favorite saying of his when he'd had enough.

We packed everything we had into a moving truck and a horse trailer and off we went up the Alaska-Canadian Highway. We were another statistic in rural Pennsylvania's population decline. Two weeks later, we pulled into Palmer, a small farming town outside of Anchorage. Dad rented a house next to a musk ox farm. Sandoz and I shared a room in the basement.

My sisters and I spent a lot of time outside as kids, but Alaska was something else. So vast and extreme in its natural splendor, each experience was like an artisan's hammer to my heart. Sandoz and I post-holed through snow-covered fields, explored mountains in Hatcher's Pass, and marveled at the northern lights. At sunset in the winter, the snow on Pioneer Peak Mountain turned pink in an optical phenomenon I'd learn was called the "alpenglow." When spring came, we purposely stopped taking the bus. It was a three-mile walk through fields and woods to school. Coming out of my first long, dark, bitterly cold Alaska winter, I was greedy for green grass and fresh air. I relished this time with my sister, the person I was closest to in the world.

I joined track and cross-country and yearbook and started to make friends. I loved learning new things and was an A student, but at home, my relationship with my dad and stepmom grew more strained. I felt like a second-class citizen in their home, and there were deeper trust issues that still hurt my feelings to this day. The stress of it all came spewing out one night, touched off by something pedestrian like, "No you can't stay over at a friend's house." After the row was over, my sister and I started packing. Dad told us that if we left, we were not to come back. We pushed off into the world.

I was sixteen.

A larger-than-life Alaska family, a husband-and-wife truck driving team, took us in. Their son and daughter were two of my closest friends. I felt relieved, and grateful.

In high school, there is often a house where kids gravitate. In Palmer, Alaska when I was growing up, that place was this one, a double-wide trailer with green shag carpeting, brown paneling and a big garage out back. Everyone called it The Castle. It was a place where you always felt welcome, were never judged, and where laughter ruled the day. Nothing and no one was too sacred to make fun of. Projects were always underway, and that was a big part of the magic, too. It was a place you could go to do something, learn something, feel useful for an afternoon fixing cars or moving equipment or preparing a burrito spread to feed a small army.

Lift the hood on a vehicle at the Castle, and it was like the bat signal; they all came running.

The summer before I showed up at their door, to practice for cross country running, I had run to the Castle regularly to escape my own home. I would write my times in pencil on an unfinished sheetrock wall at the back of the double-wide trailer, trying to beat myself each time.

53:46
52:10
49:56

Terri, the mom, wasn't surprised when I showed up for good. Mom and Piper were living back in rural Pennsylvania by then. We called Mom to let her know what happened and to ask if we could stay in Alaska. We didn't want to switch schools yet again. She said OK. The family built a wall across the living room of their trailer, and there we stayed until we finished high school. We weren't the only misfit kids they helped. Another friend of their kids moved in at about the same time. Five teenagers in that little trailer. We could eat three boxes of cereal in a single day. Terri renamed the Castle the Fishbowl.

"They saved us," Sandoz would reflect to me later in life. "We were just kids. Terri was always there to build you up. She made us safe. There was trust. There was love. And that brought so much laughter. Terri gave me the freedom to be me. And you were allowed to be you. We were accepted before we even had to prove our worth. And the laughter . . . The silliness was HUGE."

My cross-country coaches and the school principal helped me apply and get into college. My art and yearbook teacher, Sara Arno, encouraged me to write and create and when I graduated high school, she and her husband, a hunting guide, took me and their two young daughters in a Piper Cub airplane to camp and hike for a week far off the road system in the Alaskan Bush. We set up camp in the Nushagak Hills, about 250 miles from Anchorage. It was the first time I'd ever been that far from a road system, so far out I could not walk myself back. My art teacher gave me a can of pepper spray and water and snacks and sent me on a "rite-of-passage" hike walking the mountain ridgetop. I wasn't sure what a rite of passage was back then, but I trusted and admired her and did as she said, singing aloud the whole way to help ward off any bears. I had a terrible sense of direction, but the Piper Cub plane was bright and kept me on track. I reached an agreed-upon point on the ridgeline, descended the mountain, and took a bath in a crick at its base. Then I climbed back up to the plane and our camp. I'd never pushed myself like this in nature, and the experience built my confidence as a hiker. My art teacher and her family also left an impression on me. There was a lot of love between them. And in my art teacher, I saw a model for how I might live. A woman with a creative career, a family, and a life in the outdoors.

Palmer, *P-Town*, as we all called it, is where I learned to drive, got my first job, and came to understand for the first time the power of community and how the social safety net of neighbors caring about neighbors could save a young person's life.

I left Alaska for the Lower 48 for college, but I missed the mountains and the people and soon returned. I graduated from the University of Alaska Anchorage and forged a career in journalism. I'd been drawn to the profession's public service mission at a young age and pursued it with everything I had. For a young woman with few resources who moved a lot, journalism felt accessible and practical, a way I could use my experience of always being the outsider, the new kid, for some greater good.

I threw myself into my career in Alaska. I interviewed people from so many walks of life and corners of the city and beyond, flew in small planes over Alaska's glaciers and tundra, covered the Iditarod, and even got invited to take a steam bath with a family of Native women in a Yup'ik village. Every day I learned new things.

One time, my cell phone rang when I was on the top of Flattop, a popular mountain near Anchorage; it was my boss, the city editor. I was off duty at the time, but it was my work phone, so I answered it the way I always do: "Newsroom, this is Ta."

"Newsroom?" he said, puzzled. "I'm in the newsroom. Where *are* you?"

"On Flattop," I said as I looked down at the city, Cook Inlet, and Sleeping Lady, a mountain across the inlet.

He laughed. "Well, I guess in a way the whole city is your newsroom."

Some people have relationships and memories and pictures of a place that stretch back to the beginning of their lives to ground them. I've always wanted that, but I moved too much to have it. But through my reporting, I created my own sense of belonging. It's a privilege to get to know a place so intimately, like getting to know a person.

Listening to Piper through my headset, I sit up at my computer and start scanning the half-written story in front of me. Without thinking about it, I press Ctrl S for save.

"You are really leaving, aren't you?" I say.

"I have to," she says. "I'm sorry. I just have to follow my heart on this."

"I know you do," I say, as I feel my own fault lines begin to separate.

CHAPTER 3

STAND-TO

Four months later, Piper and her family were living in a camp on the Allegheny River surrounded by the Allegheny National Forest running a canoe business out of a garage on her lawn. No banks would give her a loan, so she bought the business on a land contract.

"Wait until you see it," she told me over the phone. "It's so awesome!"

My life was a mess by then. Burnt out at work, I was also in the midst of ending a years-long relationship with a friend and colleague, a hell of an editor with a family I adored, who I wasn't in love with and who I was pretty sure wasn't in love with me either. The day I ended it, I drove alone out to Beluga Point, an overlook on one of the most beautiful stretches of road in Alaska, and watched the tide come in from Cook Inlet. I often went to nature to find clarity. Since I was a kid, the rhythm of the tide or of my steps as I walked on a trail calmed me and helped me work through challenges. The mountains gave me perspective. I found inspiration in the trees, rooted deep and reaching for the sky, or in the hearty will of an alpine forget-me-not. I loved that something so dainty could be so tough, making its home on the side of a windy mountain.

I moved in with my older sister for a short time. The game show *Deal or No Deal* was big, and I'd watch it with her daughter, a toddler. When Howie would ask the magic question, she'd look up at me, her baby teeth just coming in, and slap the couch, "No Deal!" and we'd both laugh. I was grateful for this special place to land until I could find an apartment. I felt relieved to not be lying to myself anymore, but also like a complete fuckup.

At the *Anchorage Daily News*, I was still in denial about how I wasn't cut out to be a news reporter. I'd been assigned to cover the military, so

I convinced myself that the big change I needed was to go to Iraq. I'd recently been embedded with the Air Force on an overseas disaster relief mission and spent the last several months following an Army Airborne battalion as it prepared for deployment. I ran with the paratroopers early in the morning at Fort Richardson, flew with them as they did jumps from C130s, and shadowed them on practice missions at the remote Donnelly Training area.

It was unlikely my paper was going to send me to the Middle East, so I applied to papers that might and got an invitation to a training on the East Coast for reporters headed to war zones, and another program at the Army War College in Carlisle, Pennsylvania. It felt like the universe was already conspiring to bring me and Piper back together.

I calculate how long it would take to drive from my sister's riverside camp to the training. Five hours. I have vacation time and decide to take a few weeks and clear my head.

My flight lands in Erie, Pennsylvania on a sunny day in August 2006. It's an hour and half drive from the airport to my sister's and I smile as I pass familiar sights from my youth. Cornfields and weathered old barns, the Troyer potato chip factory I toured in grade school. Maples, oaks, hemlocks, cherry, and other trees cover hillsides in every direction.

I turn off Scenic Route 6 onto State Route 62, which borders the western edge of the Allegheny National Forest. Trees tower over the road, making it feel like a tunnel. The Allegheny River tracks alongside the road, the sun glinting off its riffles. This is nothing like the thinned-out flora and fauna of Alaska's alpine climbs; Pennsylvania's forests are lush, prehistoric-looking. How I loved playing in the woods here as a kid. The ubiquitous sound of cricks. A million bugs under every rock. Mayflowers and crayfish and sweet corn and McIntosh apples.

Home, I think, feeling a little sad.

Memories rush in. I think of the farm on the hill where for me the story of us three sisters started. Our house across from my dad's parents' house, hot tar bubbles sticking to my feet as I crossed the road to visit them. Black-eyed Susans. Big rocks in the pasture we called candy stones. Grandpa molesting one of us girls. Mom getting us out of there. My parents divorcing. An order not to go to Grandpa's.

My childhood felt like I was on a wooden raft on a river, exposed to the elements, never sure what danger or beauty lay around the next bend.

And when I got old enough to make decisions myself, what had I done? I'd chosen a profession that kept me in the same survival mode. Moving. Reacting. Staying close to danger and heartache.

The conveyor belt of tragedies at my job had not slowed. There was the story of the family of five killed in their sleep by carbon monoxide, little children in their nightclothes, just gone. The women raped and murdered in apartments, in stairwells, on trails. The single mom who, on her way to work, saw flashing lights and a girl's shoe and realized her only child had been fatally struck by a vehicle on the way to school. Bethany. Brandi. Gerald. Sonya. The families probably did not remember me, but I carried their stories with me. They filled me up, emptied me out. After ten years, I can't tell which. Now I wanted to cover a war? What the hell was wrong with me.

You're running, I think as I drive, and then push it out of my mind. I slow down and turn on my blinker. Two eagle statues stand at the top of my sister's steep, short driveway. Eagles stand for courage, strength, truth. They make me think about Dutch Harbor, on the Aleutian Chain, where the eagles are so great in number, picking at the fish guts and garbage at the dump that they are like starlings, a nuisance. *Good grief*, I think. *Journalism is ruining me. I can't even enjoy an eagle anymore!*

I turn into the driveway. To the right is a two-bay garage, to the left, a small, one-story house. Both are neatly painted, light yellow with brown trim and shutters. A small wooden box with hand-painted lettering hangs on the front of the house. "Brochures: Take One" it says.

I get out and stretch my arms and straighten my back, happy not to be sitting after the fifteen-hour flight and long drive. I look around. A large yard gradually slopes into the river. Rows of red, yellow, silver, and purple canoes sit atop four sets of railroad ties. It is mid-afternoon, and several vehicles are parked on the lawn. At the back of the house, a small covered porch overlooks the river. Piper sees me and trots across the yard with a clipboard in her hand. She's a runner with a lean frame and brown hair. She wears a t-shirt, jeans rolled up to her calves, and sandals. Her arms and face are lightly tanned, which is tanner than I've ever seen them.

"You look great," I say, giving her a hug and touching her taut bicep. "Look at your arm muscles!"

"Lifting canoes," she says, smiling, and starts lugging my suitcases out of the car. "Beats being cooped up in a dark radar room all day."

My niece, Lily, and nephews, Ash and Phoenix, run over to greet me. "Aunt Tee-Tah! Aunt Tee-Tah! Are you going to live with us?"

Piper takes me inside to show me around. It doesn't take long. The house is a true camp, 850 square feet of mismatched leftovers, shoddy construction, and ten types of ugly carpeting. The sunroom, where I will be sleeping, has a pull-out sofa bed and big windows that overlook the Allegheny. The room is cluttered with boxes Piper still has not had time to unpack.

"If you wake up early enough, you can watch the fog move down the river as the sun comes up," Piper says.

I stare out the windows at the water. Mom always loved the water. In moments when it felt like our family was going to explode and many times when it did not, she'd drive us down to the beach or go walk out on the Allegheny Reservoir, and we'd all clear our heads.

"This place is great," I say quietly to Piper, and I mean it. Jetlagged, I take a shower and head to bed. Later, I sit on the back porch with Piper, nursing a beer and looking at the river. I don't know if it is the Allegheny, my sister's presence, the distance from the newsroom, or the combination of all three, but something in me unravels.

I think about how I'm supposed to leave soon for a three-day conference at the Army War College in Carlisle, near Harrisburg; the war zone training is after that, farther south, outside of Washington, D.C. I take a sip of my IPA and look at the water as it flows by. I've been on a Johnny Cash kick for months, and one of his lyrics, about taking troubles and throwing them in a river, springs to mind.

I think about another song of his, "As Long as the Grass Shall Grow." It is about how the government broke its treaty with the Seneca Indians and took their land to build the Kinzua Dam in the early 1960s to prevent flooding along the Allegheny and in Pittsburgh. The dam and its resulting impoundment, the Allegheny Reservoir, flooded over 10,000 acres of the Allegheny Reservation of the Seneca Nation, including most of the 1500-acre Cornplanter Tract, which had been given to Chief Cornplanter in 1796. My family wasn't Native, but Mom's parents, my grandparents, and my mom and uncles lived in Kinzua, a small village of about 450 residents located at the confluence of Kinzua Creek and the Allegheny River. The mouth of the creek was a favored spot of the Seneca for spearing fish. The name Kinzua was taken from the Iroquois word, *genzo waa*, which meant "fish up there," and refers to a wooden fish stuck on top of a pole. When the Cornplanter Tract was submerged, so too went the village of Kinzua. All the families who lived in Kinzua, including my grandparents, were forced to leave their homes. I wondered how they felt about it, and if they'd been compensated, and realized how sad it was that I was a reporter longing for roots and had never taken the time to ask my family one question about it. How was it that I held other people's family histories and traditions in such high esteem, but somehow thought my own didn't matter?

I take a deep breath.

"I don't want to go," I confess to Piper.

Two days later, I rent a car and make the five-hour drive south to Harrisburg. It is in the high nineties and muggy. I arrive at my hotel with an hour to spare before meeting a group of Army colonels. The gathering kicks off three days of lectures and discussions that are to culminate with a keynote by the head of Iraq's security forces.

It is my second visit to the War College. I get as far as setting up the ironing board before I start to cry. I call Piper and tell her I want to come back to her house. She talks me through my breakdown. A few days later, I drive to Washington, D.C. for my war zone training. It is led by ex-special forces and is held in the country outside the capital. At one point, our group heads from the classroom to the field for first aid training, and our SUV is "ambushed." The "bad" guys put thick black canvas bags over our heads and march us through the woods in silence. They lay us on the forest floor and take our belongings. It is an exercise, but it isn't hard to imagine it could be real. At that point in the Iraq war, ninety journalists had been killed. Later that night, Piper calls, and I tell her about my day. She sounds angry.

"Your job is so fucked up," she says.

The final day of training covers traveling in warzones. Rocks stacked on the side of the road or other manmade markings can signal mines nearby or similar trouble, the instructors tell us. Always determine how to exit a hotel or other building when you enter it, they say. We take the class outside and tend to fake wounds and then talk about passport security. I share how I almost lost my passport once while entering Zimbabwe as a freelance writer, when men dressed in suits approached the vehicle I was traveling in. They looked official and were in that weird in-between space when you've left one country but not yet entered the bordering one. But they weren't the border patrol. They were running a racket. The photographer I was traveling with stopped me before I handed my passport out the window. The poor couple in the car behind us were not so lucky. When they got to the real border station, the officials told them they'd have to go back and find the men and buy back their passports. I remember how unsettling the situation felt.

When the training is over, I drive back to my sister's. On the back porch again one evening, Piper tells me about being an air traffic controller in the Navy for eight years. We came from a family of veterans, and Piper was proud of her service and appreciated the stability it brought to her life. It struck her that they call people on planes "souls," and it meant a lot to her to have a role helping to keep those souls safe until they landed. The pay was miserable, but she learned a professional skill that she knew would make her a good living when she finally moved to the private sector. For years, she relished the idea of moving to a big, busy airport like Chicago or New York City. But when it came time to make the leap, she didn't want it anymore.

Piper says she met a woman who worked as an air traffic controller for the FAA. She had a six-figure income and was always working overtime. She smoked heavily and had circles under her eyes.

"She looked like shit," Piper says. "I just think there's more to life."

I could see myself there in a few years if I didn't change my ways. Not the six-figure income but the smoking and looking like shit. I watch a stick float by in the Allegheny's steady current. Soon it is gone, out of sight.

Piper is quiet. "Maybe you should take a break from journalism," she says.

Then she gets a goofy grin on her face. "You could always move home to Pennsylvania."

CHAPTER 4

A CALLING

Warren, Pennsylvania is on the National Register of Historic Places. It has a Historic District with nearly 600 contributing structures in twenty-five architectural styles over a twenty-eight-block area of its downtown. Victorian mansions, gothic churches, and ornate government buildings line Market Street, vestiges to the oil and timber industries that helped build the town, which is home to just over 9,000 people. The National Wild and Scenic Allegheny River runs through the city, the 500,000-acre Allegheny National Forest hugs its southern border. It is one of the most beautiful towns I've ever seen.

Today, most of the mansions along Market Street are offices for lawyers, dentists, politicians, or other enterprises. When I was a kid, many were still homes or apartments. We lived in one of the attic apartments for a few months when I was in grade school. At the end of Market Street was Loblaw's Grocery and a laundromat. Mom was raising us alone and didn't always have a car, so we'd haul laundry and groceries back and forth under the tall maple trees along Market Street.

My favorite building was the Warren Public Library, a stone building with six tall columns out front that act as pedestals for words etched in stone. Above one set, it says History, above another, Philosophy. In the middle, above the entrance, it reads:

> *Literature—The Storehouse of Knowledge,*
> *And Record of Civilization.*
> *The Fulcrum for the Lever of Progress*

Back then, I had no idea what those words meant, but the grandeur of the building made me believe that books and writing were important.

Mom had a news clipping of Sandoz sitting on the steps of the library. It made it through many of our moves. It was a picture of one of my favorite people in front of one of my favorite places, and the moment had been captured by the town's newspaper. It felt special, and as a kid, it was my first recollection of thinking about newspapers.

The second impression newspapers left on me was in junior high. We had an apartment in Virginia Beach, the last place we three sisters lived together. There I walked in on Mom crying about bills. I was in eighth grade and had been to eight or nine schools. Mom worked two nursing jobs but still couldn't make ends meet. Through tears, Mom said she was going to write a letter to the editor of the newspaper. I don't know if she ever wrote the letter, but it planted a seed in me that newspapers looked out for people like us.

I knew when Mom's payday was close because we'd be living on fumes. Bare cupboards, gas tank on E, shut-off notices. I lost count how many times I was fooled that a lone jar of wrapped bouillon cubes in the cupboard were really caramels, or that we ate mustard and mayonnaise sandwiches (which I'd later learn were called "wish sandwiches" as in, "I wish there was something between these two pieces of bread"). My spirit was like a green switch back then, it could bend and bend and not break. I'd come to realize later in life that, like drought to a tree's rings, the daily stress of food and shelter and watching Mom work herself to exhaustion would leave a permanent mark on all of us.

Sometimes, when the tank was especially low, and she had to get to work, she would starch her white nurse uniform, put a stethoscope around her neck, and go to the gas station to trade her stethoscope for gas, just until payday. It usually worked. She always seemed shocked by this, but then she was beautiful, tan with long blonde hair, and didn't seem to know it.

Mom taught us at a young age that there were always people less fortunate. She'd run across kids in dire straits at the grocery store or at one of our schools and involve us in doing something anonymously to brighten their day. Often spending her last dollars to do it, she'd buy a balloon and have a store manager give it to the unkempt kid in Aisle 8. Or we'd pick a kid at school and have the principal give them a Christmas present. Other times, she'd have us go visit her patients, people with cancer or AIDS, or other life-altering medical problems. I watched Mom have long conversations with a man paralyzed from the neck down who'd spent most of his adulthood living on a vent. Where I only saw tubes and machines and awfulness, she saw the person. She was, I'd come to understand as I grew older, an extraordinarily kind person.

Moving is just what we did. It forged in me a unique closeness with my sisters that comes from shared hard experiences navigated together, particularly with Sandoz because we were only a year apart in age. Moving so much also forced me inward, developing my creativity. Always the new kid, it gave me a heightened awareness at a young age of the power structures and pecking orders that shaped my life and others.' As Smarsh put it in *Heartland*, "Attending eight schools by ninth grade taught me that, if you can hold to your center without going crazy, you're the same person wherever you go, even as the scenery changes. That scenery is shaped, in part, by money and class." Her observation made me think of how as a teen, I had a quick way of assessing where new friends I made stood on the socio-economic ladder: paper towels. A family struggling to buy food and pay basic utilities would not buy them. We never had paper towels. Many of my friends did, thank goodness. It was not that I judged poor people. Many who have hit hard times are salt-of-the-earth types like in my own family, and I loved their company. I just figured there were things I could learn from families that were a little more stable than my own to help me make my way in the world.

Paydays were epic, all of us riding around in Mom's red Plymouth Horizon with a gazillion miles on it, muffler held up by a wire clothes hanger, windows down, our hair under ball caps or spinning wildly in the breeze, Huey Lewis and the News' "Hip to Be Square" blaring. Mom taking her hands off the steering wheel for one hot irresponsible second to pump them in the air in front of her to the beat of a song while we sang at the top of our lungs. Our first stop was usually a check-cashing joint where she'd swap her paper check for cash, then we'd drive to the gas station where she'd left her stethoscope. "I'll be right back," she'd say, all smiles, and run inside. A few moments later, she'd emerge with the stethoscope and hop back in the car. If Mom had to pawn a ring or Sandoz's flute or something else of value to get us through until payday, we'd make that stop too. We'd celebrate with a Little Caesar's pizza on the beach, which my sisters and I would descend on like hungry locusts and then splash in the ocean.

Even as she struggled with money, Mom was big on accountability. Once, when I was twelve or thirteen, I spray-painted my name across a wooden foot bridge. I can only assume I thought of it as art, because with such a weird first name, it wasn't like I was going to get away with it. When Mom discovered the vandalism, she had a cop come to our apartment and made sure I got community service sanding the graffiti off the bridge.

By sixteen, I was living with the Alaskan family in Palmer whose generosity allowed me to finish all four years of high school in one place. It was there I truly began to fall in love with journalism. My art teacher, Sara Arno, was also the high school yearbook advisor. She sought me out and asked me to join the staff. She was picky and thought I had it in me to be editor one day. It was the first time I'd been recruited for anything. I spent the next two years trying to become the person she thought I was.

Yearbook class was a place I felt I excelled. I loved the responsibility, the creative collaboration, the way I could issue myself hall passes to do things I found interesting. On a visit home to see my Mom, I found a book she had of Anna Quindlen's *New York Times* columns called *Living Out Loud*. I read it cover to cover, amazed and inspired that a woman could go so far in journalism. I wanted to be like her.

My confidence plummeted the moment I got to college, at the University of Montana, on scholarship. All around me were kids who seemed to have everything: the right clothes, the right parents, the right education. I felt alone, ill-prepared, and angry. I dropped out after one semester and used my scholarship money to travel around the country.

My cash ran out at the end of I-40, in North Carolina, where I got a job as a lifeguard. For a while, I slept in my car in a hospital parking lot. I joined a health club so I'd have a place to shower and get ready for work. I picked up a second job as a cashier at a chain grocery store. People said I was pretty and sweet, but I was still angry, and when no one was looking, I gave away boxes of diapers to WIC moms who came through my line.

Eventually, I stopped feeling sorry for myself, put myself through counseling, and although I'm not Catholic, I applied to a women's Catholic school, Carlow College, in Pittsburgh. I got a small scholarship and some federal grants. Loans and a job at a record store made up the difference. I wrote a few columns for the campus paper but was afraid to commit to journalism. What if I wasn't smart enough? What if no one would hire me? How would I pay back my student loans? I'd seen how stressful debt and a lack of resources could be. This, more than anything, was the demon I ran from.

I hid from journalism for another two years. I moved back to Alaska and enrolled at the state university as a biology major, thinking it would be easier to become a doctor. Then, one night, a column ran through my head, and I couldn't sleep. I kept arguing with myself about the kind of person who gets up at 2 a.m. and starts clacking away at a computer until I finally got up and did it. I wrote most of the night. The next morning, I walked into the campus paper and told them I wanted to be a reporter.

I was an introvert with a curious and creative spirit, a young woman with a strong sense of fairness who wanted to be taken seriously. Journalism forced me to the edge of my comfort zone and helped me grow as a person. It gave me a respectable way to question authority, a reason to enter people's lives, see things from their perspective, and try to share that story to build understanding. Most problems, I thought, could be overcome with a little more empathy and better communication.

I thought I was talented, but when I got my first real job in 1999, at the city's feisty alternative weekly, the *Anchorage Press*, I realized I couldn't write worth a damn. The editor rewrote my stories from top to bottom. He didn't have a choice: I was all the paper could afford back then, and little I wrote hung together. I kept at it. I compared "before" and "after" versions of my stories and tried to figure out how they got better. I watched more experienced reporters and tried to imitate them. I made vocabulary flashcards and flipped through them while I hiked Flattop. I wrote and wrote and wrote some more. Perhaps most importantly, I discovered reading. Fiction, non-fiction, newspapers, magazines—I devoured everything.[1]

After I thought I had developed some writing chops, I started applying to the *Anchorage Daily News*, then the big daily in the state. I kept pestering the *Daily News* city editor for a job, and he politely told me to keep trying. I emailed him from the Aleutian Chain, where I worked

---

1. Parts of this chapter originally appeared in "Reporting Alaska," a story I wrote for the *Anchorage Press* in 2007.

as an editor for a short time, and from Dillingham, a village in Western Alaska, where I ran the *Bristol Bay Times*. Finally, back at the *Press*, I scooped the *Daily News* on a story. The city editor called me. There was an opening on the news desk, on the cop beat, he said. Was I interested?

Alaska was a place of extreme temperatures and geography that drew wild characters into all manner of predicaments. Most days there was a chaotic, sink-or-swim quality to the cop beat. My job included more than stabbings, rapes, and murders. I wrote about people who fell down mountains and got thrown overboard in rough seas. Alaska has volcanoes, earthquakes, avalanches, wildfires, floods, tsunamis, animal attacks. Small planes, a ubiquitous sight in a place with so few roads, sometimes never made it out of the city. They crashed into people's houses, landed in backyards, made emergency landings at sports fields while kids played baseball or soccer. "Only in Alaska," neighbors would cluck as firefighters hosed down and cleaned up the wreckage.

I usually had no more than a few hours to get to a scene, interview folks, get back to the office, write a story, and go over it with my editor. I worked in a pressure cooker, and part of me loved it.

But a decade in, my front row seat to all the ways in which humans can harm and be harmed left its mark as distinct as the years I spent looking at empty fridges and watching Mom suffer stress migraines from raising three girls alone.

By then, I had collected a stack of writing awards, was elected president of the state's press association, and owned a house. From the outside, I was a success. But inside, I felt numb, trapped.

To drown out the dissonance, I ran mountains, I drank, I smoked cigarettes, and I put in longer hours at work. A Libra, always striving for balance and fairness, I hoped the mountain runs countered my poor lifestyle habits, but my internal scales told me different. I knew there was only so long I could avoid dealing with the change I knew I needed to make and the uncertainty it would bring.

CHAPTER 5

NATURE'S PULL

In August 2006, while I am still visiting my sister, a storm blows through Warren County. Lightning. Thunder. Driving rain that no one thought would last but does. Early the next morning, Piper walks onto the porch and peers over the railing at the railroad tie steps that lead into the river. Water covers all but the top one. The rain has stopped, but the high water is a major safety risk.

"No one's going out today," she says and walks back inside to start canceling reservations she had spent hours helping customers plan.

During the storm, three canoes wash downstream from Allegheny Outfitters, the livery Piper originally wanted to buy. Piper calls the owner to let her know. She mentions that she is still interested in buying the business if it comes down in price. The owner invites her out to dinner to discuss a potential sale. "I'll make you an offer you can't refuse," she tells Piper.

I offer to babysit the night of the dinner. I am sitting on the living room couch, reading a paper on counterinsurgency warfare that I've been trying to wade through for a month, when my four-year-old nephew, Ash, walks in wearing his Spiderman pajamas, his younger brother and sister trailing behind him like he is an emissary from another country.

"Aunt Tee-Tah," he says with a worried look on his face. "There's a hummingbird in the kitchen."

It is dark outside, around 9 p.m. A hummingbird seems unlikely. I put down my paper and go investigate a bat, I think.

I creep into the dark kitchen. Ash, Phoenix, and Lily stand in the entryway between the kitchen and the living room holding their blankets, watching me. I kick myself for not asking my sister where the light switches are. As my eyes adjust, I see dark shapes fluttering outside the screen door in the kitchen. Relieved, I point to the bats and tell the kids, "See, nothing to worry about, the hummingbirds are outside."

Ash smiles. "Boy, that was scary," he says. "Good thing they're outside because those aren't hummingbirds, Aunt Tee-Tah. They're bats!"

Crisis averted. Ash asks if he can have a drink. His brother and sister follow suit. The younger two have a habit of asking for things in a rush, running all their words together except the last one, which they say with as much force as possible, sometimes adding a hop and a wide grin for extra emphasis.

"MayIhaveadrink, *PLEASE!*" (grin, hop)

In the dark kitchen, I fill three cups with juice. I turn to hand the cups to the kids. All three of them are looking over my shoulder in terror. Lily, the youngest, looks like she is riding a fast motorcycle, her face stretched in a painful grimace ready to give way at any moment to a torrent of tears. Ash and Phoenix are wide-eyed, pale, and frozen. I turn to see what they are looking at. A bat dives at my head.

"Ah!" I scream and swat my hands through the air. My panic panics the kids. They cry and bump into each other as they try to escape. "Get in your bedroom and close the door!" I yell.

Lily shrieks, trips over her blanket, and falls to the floor, begging her brothers not to leave her behind. Ash goes back to help her, crying the whole time. He seems certain they are going to die.

I hurry everyone into the bedroom and close the door. Phoenix screams and blubbers something. I stick my head back inside. Ash translates that Phoenix is saying not to close the door, they are scared. I explain that I must close the door to keep the bat out. That seems to register, but when I closed the door Ash yells in a high-pitch voice, "We need our flashlights!"

I open the door back up. "Flashlights?"

"Yes," Ash says, pulling his out from under his covers on the top bunk. "Lily and Phoenix's flashlights are in the toy box in the living room. They have to have them."

Lily and Phoenix sit in their beds, nodding their heads in agreement: Every word he says is true.

In the living room, Skywalker the cat is chasing the bat. I crawl as fast as I can across the floor, dig the flashlights from a cardboard box in the corner, and crawl back to the kids' room.

Phoenix cries that his flashlight doesn't work. I apologize. Hunting for batteries would have to wait. I tell them Skywalker is chasing the bat. I close the door and listen for bat and cat sounds. A few seconds later, Ash opens the door.

"Phoenix has to go to the bathroom," he says.

I say okay, and after Phoenix comes out of the bedroom, I go to close the door behind him, but Ash resists, pleading, "We have to stay together!"

Okay, I say, everyone into the bathroom! When everyone is in, I start to close the bathroom door. The kids scream. I open the door back up. They are scared, they say. I explain again the logic behind closing the door. Suddenly, they remember it is a good idea and abruptly swing the door shut in my face. A few minutes later, they scamper back into their bedroom.

"Close the door!" Phoenix yells.

Skywalker chases the bat into the sunroom and pounces on it. The two tumble underneath the couch, hissing and screeching. A few minutes later, Skywalker walks out with the bat in his mouth. He drops it in the center of the living room and licks his paws.

I scoop the bat between two paper plates and go to tell the kids the news.

"Skywalker is the hero!" I say, holding the paper plates tightly closed. "He killed the bat!"

"Skywalker's the hero!" Phoenix says.

"Skywalker's the hero!" Lily repeats.

Ash shakes his head. "His mom and dad are going to be really sad," he says solemnly.

I am sitting on the back porch again when Piper gets home. She laughs as I recount my night. "It's like that movie *Adventures in Babysitting*," she says, tears rolling down her cheeks.

It occurs to me during the chaos of the night and in the boisterous retelling of it that for the first time in a long time, I am happy. I was a career woman, like my mom and sisters, and proud of that. But I'd always dreamed of getting married to someone who felt like a true love, too, of having kids and notching their height into the wall with each passing year. To create a home life where there were snack times and bedtimes and funny surprises like a bat dive-bombing my head while I pour cups of juice. It felt good to reconnect to that vision. Maybe I wasn't so different than the salmon, I thought, pulled back to the place where I got my start by some invisible force.

Piper tells me she negotiated a deal to buy Allegheny Outfitters. Half the money up front, the other half at the end of the first season. It is another leap of faith.

"Screw it," she says. "Sometimes you just have to go for it."

***

I had this idea when I booked my trip home that I would look up Leonard, an old friend, and maybe we'd fall in love.

It was stupid, crazy: we hadn't seen each other in a decade.

Just as I had gone to high school in one place, so had Piper: she'd moved back to rural Pennsylvania with Mom. Leonard was one of her close friends. We'd hang out when I came home to visit. I never forgot how special he made me feel when I walked into a room, like I was the most beautiful thing he'd ever seen. He knew my mom and sisters and this place. That shared history was so rare and special to me, I thought, maybe it could work.

Leonard grew up on his dad's forty-five-acre farm not far from some of Mom's apartments. His mom left when he was a young boy. As a kid he spent a lot of time alone in the woods, hunting, riding his dirt bike, and playing in a creek that ran through his dad's property. I knew he had been through some tough things in his life, and come out the other side a good person. He worked in the oil fields and spent countless hours in and under vehicles and equipment of every shape and size. Piper looked him up as soon as she moved back and bought the canoe business. "He is the realest person I know," Piper tells me when I ask how he's doing.

Leonard is on the phone the night I get back to my sister's house from the War College. Piper has called him. I feel spacey from driving five hours as she hands me the phone. I am dying to talk to him, but now

I don't know what to say. Ten years is a long time. Piper hands me the phone. "Leonard?"

"Hi, gorgeous," he says coolly. My heart beats faster. I sit down on the hideaway bed in the sunroom and look out the window at the river.

We talk for a few minutes. He spends his days riding a four-wheeler alone through the woods checking oil wells. His spare time is devoted to his dirt-track racecar. It's expensive, but something he's wanted to do since he was a kid and saw his dad racing. It keeps him out of trouble, he says. I smile. Even as a teenager, Leonard was a good mechanic, the person friends would turn to when something wouldn't start. I tell Leonard he should take me to the races while I'm home.

"I never stopped thinking about you," he says before we get off the phone.

I know he means it.

A week goes by, then another. Leonard never calls. I realize I never told him how I felt. It is hard for me to trust him with my feelings. What if he rejects me? I finally find the courage to call him. I realize the reason he's been avoiding me is not because he doesn't like me, but because he does.

"Do you have a minute?" I say.

"Yeah, I have a minute."

"Well . . . um . . . you only live once so I'm just going to say it. The whole reason I came home as long as I did was to see you. I like you in the way that . . . um, um —"

"Say it."

"That when you tell me 'Hi gorgeous,' it makes me dizzy."

Leonard lets out a quiet moan. "Do you know how goddamn happy that makes me?"

I ask him to please spend some time with me before I leave.

"Then what, I fall in love with you, and you move back to Alaska?"

"I don't have to stay in Alaska," I say.

"No, you don't."

Another silence. I am sitting outside on the stone steps near the water. I pick up a pebble and toss it into the river. He asks me to come see him tomorrow on his lunch break so we can talk. Just before he hangs up, he says, "Are you smiling? Because when you smile, I smile. You smiling?"

"Yes."

"Good."

I meet him at Washington Park, a city-owned picnic area high on a hill overlooking downtown Warren. The woods around the park are crisscrossed with trails. Throughout them are oil well jacks that pump up and down. It is in the mid-nineties and muggy, one of the hottest days of the summer. I wait in the shade under a towering oak tree. I hear the four-wheeler before I see it. Leonard whips around a corner, throwing a few pebbles as he pulls into the empty parking lot. A person who grew up in wide open spaces.

He is dressed in a dirty white t-shirt and blue jeans that hang on his thin muscular frame. He is taller than me now and his brown hair is cut short. His face is still cute in the boyish way I remembered, but his eyes are older.

I walk over and give him a hug. He holds me close.

"How are you doing?" he asks softly.

He knows I'm a wreck. I heard Piper telling him about my breakdown over the phone.

He swings a leg over the seat and starts it back up. "Get on," he says, and I do. I'm wearing jeans and a white top. I wrap my arms around his waist, and he drives us into the woods where it is cooler and shuts off the engine. He climbs off, walks to the front of the four-wheeler, and faces me. He looks up at me and then down at his feet. He kicks the left front wheel lightly with his boot and then looks back up.

"So, talk," he says.

These two little words undo me. Have I ever heard anything so perfectly straightforward? I sit on the four-wheeler, speechless and embarrassed. I smile, not knowing what else to do. I'm a complete coward. *Tell him you've been thinking about him nonstop! That you wish he'd take a chance on you like you're willing to take on him!*

Leonard seems annoyed. He asks me about my job, my travels.

"What do you want with a guy like me?" he asks finally. He lifts his arms and turns in a circle so I can get a good look at him. His pants and shirt have oil stains on them.

"I've never been away from here, you know that."

I do know. He loves rural Pennsylvania, has never wanted to live anywhere else. I might be from here, but I don't know the landscape anymore. He's as much of this place as the rocks and trees.

I tell him I like him just the way he is. He softens.

"I clean up a lot better than this," he says.

He tells me that if we are together, he will take care of me. I know it's true. Leonard can cut and weld metal, fell a tree, raise an animal, harvest a deer, dig a well, fix just about anything. He has more common sense than I ever will. Society seems not to value these skills much anymore. But I do.

"You and your sisters were always so smart and hardworking and just good people," he says. "I always loved that about you."

I ask him what he wants in life. He looks right at me. "I want to be with someone who loves me as much as I love them and shows it."

This guy is fearless! He just says things, comes right out and says them! I smile. I don't know what to say or how to act. Was I in love with him already? My heart is racing.

I get off the four-wheeler and walk over to him. His hands are on the handlebars. I duck under his arms, stand up inside them, and kiss his lips.

"You have no idea how long I have wanted to do that," he says and pulls me close. He smiles, takes a step back, and shakes his head. I've always loved his smile. He wipes some grease off my elbow and swats away a mosquito that lands on my arm.

CHAPTER 6

STARTING OVER

Back in Alaska, Leonard and I date on the phone for four months and then I put in my notice at the newspaper, shrink-wrap my belongings on a pallet, and ship them across the country to Pennsylvania. Colleagues at the paper make me a front page with fake stories about me as a going away gift, and I cry as I walk out of the newsroom for the last time.

It is late December when I fly back home, for good this time. I have some money saved, and my plan is to decompress and help Piper with her business while I figure out what to do next.

It is Piper's first winter owning a seasonal business, and it is a lot harder than she thought it would be. The money the company made over the summer all went to expenses, and now there is a ton of work to do to better position things for next year, but no money coming in to support her and her family while she tackles it. Bill collectors are calling, there's little money for groceries, and my sister has been wearing the same pair of disposable contacts for six months because she doesn't have the money for a new pair. Piper is finishing her master's degree in professional aeronautics online through the GI Bill, and that brings in some income. She starts selling off her record collection on eBay to make ends meet.

"I don't know how Mom did this, for like twenty freakin' years," Piper says one day, crying.

It is a brutal February. Piper's pipes freeze. Huge ice jams form on the Allegheny River and back up onto her lawn, nearly crushing her fleet of canoes.

At the first sign of decent weather, Piper and I plan for a ten-mile run through downtown. Piper is in a bad mood when she picks me up. She says nothing, won't look at me. I try to ignore it, thinking she'll snap out of it once her blood gets pumping. A light drizzle falls as we drive to Perkins, our starting point on the west side of town. On the way, Piper says she wishes I hadn't come; she wants to run alone.

"Why the hell didn't you tell me that earlier?" I ask. I tell her to run as fast as she wants. Secretly, I vow to keep up.

At Perkins, Piper gets out, turns on her iPod, and takes off down the block at what looks like my 400-meter pace. She hangs a right onto Pennsylvania Avenue and heads for downtown Warren, her legs pumping fast.

I take off after her, gasping for air as my feet pound the wet sidewalk. *She can't keep this pace*, I think. I am wrong. She runs over the railroad tracks and along the Allegheny River. I lose sight of her near "The Point," the town's landmark flatiron building with a steeple clock on it.

I slow to a jog and smile. What was I thinking? Had I forgotten she was once a cross-country star? How hard times could fuel a person?

Up ahead, a statue of General Joseph Warren, the Revolutionary War hero the town is named after, marks the entrance to Third Avenue. I turn down the road and head toward Market Street to cut Piper off.

I pass the old stone church, where my grandfather's funeral was held long ago, and the Struthers Library Theatre, one of America's oldest theatrical venues, which my grandma used to clean.

I spot Piper under the bare oak and maple trees along Market Street. I run faster. Finally, at the three-mile mark, she stops and lets me catch up. She is red-faced and winded. She clasps her hands on top of her head and looks at me.

"I'm sorry," she says. "I just had to get that out of my system. Running is all I have right now to keep me sane. I'm sorry for being a jerk. You kept up pretty good."

"I cheated," I confess, equally winded.

We walk and talk about the feast-or-famine nature of a seasonal outfitting business.

"We will never go through this again, ever," Piper says as we pick the pace back up. "I'll get a job with the FAA and move if I have to."

Piper sees a lot of ways to grow her business. This winter we are working on one of them: a river guidebook. All through her first season, customers asked for a guidebook. Piper figured one existed, the

Allegheny being a National Wild and Scenic River and all, but when she investigated, all she found was a brochure map of the river published by the PA Fish and Boat Commission, and the *Allegheny Pilot*, a fascinating map book from 1855 geared toward helping people in the region's early timber industry move lumber rafts down the Allegheny.

We start reporting the guidebook that summer, setting out from Kinzua Dam one sunny weekday in our kayaks with notebooks and camping gear. It is one hundred ninety-six miles from Kinzua Dam to Pittsburgh via the Allegheny; our goal is to document the upper forty-five miles for the book, including the river's seven federally protected Allegheny Islands Wilderness.

One day we paddle for seven hours. Piper had done scores of trips like this over the last year, solo and with her family, to learn the river, but this is a first for me. My arms ache, and my butt is numb when we finally reach Crull's Island, a ninety-six-acre wilderness island with a jungle-like forest, to camp. Piper eyes a gravel bar with a path she knew well, and we pull in. The path leads to a fire ring and a flat, cleared area. We set up our tent, build a fire, and then devour sandwiches we'd picked up earlier that day in Warren.

It turns dark quickly. The tree canopy is high and throughout the night, after the fog moves in, water condenses on the leaves and drips, sounding like it's raining when really it isn't. Pennsylvania's forests have their own weather system, similar to how mountains in Alaska do, I think. My mind wanders to small bush planes I'd flown in over the years in Alaska and how intimate the experience was, flying so close to the mountains. I remember more than once looking out the window and wondering if a human foot had ever touched the earth below. I also wonder what I'd do if I got stuck out there. Probably die.

In the morning, we drink coffee and wait in silence on the riverbank as the fog moves downstream. By the time we get to our pickup point, farther downriver, I am sunburned, thirsty, hungry, and relaxed. There is something beautiful about the accessibility of the wilderness in rural Pennsylvania that I had not considered until now. My time in Alaska made me think that somehow a 500,000-acre National Forest wasn't really wilderness because it had logging roads and towns nearby. How arrogant and wrong I'd been. It was amazing what an overnight trip on the river could do for a person. I felt restored.

From that trip, the guidebook took shape. It would be slim, for easy pocket storage, and waterproof, each page encapsulated in a five-mil lamination. There would be an introduction section with river history, safety information, paddling terms, vessel diagrams, and maps showing where paddlers could find hiking trails, camping spots, historical sites, and other major landmarks, which included oil refineries, factories, and towns, which were also part of the area's unique history and the river experience.

This "Pennsylvania Wilds" thing was sparking a lot of new conversations about nature tourism. Piper was getting excited about what the guidebook could do for the area, despite some people giving her the brushoff.

"All these tourist meetings I've been going to, some of these people just don't see the river as anything special," she tells me one day. "Wait till you get on the river again this summer. There's all this cool stuff. There's this pile of rocks in the water and it looks like a person put them there, but they're fish houses. Fish push all these rocks into a huge pile to lay their eggs in them."

Piper took a few graphic design classes at a tech school in Pittsburgh before joining the Navy, so while we wait for the weather to break to finish our reporting, she starts laying out the book. Her computer is hooked up in her uninsulated sunroom, the only space in her tiny house where she can work uninterrupted. It is 19 degrees out. Piper puts on her Navy foul weather jacket and gets to work. A few hours later, she emails me a picture of the book's cover.

Leonard and I are living in a small brick house in Warren. I am making soup when Piper calls to tell me to check my inbox. I'm anxious. My sister has a hippie design style, she likes peace signs, flowers, and smiley faces.

I sit down at my computer and open the attachment. Piper has changed the name to *Allegheny River Paddling Guide*. The title is framed between two paddles at the top of the page. Below the title is a single picture of a kayak on the river. It is a simple design, not too slick but not amateurish, either.

"It looks so . . . *professional*," I say.

"Really? Thanks!" she says.

Piper vows to get cracking on the rest of the pages. April 1, opening day, is just a few weeks away. In addition to the paddling guide, Piper has overhauled and relaunched her websites. Already reservations are piling up. Just that day, a Boy Scout leader booked a trip for sixty boys; they planned to camp on Piper's lawn the night before their trip began.

"It's going to be absolute chaos around here," Piper laughs.

Piper joins the board of the local visitor bureau whose mission is to promote the county. The organization has retained a consultant to look at how to grow place-based tourism. An earlier study had found that the area had some incredible natural and cultural assets, and great opportunities to increase tourism through the Pennsylvania Wilds Initiative and other regional efforts.[1] It also said the industry was not flourishing because of a "self-limiting cycle of weakness" that includes "a frontier spirit of individualism that has never been focused on sharing the qualities of the place with visitors" and a "lack of entrepreneurial businesses and a business culture to support them." It concluded that however much potential there is, ". . . it will not grow readily in the cultural soil of the county," unless changes are made.

Meetings with the public are now underway to establish a new direction. Many businesses and organizations in the county participate. At one, the facilitator asks people what the county's greatest asset is.

"It's our golf courses," someone from the visitor bureau says.

Piper is annoyed. Golfers stay at the hotels, which fund the visitor bureau through hotel taxes. "Don't get me wrong," Piper explains to me later, when I ask how the meeting went, "we have some really nice golf courses. But come on, we are the gateway to Pennsylvania's only national forest. We have the National Wild and Scenic Allegheny River running through an incredible historic downtown. We have endangered species, bald eagles."

The facilitator asks about some of these natural assets.

"Who would ever come here to canoe the Allegheny River on purpose?" says a man at the table.

The facilitator looks at Piper, who shares that she just bought Allegheny Outfitters, and that people *are* coming to Warren to paddle the river and spend time outdoors. Piper is the youngest person in the room. She hears chuckles. It hurts her feelings.

---

1. The State of the County: Tourism & Character of Place in Warren County PA, August 2006.

"Everyone just looked at me like I was inexperienced," she tells me. "That I would settle into the fact that Warren is what it is. I think part of the issue was a lot of people had never paddled the Allegheny before. They had never been out there."

Not everyone thinks she's wrong. A county commissioner and the director of the local chamber tell her they appreciate her vision, and the next day, the county planning director makes the twenty-six-mile round trip drive out to her house to make sure she didn't take the meeting too hard.

"He told me, 'You are a real firecracker. You are doing a great job. You just keep doing what you are doing.' It meant a lot to me that he took the time," Piper tells me.

A few months after I move home, Piper invites me to a local tourism meeting. She's encountered so much negativity and gossip volunteering at the local visitor bureau she is thinking about quitting the board. Piper is coaching basketball at one of the local high schools and picks me up after practice. We arrive at the Warren library and head upstairs to the Slater Room. It is still surreal to me that I am here, in the library I loved as a kid.

About twenty-five people sit in rows of chairs. Piper and I take seats in the back. The head of the chamber wears a black suit and red tie and addresses the group. He tells everyone there is going to be a three-week period this summer when several events—a national canoe race, a popular bike race, and the county fair—will bring thousands of visitors to the area. The goal of this meeting is to find ways to help local businesses take advantage of the influx, he says.

Next, a woman with long brown hair and wearing a tan pantsuit with a blue button-down shirt stands in front of the crowd. She says she came to Warren County more than two decades ago for a job. She says she'd been living in Manhattan at the time. The switch from big city to rural Pennsylvania was a real shock.

"I felt I had been invited to another planet," she says, drawing laughter. Piper and I look at each other. We like this lady.

The woman says it took some time to fall in love with Warren County because many of the great things about living here—the Allegheny National Forest, the river and reservoir, the festivals, and outdoor events—weren't really promoted. One recent tourism report went so far as to say there's "no entrepreneurial spirit" in Warren, she says.

Piper leans over and whispers, "That's why everything I say gets beat down."

The woman continues, "So, when I read these tourism reports and hear from these tourists who say they can't find all the wonderful stuff that Warren has to offer, I can relate, but I know all the wonderful stuff Warren has to offer, which is why I'm giving this presentation."

She wants to make a list of all the interesting things going on this summer and brainstorm ways the group might market them to this influx of visitors. People suggest doing surveys, handing out maps and calendars. A man asks where people should send calendar listings, and the visitor bureau chief gets defensive and says they have an events calendar. I'm not sure that will help. The visitor bureau's website at the time was a hodgepodge of clip art, random boxes, white space, and more than eighteen different fonts in purple and black text. Piper has tried for months to get the board to upgrade it, even offering to build a new site for free, but has made little progress.

Piper pushes her notebook toward me and scribbles, "HERE IT COMES." She sits back and crosses her arms. People start squabbling over calendar listings.

The meeting adjourns and Piper and I head to the parking lot.

"I need a vacation, and the season hasn't even started yet," Piper says as she climbs into her vehicle. I tell her I didn't think the meeting went all that badly.

"Wait till you go to a bunch of these. You just get so tired of it," she says. "People get afraid of new ideas, of change. They can't see past their old beefs. I should stop coming. It just sucks the life right out of you. And I'm sacrificing time with my kids for this."

There is weariness in her voice. I am down when I get home. Between the meeting, another person calling Piper's business "an experiment," and Leonard telling me he hopes our dreams come true considering how hard we are trying, it all suddenly feels like: Maybe people are right. Maybe it can't work.

In the morning, I call Piper and confess that the meeting got me down too. Trying something new is a balancing act, we agree. You have to stay open to constructive criticism, but a big part of you is operating on faith, so you have to limit your exposure to people that make you doubt yourself or your idea. Piper tells me about a documentary she watched on TV about a famous entrepreneur.

"I started watching it and he's like 'I didn't have a chair to sit in,'" Piper says. "And that's when I realized: Things don't happen overnight. They just don't. We've got to be in it for the long haul. That's how people get to where they're at. They figure out what's got to change, and they do it."

CHAPTER 7

BUILDING OUTDOORS

By mid-March 2007, it looks like spring is finally on its way. Snow still covers the ground, but the days are getting longer, and the sun is warm enough to heat the inside of my car. Piper calls me on her cell phone as she takes her oldest boy to kindergarten.

"I'm driving to Youngsville, and you know what I saw?" she asks, sounding excited. "Two vehicles with canoes strapped to them! It's beginning!"

The next day the temperature plummets, and by evening, huge snowflakes fall across the countryside. It snows all day the following day too. And the next. Any hope of an early April opener disappears.

Piper and I are in intense paddling guide edits. It is a slow, sometimes agonizing process, especially for Piper. She is learning her design software as she goes and working in her unheated sunroom. Pages are written and designed and then tossed. Others work on the first try. One night, Piper posts a blurb on her website that says people can sign up to be notified when the *Allegheny River Paddling Guide* rolls off the presses. Within two hours, two people sign up. Others join them as the days go by, buoying our spirits.

Finally, on April 19, spring arrives. It is sunny and in the mid-fifties. Piper takes her kids scouting for trails we needed to locate before we felt comfortable including them in the guide. She finds the Tanbark Trail, which follows an abandoned logging route for eight miles, and Anders Run, a flatter, shorter trail that winds through some of the very few old-growth white pine and eastern hemlock remaining in Pennsylvania. Some of the trees are believed to be around 400 years old.

Texting doesn't exist yet, so Piper emails me pictures of water running over moss-covered rocks on the Tanbark Trail. "IT WAS AWESOME!" the email says. She leaves me a telephone message after they find Anders Run. "We are victorious!" it says.

The next day, Piper and I set out to paddle the last stretch of river for the *Paddling Guide*. I drive to my sister's house around 5:30 a.m. in thick fog. Four whitetail deer jump across the road in front of me on the way. Finally, her sign comes into view. I slow and turn down the driveway. A long white passenger van is idling in the yard. Inside, two kayaks are balanced across the top of the seats, not the usual way of transporting them, but good enough for today.

I walk up the front steps. Piper is in the kitchen packing a dry bag and waves to me through the window in the door. I walk in. We whisper hellos so as not to wake the kids. Piper motions out the kitchen window and smiles. "God it's good to see that van running," she says.

Piper drives the van. I follow her in my car. Our starting point, the George Jones Memorial Park, is five miles away, in Tidioute, a picturesque village of about 800. We cross the town's old iron span bridge and make our way to the boat launch. I can't stop grinning as we unload the kayaks. Piper laughs when she sees my expression. "I know!" she says, "Just the smell of the van with this kayak next to my head and I was like 'Yes! Summer's here!'"

We leave the kayaks in the grass and drive the two vehicles to Tionesta, a larger riverside town about fifteen miles south. Tionesta is our end point for the trip and the *Allegheny River Paddling Guide*. We leave the van at a boat launch there and drive back to Tidioute in my car. It is still foggy when we arrive. We walk over to the water. It is high, too high to send customers out. At Piper's, the water covered all but the top step. It seems too risky to paddle in water that fast without better visuals, so we walk into town to grab some breakfast and wait for the fog to pass.

Piper suggests we eat at Montana Pat's, a gas station and convenience store that doubles as a restaurant and fitness center. It is the sort of quirky amalgamation one finds in tiny towns in rural PA. Fit as a Fiddle, the fitness center, is in a side room off the gas station and restaurant; a spunky middle-aged woman who owns all four of the enterprises insists on giving us a tour while we wait for our eggs.

After breakfast, we walk back to the park and I scribble a few notes in my notebook about the basketball courts, picnic tables, and other amenities. It is around 9 a.m. when we slide our long yellow kayaks into the swift, muddy water. The forecast calls for temps in the 60s but for now it is still chilly. I am wearing pants, gloves, two shirts, a lifejacket, and a windbreaker.

We sail under the iron span bridge and past the Trading Post convenience store. Next, we see a house perched high on a steep left bank of the river. A large handmade sign on it reads "Pie on the Porch." A trail leads down to the water. We'd later learn a woman owns the bakery (which doubles as her home and a greenhouse); if customers call ahead of time, she'll make them a pie and let them eat it on her porch. It is just the sort of amenity we want to tell paddlers about.

Farther downriver, Piper snaps a picture of a riverside sign for Tippy Canoe Inn, a bar and restaurant. Then we are out of Tidioute and for long stretches see nothing but trees, rocks, and grass. By the time the sun comes out, we are both shedding layers. Piper rolls up her pants, props her legs on the front of her kayak, and leans back in her seat. We talk about family and how exciting it is to be trying something new. Piper says it is interesting how all three of us sisters have always been driven. We didn't have a lot of choice. Who would be there if we failed? You always must have a backup plan, Piper says. Hers is still the FAA. They'd recently offered her a position in Antarctica. It was good money, but Piper found it so extreme as to be comical.

"I feel like I'm on *Bill & Ted's Excellent Adventure*," she says, and then breaks into her best surfer voice, "'Dude! We've got to get the business going so I don't have to go to Antarctica!'"

We pass six more Wilderness Islands, all smaller than Crull's Island, where we had camped the previous season on our first river reporting trip. I make notes about the Hall Barn, an old wooden structure the U.S. Forest Service turned into a bat maternity ward. According to interpretive panels, some 1,000 female bats take refuge in the barn each year to give birth. Boaters can't see the barn from the river, the trees and brush are too thick, but anyone paddling around dusk is likely to spy a stream of bats overhead as they leave the barn through a single open window in search of food.

With the water so swift, the five-hour trip to Tionesta only takes three hours. We pull into the town's public boat launch around noon. Nearby is a blue seventy-five-foot-tall lighthouse. A local businessman built it to honor his community and family. Inside, it is decorated with photos and quotes.

"If you enjoy what you do you don't have to work a day in your life," one reads.

Back home, Piper and I slog through round after round of edits. Piper has photographed wildlife along the river all year—snapping turtles, muskrats, eagles, blue herons, water snakes—and we are trying to figure out how to make everything fit.

By late April, people are calling Piper's house asking for the guide so they can plan their summer paddling trip. We finally ship the book to be printed. A few weeks later, we drive to Erie together to pick it up. We are smiling our faces off.

"I can't believe it!" Piper says, holding a copy in her hand. "We did it! It's finally here!"

When the customer faucet turns back on, it is like a fire hydrant. I've helped Piper with strategy and tactical writing projects, but it is Piper's love for the outdoors and excitement about connecting people to nature that drives her business growth. Her passion comes through in her pictures, in how seriously she studies the river, forest and local wildlife, and in the hours she spends on the phone helping people plan trips.

This is Piper's first season with two locations. My job is to run Allegheny Outfitters, which at the time consists of a shack next to the river, a few beat up old vans, and a stack of patched canoes. The place is a powerhouse of activity, but the equipment is in rough shape, and I am not easy on it. The door falls off Big Red, one of our passenger vans, one day while I'm trying to load gear to shuttle paddlers up to Kinzua Dam. I blow a wheel bearing in another van, run out of gas once, and forget to latch a bungee cord on the top rung of a canoe trailer and nearly lose a boat turning into the parking lot at Kinzua Dam. At one point, a van overheats. I call Leonard to ask what to do.

"Do not drive it," he says.

It's a busy Saturday and I have one more run left, so I take that as, "after this one last run, don't drive it."

I fry the engine. An entire fifteen-passenger van, gone.

I work for minimum wage in muggy, sunny ninety-degree heat and in between runs, read an accounting book with a cartoon picture of a lemonade stand on the front of it, trying to remember from the accounting classes I took in college what a profit and loss statement is and why it matters and how I could possibly piece one together from the metal cashbox we use to check in customers. Half our canoe fleet sits in an area we designate "sick bay," and each day, the pile grows bigger.

One July morning, I unlock the shack and hit play on the answering machine. "I'm calling to complain about service," a woman says. "There was a hole in my canoe the other day and I'm very upset about this. I'm rating your service as questionable at best."

Piper reinvests everything she makes into improving the business and its systems and equipment. I'm in awe at how genuine she is with her customers, even when money is on the line. She puts safety ahead of profits, always. In day-to-day operations, if something is the company's fault, she tries to make it right. If it isn't, she holds her ground. More than once, she blacklists local clubs for bad behavior. I think, *this isn't something you do in a small town!* But in almost every case, someone from the group calls a week later, apologizes for being drunk and rude, and makes amends. Another time, while Piper is checking people in, a customer chucks an empty pop can in the river. Without hesitation, Piper drops her clipboard and wades into the river and grabs it.

"We do not throw trash in our rivers," she tells the person as she climbs back up the bank, her pants soaking wet. She picks up her clipboard and walks off toward a recycling bin. My hero.

And then one day, I am walking across Piper's living room, carrying a stack of accounting papers, when I hear someone talking on the TV about how rural Pennsylvania needs to stop chasing smokestacks and invest in what differentiates it from other places: its unique locally-owned businesses, public lands, cultural and recreation amenities, and small-town charm.

It is such a fresh perspective; I stop to listen. Growing up here, the message many in my generation heard was "get out, save yourself, there is no future here." I flip over one of the papers in my hand and start scribbling notes.

"We have 25,000 incorporated communities in the United States, and they are all in competition for jobs, people, and investment," the man on TV says. "Why does place matter in the world we live in today? Because in a world where capital is footloose, if you can't differentiate your place from others, you will have no competitive advantage."

"Are you hearing this? Who is this guy?" I ask Piper.

"That's the PA Wilds," she says.

CHAPTER 8

WHAT HAVE I DONE

When I was in my early twenties, I met one of *National Geographic's* legendary whale photographers when he came to speak at the University of Alaska, and I interviewed him for the campus paper. I told him if he ever needed an extra hand to swab decks or carry gear, I'd gladly do it for a chance to go on a reporting trip with *National Geographic*.

Unexpectedly, the photographer called some months later and said he had an opening to join him and a well-known wildlife writer as they shadowed a team of researchers studying humpbacks in Southeast Alaska. I was ecstatic. I'd loved the magazine since I was a kid, leafing through it with my mom's dad, a World War II veteran we all called Grumpy.

On the boat in Southeast Alaska, we'd go long stretches without seeing any whales, and then the humpbacks would appear, and everyone on the boat would swing into exciting action.

This is how the PA Wilds Initiative felt to me as I helped my sister build her outfitting business. It was this unique, special thing we knew was out there, but there'd be long stretches when we didn't hear anything about it. And then suddenly it would blast out of the water with a double breach that wowed and inspired us and helped keep us going. Then it would disappear again.

The man I heard talking on the television at Piper's house, an international expert on sustainable community development named Ed McMahon[1], was one of those sightings. Little did I know that four hours away, McMahon was a keynote speaker at one of the first summits for the fledgling PA Wilds Initiative.

---

1. Not the big check guy. The author of fifteen books, McMahon was a Senior Fellow at the Urban Land Institute in Washington, D.C., where he was nationally known as an inspiring and thought-provoking speaker and a leading authority on topics such as the links between health and the built environment, sustainable development, land conservation, smart growth, and historic preservation.

Nor did I know that the *New York Times* had published a story that same day about how the Pennsylvania Wilds had some of the best opportunities to view the Milky Way in America because of its large, forested landscape and lack of light pollution.

Having a great view of the stars wasn't news to people who lived here, but the idea that outsiders would travel great distances to experience it was. One man at the conference, David Brooks, a visitor bureau director from one of the region's most rural counties who was helping to raise awareness locally about the economic potential of outdoor recreation, walked to a nearby grocery store and bought its entire stock of *New York Times* and brought them back to the conference.

"Everybody was just thrilled to get that kind of exposure," Brooks would explain to me years later. "To buy that type of space in the *New York Times* at the time was equal to four years of my annual budget. We did the math and column inches. When you put it in that perspective, that value, the prestige that goes with the *New York Times* as well, it added a lot of credibility to the idea. It really sold people that it was legit, and it worked with the outside world."

I was also completely unaware that in other parts of the region, locals were already pushing back against the state's aggressive marketing of the Pennsylvania Wilds as an outdoor recreation destination out of concern that the region's economically distressed rural communities needed more time and resources to prepare for thousands of new visitors.

From my field-level view in Warren, what I do know is that my sister's business is growing. Allegheny Outfitters has gone from serving 1,200 paddlers a season to more than 10,000. Piper launches an annual weeklong river cleanup that brings out hundreds of volunteers and removes tons of garbage from the Allegheny and its tributaries. Like-minded people and organizations start rallying around her with their own ideas. What about a mountain bike course on the National Forest? A brewery? A bike shop?

As a crime reporter, I learned about the "broken window syndrome," the idea that if you don't respond to small acts of vandalism in a community, it sends a message that no one cares and can lead to more not caring. Before long, the whole place can go to pot. But the reverse can also happen. Success can breed success.

Watching my sister and seeing how contagious the entrepreneurial spirit is, and how the PA Wilds work is sparking new conversations, gives me hope. *This is how a rural place can make a comeback*, I think, *with one small win*. And then another, and another.

I work at Allegheny Outfitters during the day and help Leonard with his racecar at night, learning the difference between a ratchet and a wrench by fetching him tools while he's under the car.

Leonard's garage is on a one-acre lot in the country next to a dairy farm. He and his dad bought the property before I moved home. At the time, the building was missing part of its roof with a wall caving in. Leonard was bringing it back cement block by cement block.

My Alaska family had introduced me to muscle cars and dirt bikes, but auto racing was not a sport I followed. At first, I had found it puzzling. A bunch of cars going in circles? But after a few races I start to appreciate the variables that go into setting up a dirt track car for success under different track conditions, the skills and confidence it takes to drive dozens of laps at high speed with big horsepower, the dedication and sacrifice it takes to run a competitive race team, and the rich history of auto racing in America. A lot of people followed NASCAR, but to me, dirt was where it was at. The gritty roots of racing, it was still accessible to a blue collar worker driven enough to try; but also where, on certain nights, such as bigger money races that drew in national talent, local drivers who made the show had a chance to test themselves against the sport's top competitors. It was rare to find articles about dirt track racing in national mainstream media in the early days of Leonard's racing, but a few years in I ran across one, "The Beauty of Dirt-Track Racing," from Dan Neil, an auto columnist for the *Wall Street Journal*. "There are these perfect moments of perception you get at a dirt track late at night," Neil wrote from Fayetteville Motor Speedway in North Carolina, reminding me of the many nights I watched Leonard race. "(A)s dark as a theater, clouds of red dust boiling through the feeble lighting, the cars bawling, chain-sawing ass-ways at 100 mph around the rim of a dirt-clay saucer, the announcer's patter . . . This is totally the best way to spend Saturday night in the U-S-of-A."

Incredibly, we lived only a few miles from Stateline Speedway, a storied one-third mile clay semi-banked oval track that opened in 1956. The track had a rich history and had helped to cultivate national racing talent like Chub Frank (Chubzilla), Max Blair, and local legends like Dick Barton.[2] Over the years it had hosted Lucas Oil and World of Outlaws late model events. Dale Earnhardt Sr. even came to the track once.

We spent most Saturdays at Stateline, first in a cadet car, then in an open class E-mod. Up in the stands I would hold my breath as the cars bunched up for the start. The flagman would throw the green and the drivers would race wide open down the straightaway, chucking their cars sideways into the turns for twenty-four wild laps. Leonard's crew chief and best friend, whose nickname was Snoopy, watched from behind the pit fence, ready to change a flat tire or load up the car if it got wrecked. Auto racing is wildly expensive, and we had to race with our wallet between Leonard's foot and the gas pedal. But on the nights it all came together, it was like poetry in motion. The car connected to the track, nothing broke, Leonard wove through all the wrecks, and we were a top finisher.

Leonard leaves the oil field to work at his uncle's feed mill and we move into a beat-up trailer behind his race garage to save for the summer and continue fixing up the building. I help paint the garage walls and put insulation on the ceiling.

Leonard proposes to me under an apple tree in his dad's pasture. I am happier than I've ever been. We start trying to have kids right away given that I am thirty-two, and before long, I am pregnant with a boy.

I am in love, excited to be a mom, and super proud of what Piper and I have accomplished. I am also beginning to panic about my decision to quit journalism. My savings are running out, and it is clear that at this stage, Allegheny Outfitters can support one family, not two. I scour the classifieds daily. Nothing I see feels remotely like a fit.

I admired people who could clock in, apply their talents, and when work was done for the day, it was done. They could let it go. All my years of moving, of not owning a television, of writing and asking questions, of witnessing human tragedy and triumph so close, so repeatedly, of respecting authority but also questioning it, had hardwired me in a different way.

---

2. Find the track online at StatelineSpeedway.com. The track has had a few owners over the years, but as the newest one, Bill Catania, acknowledged to a group of drivers at a meeting in 2025, "You can own the dirt, but no one can own the legacy." Learn more about the track's history at StatelineLegacy.org.

"Defective" is how I sometimes thought about it. Other times I am kinder to myself and go with "passionate." I find work I care about, and I do it with everything I have. My work has always been more of a lifestyle than a job. I know whatever I do next, I need to set better boundaries, but the 9-to-5 openings I see in the classifieds feel extreme. Suffocating.

I have no professional network here. I didn't think through the consequences of that when I yanked up my roots in Alaska and moved home. In Anchorage, I could have walked into any interview and the starting point would have been, "So you're Ta from the *Daily News*." There would have been some frame of reference about me as a professional because of the visibility of my work. I would have heard about interesting job openings through the professional grapevine and been able to ask colleagues to make introductions.

I envisioned myself at an interview here and the person trying to make sense of my story. "So, you ditched your career to move home to rural PA to work for minimum wage for your sister at a seasonal business where the doors are falling off the vans, and now you're pregnant, unwed, unemployed, and camping in a trailer with no heat or kitchen?"

That wasn't my story, of course, but I could see how it might come across that way. I thought of my years writing stories and wondered if I ever got one that wrong.

All summer and fall, Leonard and I save to buy the house next to his garage. When it doesn't look like the deal will go through, we sell the old trailer we've been camping in for $500 to a local farmer. We buy a new trailer and park it in the same spot before winter sets in. It is the largest single-wide on the market, bright inside with a skylight window and an island in the kitchen and a big garden tub. As the snow starts to fall, we set up the baby room and next to it, an office for me. By March, I am nine months pregnant. Sandoz sends me her old maternity clothes in the mail. Leonard is working two jobs—the feed mill during the day and at a nearby race shop at night.

Days before I am supposed to go into labor, Piper calls to tell me about a job opening she heard about through the local visitor bureau. She forwards me the ten-page "Request for Proposals."

I waddle down the hall of my trailer to my office and print it out while Piper gives me the highlights: a place called the Pennsylvania Wilds

Tourism Marketing Corporation is looking for a contractor to be a "PA Wilds Small Business Ombudsman." The person will travel the Pennsylvania Wilds region working with rural entrepreneurs and small businesses, helping them understand how to leverage the PA Wilds Initiative and connect to resources.

"Are you serious?" I say.

After seeing Piper's business growth, and the way outsiders responded to the area's natural beauty and small-town charm when they came to paddle, I'm more convinced than ever that the concept of the PA Wilds is a good one, even if the implementation feels off. The effort needed more buy-in at the local level if it was going to make it. Most people in Warren that Piper and I talked to didn't know what it was or why it mattered, or they thought it was just another state thing that wouldn't last beyond the governor it was launched under. I wondered the same myself.

My gut tells me if they don't get a local in there with a real example of an outdoor recreation business working in a small rural town, the effort is going to die, making it harder for businesses like Piper's, and towns like Warren, to make a comeback.

"You have to apply," Piper says. "Can you imagine what will happen if they get the wrong person in there?"

The baby kicks, and I rub my hand across my big hard belly. The proposal is due in ten days. I'm due in three. I hang up with Piper, staple the proposal together, grab a pen, sit on the couch, and start reading.

"There are significant opportunities for citizens with entrepreneurial attitudes to start businesses that will bolster the local economies and provide products and services that will enable the region to capture more tourism dollars from the visitors that come to enjoy the natural beauty of the Pennsylvania Wilds," the proposal says.

Yes! I think, *There are!*

They want someone with a small business development background who is familiar with rural PA. Not exactly me but I could make a case for it. The document includes a long list of programs that exist to help entrepreneurs, most of which I've never heard of. "The relative complexity of the service provider network caused by the large geographic area of the Pennsylvania Wilds can make it a daunting task for an entrepreneur to find the appropriate service providers to serve their needs," it says.

I think of Piper's experience. How she saw the potential for growing an outfitting business along the National Wild & Scenic Allegheny River. About the thousands of new paddlers she's attracted to Warren over the last two years and how those visitors spent money at other businesses when they were here. How she'd created a paddling guide to intentionally pass her foot traffic to others, at no cost to them. She couldn't find financing to help her do any of what she had done. I thought of the struggles that caused, was still causing.

I call Piper back. "I have to do this," I say. "But I'm going to need your help."

I open a Word document on my computer. I've never been good at selling myself. I start writing in a way that feels fake and gimmicky and then delete it. *Just be real, Ta.* I start again. I share how I watched my community decline as I grew up, how I left rural PA, and never thought I'd return. How my sister moved home and bought an outfitting business and how I joined her. How inspired we both were by the PA Wilds concept and its focus on the outdoors, conservation, and growing local businesses. How we wrote the paddling guide. I share how Allegheny Outfitters' customer base had grown and how Piper's business had inspired others in our small town. I share her hardships.

"My sister's fleet of passenger vans needs replaced," I type. "Where will the money come from? She's not sure. And so far, in the rush of everything else, she hasn't had the time to explore what agencies might be able to help her, let alone make the long drive to visit them and start on the applications. I don't bring up her experience because I think it is unique. I bring it up because I'm pretty sure it's not."

I admit to knowing very little about all the grants, loans, and financial and technical assistance available to small businesses, but that I'm a quick study. I lay out how I'd tackle the first two years on the job and include a budget. I tell them I'd hire my sister in her off season as a contractor to help me build a website to be a clearing house for locals to better understand the Pennsylvania Wilds Initiative and connect to resources.

I write and edit until Leonard gets home, around midnight, and then fall asleep thinking about whom I can ask for a recommendation. My habit of never keeping in touch with people after I leave a place—a coping mechanism I learned growing up—is a professional hazard, I realize.

The next morning, I email the reporter from the *Daily News* I was closest to, who had since switched jobs to do internal communications for the company that maintains the 800-mile trans-Alaska pipeline. We chat on the phone. It is good to hear her voice. Outside of my sisters, work friends are the only kinds of friends I've ever had, and I miss having them. It was depressing not having any girlfriends around for my first baby shower. My friend happily agrees to write me a letter of recommendation. I am grateful.

I still need a letter from someone locally, but who? The only people I knew were family. My two uncles who live here, both veterans and self-described "river rats," were just as goofy as Grumpy had been, calling us different nonsense names each time we saw them. I imagine what their letter might say: *Listen here, you rascals, you should hire our niece, she is the best squirrel lobster ditch digger you ever met. She is a good goddam writer too and comes from good people.*

I remember Mom has a friend who is an attorney. I call and ask if she thinks he might write me a letter of recommendation. Turns out he is a prominent attorney, and a fan of our *Allegheny River Paddling Guide*. He agrees to meet me for lunch. We hit it off, and he writes me a letter.

I print five copies of everything and put the stack of papers in an envelope and mail them to the Marketing Corporation.

Six days later, I am sitting at my desk early in the morning, taking care of bills, when I feel the faintest flutter in my midsection. It is unlike anything I've felt before. I call my doctor's office, and they agree it is probably the start of contractions. The flutters grow stronger and by that night, they are blackout painful. Leonard takes me to the hospital around 11 p.m. Our son, Max, is born the next morning around 5 a.m. We take turns holding him in the hospital room. My mom, Leonard's dad and stepmom, and Piper visit and hold him too. From the minute he is born, it is like he has always been there, a part of our family. I adore him.

A few days after I get home from the hospital, I get an email that I am a finalist for the ombudsman position. They'd like me to come to the Capitol Complex in Harrisburg for an interview. I am excited and panicked.

Max is asleep in his car seat on the floor next to my desk as I read the email. I think about how tough it was for kids in my socio-economic class growing up in rural Pennsylvania. The trouble we found and the trouble that found us. How many people did I know who had lost their lives to drugs, alcohol, suicides, car accidents? So much sadness and self-destruction. I want the next generation to have more opportunities, more hope. Surely it was possible to build a rural economy that had more pathways to success, that was a little more inclusive? An economy that didn't send the message that if you want to succeed, you have to leave.

It sounded cliché, like something dark-humored reporters would make fun of in the newsroom, *we have to do it for the children!* But the Wilds' work seemed different to me, something that actually *could* make a difference. It had already reached and resonated with someone like my sister and inspired the hell out of her. To me that was power.

Getting involved in something like that would give me a chance to finally help build something. It felt purposeful, like journalism did to me.

I respond with some dates that will work for the interview, and then wonder how, tactically, I am going to pull it off with a nursing newborn. I hit send on the email and then sit down on the floor next to my son. I smell his head and kiss his cheek.

"We are going to figure this out, little buddy."

I had kept up my running routine until I was eight months pregnant, but with a newborn, none of my old work clothes fit so I drive to the Warren Mall to see if I can find something other than my best ratty sweatpants to wear to the interview.

The mall is depressing, with 1970s decor, broken doors, many empty, gated storefronts, and potholes in the parking lot big enough to swallow your car, and as I pull in, I wonder again how long the two anchors, Kmart and BonTon, can hold out.[3]

I get the stroller out of the trunk, snap the baby seat into it, and head into BonTon. The store is mostly empty. I find a light turquoise button-down shirt and a pair of black slacks and then head to the shoe department.

My blood sugar is up and down. I feel lightheaded and sweaty and dig in my purse for a nut bar. A salesclerk, an older lady, offers to help me. I wonder what she must think of me standing here with disheveled hair, on the verge of crying. I share that I am trying to find an outfit

---

[3]. Eight and ten years, it turned out. Both chains went bankrupt. The Kmart in Warren closed in 2016; BonTon in 2018.

for an interview in Harrisburg. I hold up the shirt and pants to get her take. She looks at the baby and back at me. "Don't worry," I say. "The actual job doesn't start for three months. I just need to get through this interview."

It is a five-and-a-half-hour drive to Harrisburg. As I learn to navigate my postpartum body, I often feel clumsy and emotional. I decide to go down the night before, so I am at my best for the interview. I am still trying to figure out nursing, and I don't own a breast pump, other than the free handheld one the nurses sent me home with in my bag of hospital goodies. I decide it will be easiest to take my son with me. I have an aunt and uncle who live just outside the capital. I call Mom and get their number and ask to stay at their house and if they can watch my newborn while I'm at the interview. They are happy to help. It dawns on me, not for the first time, how incredible it is to have a state capital connected by road (in Alaska, it is not), and to have extended family so close again.

Ordinary activities are a big deal when you have a fragile newborn. Leonard is worried about us driving south and has me call him at work at regular intervals to let him know we are okay. I make it to my relatives before nightfall and set up a portable crib in their living room. Max has started making funny screeching noises.

My uncle looks at him and smiles. "We are going to call you T-Rex," he says.

My aunt and uncle help me gauge how long it will take to get to the Capitol Complex in the morning with the traffic, and as I lay in bed, I calculate for the twentieth time how long I will have to make the drive and do the interview before my boobs start leaking. I think about the new moms I worked with over the years at the *Daily News*. I never understood this part of returning to the newsroom. It would have been tough with breaking news.

I sleep terribly. In the morning, I do all the math again. I wonder if they will have me sitting in a waiting room. I stuff extra nursing pads in my bra, feed the baby one last time, and tell my aunt and uncle goodbye. My son is maybe ten days old. It is the first time I've left him, and it feels unnerving.

"Good luck," my aunt Jean tells me. "You are going to do awesome. And don't worry about T-Rex. We will take good care of him."

The morning rush hour is over, but it has been so long since I've driven in a city that I white-knuckle it most of the way. I cross the Susquehanna Bridge, and before long, the Rotunda comes into view. I head toward the Capitol Complex, find a parking garage, and do a couple of loops inside. I find a spot, pull in, and turn off my car. I take a deep breath. *Made it.*

I grab my purse, lock my car, and walk out of the dark garage into the sunlight. I head toward a tall, square fortress on Fourth Street, the Keystone Building. I walk through the doors into a huge bright lobby. Everything about the place says power: concrete and marble floors, glass ceiling, stone pillars. A few people in business suits walk across the quiet, empty lobby.

I spot the elevators. My footsteps echo as I walk toward them. My ego warns me to turn back, that this will never work. Me, this job, rural PA making a comeback.

A feisty inner voice pushes back: *Be brave, Ta! Think of all the things you've done! You moved out at sixteen, put yourself through college. Who cares if it took a decade to get the four-year degree. You did it. Forged a reporting career. Traveled to eight countries on four continents. Your roots are in this region. Your family appreciates its beauty, has lived its hard times. The Pennsylvania Wilds is part of the reason you moved back home! And it is a good idea that is going to die if they don't get a local with some grit and communications skills and a relevant story as the messenger!*

I get in the elevator and push the fourth-floor button. My boobs already feel like they are going to burst. I think of the baby and then immediately try to put him out of my mind as just the thought of him can make my milk release.

The elevator doors open, and I walk toward a glass entrance that says, "Pennsylvania Department of Community and Economic Development." Inside, I check in at the front desk. A few minutes later, a tall man in a suit comes out to greet me. We shake hands, and then he shows me to a conference room. Half a dozen people sit around a long table. A large glass window overlooks the lobby below.

There is one empty seat, at the head of the table. I smile, pull out the chair, and sit down. I wonder if they can tell I've just had a baby. I remember hearing men at past jobs talk about filling a woman's position after she'd left on maternity leave because they figured she wouldn't come back. Sometimes she didn't, but that wasn't the point. I worry they will think I'm not up to the job if they know I have a newborn.

The people go around the room and introduce themselves. They are state and local government and nonprofit leaders representing different aspects of the Pennsylvania Wilds Initiative: tourism, business and community development, and conservation. They start at one end of the table with each person asking me a question. Before I know it, the interview is over and the tall man is walking me out.

I feel it went well and am relieved it is over but then immediately second guess myself and think about things I forgot to say or wish I could reword.

"How do you think I did?" I ask as the tall man shows me to the door.

He smiles.

"I thought you did great," he says. "We'll be in touch."

CHAPTER 9

THE HIGH PLATEAU

A few weeks later, the head of Business Financing for the Commonwealth of Pennsylvania, Scott Dunkelberger, calls and says he'd like to come to Warren to meet with me about the ombudsman job. My heart is racing. *Holy crows*, I think. *I did it!*

He hasn't offered me the job yet, so I try to temper my enthusiasm. Scott asks if we can meet at Allegheny Outfitters. I picture him showing up at our unheated ten-by-twenty shack by the river. The building is on runners, positioned between foundation pillars for a hotel that was never built. Allegheny Outfitters leases the space from a private fraternal club located in a building nearby. Our lights and refrigerator are powered by an extension cord that runs from their main building through the weeds to our shack. Piper has been replacing the livery's equipment as fast as she can, but the place still looks pretty rough. We've also been having issues with some of the fraternal club's bingo players. One got so mad that our shuttle vans were in her way that she drove her car onto the small step that leads into our shack and left it there, blocking the door.

I decide some details are best left until after I get the job. I tell Scott it would work better if we met at a coffee shop.

When we get off the phone, I call Leonard at work and tell him the news. Since I submitted my proposal, I have been thinking a lot about work and motherhood. My son and I are inseparable, and I've loved the two months I've had off with him. But I know I have to go back to work. I need a steady paycheck, and I miss having a professional life.

I call Leonard's cousin's wife, an amazing homemaker who lives up the road, and ask her if she'd be willing to watch T-rex full-time if I get the ombudsman job. She says yes. It means so much to me to know he will be in great hands during the day.

I am driving a used Jetta with a pile of miles on it and decide to borrow Piper's newer Jeep Cherokee to meet Scott. Some people put a lot of stock in first impressions. I figure it is best to err on the side of appearing extra put-together.

I recognize Scott from the interview in Harrisburg. He reminds me of someone who did elite military service. Disciplined is the word that comes to mind. His mustache and hair are graying and neatly trimmed. He is tall, in shape, and wears a dark, fitted suit with pressed creases. He is calm, polite, doesn't say a lot, and seems to watch everything. He is not afraid of silence. I find him intimidating.

Scott and I sit on sofa chairs in the coffee shop. An espresso machine hums in the background. Scott says he'd like to offer me the job. I break into a huge smile and start battering him with technical questions. He smiles and says he has people who can answer those questions once we get the contract in place.

"The important thing will be for you to show results," Scott says. "And to track those results so that two years from now, we can make the case to keep your work going."

It is a sing-for-your-supper set up. I get it, and I am not intimidated. If there is one thing I know how to do, it is work.

Scott asks me for a ride to his next meeting. I am surprised, and it strikes me that for as high up in state government as Scott is, he values spending time in the field and seeing things with his own eyes. I am pretty sure that this visit, the car ride, and meeting me in person are all ground truth, part of his decision-making process. Some of the best leaders operate this way, and it makes me trust him.

"Sure thing," I say, and we head to the parking lot. It is sunny outside, and I am feeling great until I go to unlock Scott's door and look in the window and realize Piper's car is a mess. Papers and toys are strewn across the front and back seats and floors. There are empty drink cups and water bottles, a pair of muddy sneakers, and a sticky piece of candy on the passenger seat. Three kids, two businesses, few resources, I get it. But how did I not notice it before now? I open the door and reach inside and start scooping things up. I turn back and smile at Scott and apologize while also trying to act like it's no big deal, just borrowed my sister's car. Inside I am dying at how badly my first impression plan is backfiring, and the thought of a jolly rancher sticking to the behind of this respectable titan of industry.

***

The Pennsylvania Wilds is big. It takes four hours to drive from one side of the region to the other using either of the east-west highways that traverse the region; Scenic Route 6 in the north, or I-80 in the south. If you are not going that far, just driving from one small town or village to another, your trip is likely to go through the woods, climbing up and down ravines and across flat stretches on windy two-lane roads with very little shoulder and even less cell coverage. It is not uncommon to see whitetail deer, turkey, elk, fox, or even the occasional black bear.

People sometimes say the region has mountains, but its defining geologic feature is a high plateau on the western side of the Appalachian Mountains carved over the centuries by water to form channels, valleys, and canyons. Look out from Rim Rock or Hyner View or most any other high vantage point in the region. What you will see are hills of equal heights, covered in trees, rising and falling into the distance.

It is here, in this most rural quarter of the Commonwealth, that lies the greatest concentration of public lands in Pennsylvania. At 2.4 million acres of public land, it is one of the largest contiguous blocks of forest between New York City and Chicago. Tens of thousands more acres of forestland are privately owned.

Major river systems, and some of Pennsylvania's finest headwaters, begin here. As one summary put it, the region is "unrivaled in Pennsylvania for the amount and quality of water it produces; the timber, mineral, and gas deposits it holds; and the incredible outdoor recreation opportunities it offers."[1] Over the centuries, people have exploited it and restored it, in equally stunning measure.

The Pennsylvania Wilds has a lot of small communities in its big woods. About 500,000 people total are scattered across an area the size of Massachusetts. Many families have lived here for generations, and by the time the Pennsylvania Wilds effort was launched, many of the region's

---

1. *The North Central Highlands: A Sketch Plan for a Special Place.*

communities were economically distressed and experiencing what one study would label a "rural exodus."[2]

The region had a history of innovation and of working with its hands. The Holly carburetor, the Zippo lighter, the Piper Cub airplane, so popular in Alaska, all were invented here.[3] Before Woolrich "The Original Outdoor Clothing Company" was in Milan and Tokyo and New York, its roots were in Clinton County, on the eastern side of the Pennsylvania Wilds. Even the St. Louis Arch (or eighty percent of it) was fabricated in my home county.[4]

While there was a diverse mix of industries in the region's core communities—resource extraction, agriculture, health care, financing, government, transportation, utilities, construction, retail, and wholesale trade—manufacturing was still the heavyweight employer in almost every county of the Pennsylvania Wilds.[5] And like other parts of Pennsylvania, the region "has had to make a long, challenging, and in some cases painful transition over the past few decades from a manufacturing-heavy economy to a more modernized, knowledge-based economy," as another report summarized it, concluding, "Geographic isolation is increasingly becoming a competitive disadvantage in a globalized and mechanized economy."[6]

Globalization, tectonic shifts in technology and digitalization, urban migration, systemic underinvestment in rural areas, an aging workforce, and other macro forces gutted the region's once-vibrant rural communities. While there were nuances from community to community, the collective story of the region's population loss, charted on a graph, is a downhill story, from a high of 539,497 in 1980 to 492,903 in 2020.[7] It was a lot of loss for a region that, to begin with in some places, had fewer than twenty people per square mile. Many young people left, which made the situation even more dire. Schools and businesses closed.

---

2. How Migration Impacts Rural America, 2016. https://w3001.apl.wisc.edu/b03_16
3. Many of these inventions were from Bradford, PA and are captured in interpretive exhibits at the Kinzua Bridge State Park visitor center. The Piper Aviation Museum, in Clinton County, is also a must-see.
4. Commemorative mini arches were installed outside Warren's visitor bureau and local chamber offices to celebrate the Boilermakers Local 659 who in the 1960s fabricated the steel for the arch at the town's now defunct Pittsburg-Des Moines Steel Plant.
5. County Profile Reports, PA Department of Labor and Industry, December 2024.
6. Pennsylvania Wilds Initiative Program Evaluation, Commissioned for PA DCNR, Econsult Corporation, April 2010.
7. Decennial Census: 1900 to 1990, compiled and edited by Richard Forstall, Population Division, US Bureau of the Census. 2000-2020 Data: US Census. 2030 Projection: Center for Rural Pennsylvania.

Many people who live in rural places live there because they appreciate living in a place with a smaller population. Small towns often offer less traffic, a lower cost of living, greater access to the outdoors, and a strong sense of community. As the CEO of one local manufacturing company explained when asked if he'd consider moving his company elsewhere, given the challenges of local workforce issues, "Hear that helicopter outside? That's a life-flight. I'm not sure who got hurt, but tonight the churches are going to be filled with people praying for that person. And tomorrow they will be dropping food by their house. This community cares so much for each other. I appreciate having my business in a place like that."

Others, too, like rural life because they just want to be left alone. In conversations, I've even had a handful declare, "People are leaving? Good!" But there is a tipping point. Rural communities with an aging and declining population face compounding problems, according to an economist for the Federal Reserve Bank: a shrinking workforce, making it more difficult for employers to find workers; an increasing need for health services as more rural hospitals and other care facilities close; and a shrinking tax base, which puts pressure on local government to fund essential services such as infrastructure and public schools, that may help attract businesses and workers.

"In short," the author writes, "as people leave, the people and businesses that remain are generally worse off."[8]

If projections hold, the Wilds region will have fewer people in 2030 than it did in 1900, and more people with gray hair than young people.[9] Bold action was needed, or some rural communities might not have a tomorrow.

The PA Wilds Initiative grew out of this soil. The thinking was that if rural PA could better leverage its vast public lands and other natural assets to grow its tourism economy, the influx of visitor spending could help grow local businesses and make rural communities more vibrant and competitive to attract and retain families, residents and workers that

---

8. From the 2020 article "Rural Population Loss and Strategies for Recovery," by Alexander Marre. Find it at https://www.richmondfed.org/publications/research/econ_focus/2020/q1/district_digest.

9. Decennial Census: 1900 to 1990, compiled and edited by Richard Forstall, Population Division, US Bureau of the Census. Also, Looking Ahead: Pennsylvania Population Projections 2010 to 2040, Center for Rural Pennsylvania, March 2014; Also, Pennsylvania Population Projections 2050: A First Look, Center for Rural Pennsylvania, October 2023.

support the region's various industries. All while helping to inspire the next generation of stewards for the region's tremendous natural and cultural assets.

I had a sense of the magnitude and experimental nature of the initiative when I applied for the ombudsman contract, but it wasn't until I got the job and started traveling the region that I truly began to understand the journey ahead. It was as though I had crested a first mountain and upon reaching the summit, saw before me a wide expanse of peaks, valleys, and rivers, and beyond them, at some far point in the distance, the place we were trying to go. There were countless ways to get there, and no road map.

The lack of a map surprised me most. The Request for Proposals for the ombudsman job asked how I would tackle things, but I assumed the question was a thought exercise. I was wrong. I am given a true north and a compass. Charting the course is up to me. There are a lot of people watching to see if this grandiose initiative launched by a Democrat from Philadelphia in the most rural, Republican part of the state is going to fall flat on its face, and by extension, watching me, the first and only non-government staffer devoted to it. News of my hiring is covered by media outlets across the state.

Thankfully, I have guides. Meredith Hill, the director of the PA Wilds Initiative for the PA Department of Conservation and Natural Resources (DCNR), is one of them.

DCNR manages most of the public land in the Pennsylvania Wilds, and many facilities at those lands. It also has an annual grant program to support locally-driven conservation and recreation projects, so it has a real, every-day presence in many rural communities. Gov. Rendell has tasked DCNR to lead the PA Wilds Initiative, in coordination with its sister agency, the PA Department of Community and Economic Development (DCED), where Scott Dunkelberger works. Meredith is the only state person devoted to the PA Wilds full-time. It is me and her, covering a place bigger than some states.

Shortly after I'm hired, Meredith calls and asks if anyone is helping me learn the region and introducing me to people.

"Not really," I say.

My contract is technically with the PA Wilds Tourism Marketing Corporation, a new nonprofit that is governed by the directors of the region's local visitor bureaus. The Marketing Corporation gave me a list of "outputs" and "outcomes" to strive for, and a few of its members are helping me set up presentations in their communities. Scott set me up with weekly check-ins with his office. I am working with his staff to set up a database so I can track businesses I meet with and referrals I make to other organizations.

On the other end of the line, Meredith sighs, frustrated. "OK. I'd like to take you to meet a few folks."

Meredith takes me on several whirlwind trips that help me begin to understand the landscape and build my network. I am grateful. She introduces me to small business owners, teachers, county commissioners, economic developers, public lands managers, and other rural leaders.

Some of the people Meredith introduces me to do not seem to be fans of hers and are suspicious of the Pennsylvania Wilds Initiative, but she doesn't let this deter her, even when some of them are from her own agency. Some people pull me aside and tell me to be cautious, that Meredith has an agenda, which is curious to me because she doesn't try to convince me of anything, letting me draw my own conclusions, or when she does advocate for something, she is transparent about it. Her approach makes me like and trust her and reminds me again what happens when a powerful woman comes on scene, even when theirs is a humble power like Meredith's. On one trip, we find several fawns frolicking on a playground at an empty camp in the middle of the woods. She pulls over and watches them, smiling and fumbling with her camera trying to capture the moment. This makes me like her even more.

At one meeting, the executive director of a local visitor bureau gives us a disapproving look when we show up, and wants to know what I'm doing with DCNR when my contract is with the Marketing Corp. The woman asks me if I even know what the P-R-S-A is. It is the Public Relations Society of America, she tells me, and she is a member.

When we climb back in the car, I look at Meredith with an incredulous smile. "What the hell was that?"

She shakes her head, looking a little defeated. "I was hoping that would go better," she says as she puts the key in the ignition and starts the car. "Some of these visitor bureaus can be tough. What I do is, when I'm in their area, I just try to give them a call and make a connection."

I think about Piper's experience with her local visitor bureau and wonder what I am in for. There are eight visitor bureaus in the region, and now I technically work for them.

Over the next year, I take numerous multi-day trips like this, getting to know rural towns and people in the Pennsylvania Wilds and learning to navigate the region's complex parochial shoals. At DCED, there is concern that I will be seen as a threat to the state's network of business service providers, so Scott takes me on a trip to meet people at the region's Small Business Development Centers, Local Development Districts, and similar organizations to help send the message that I will be sending them referrals, not competing with them.

The sheer size of the region and number of partners involved are dizzying. It didn't take long before I realized my job was going to be a lot harder than I thought.

Meredith introduced me to Ed McMahon, the guy I saw on TV at Piper's, and I'd eventually meet him in person at a "Balancing Nature and Commerce" workshop in West Virginia held by The Conservation Fund, a national nonprofit with a dual charter to pursue environmental preservation and economic development. The workshop attracted communities from across the country that were trying to do a more holistic, sustainable type of tourism development, like we were, rooted in a community's sense of place.

"We spend way too much time in this country fighting about what we disagree on and not nearly enough time sitting down, community by community, and figuring out what we do agree about," he told us. "I tell you when you do that, you can reach consensus about place. Because most Americans care more about the place they live than the political party they belong to."

For my sake, I hoped he was right.

CHAPTER 10

A BRAND AND A STRATEGY ARE BORN

What were the origins of this experiment that I'd first heard about that day in the newsroom in Alaska, and that was now employing me?

I decided to tackle this question the only way I knew how, as a curious reporter, interviewing people, reading past stories and reports, and taking trips to see certain things firsthand, including, one day, kissing Leonard and Max goodbye and driving two hours south to the unincorporated community of Benezette, ground zero for viewing Pennsylvania's wild elk herd.

Many months later, here is what I stitched together:

The PA Wilds Initiative started the way a lot of opportunities do: with a problem.

Nestled in the mountains, miles from any major town, Benezette, which is home to fewer than 200 people, reminds me of Talkeetna, the quirky gateway town to Denali National Park in Alaska. Only here, instead of the largest mountain in North America, the attraction people are coming to see is the largest wild elk herd in the Northeast.

In this valley, the seed of the PA Wilds Initiative took root. Pennsylvania's native eastern elk were declared extinct by the U.S. Fish and Wildlife Service in 1880 following colonization and exploitation by settlers. Three decades later, in 1912, the PA Game Commission decided to reestablish an elk herd, buying fifty of them from Yellowstone National Park for fifty dollars each and transporting them to rural Pennsylvania by train. Additional shipments followed.[1]

By the 1990s, the herd's range spanned three forested counties in northcentral PA. The elk were most visible to the traveling public in

---

1. Mario L. Chiappelli, who came from a coal-mining family in Bennetts Valley, wrote a wonderful book about the history of elk in the region, *Preserving the Pennsylvania Wilds: The Rebirth of Elk Country* (The History Press, 2023).

Benezette. Word started to get out that you could drive up the village's Winslow Hill and see the elk spar and hear their haunting bugles. Benezette was not prepared. Neither were many of the thousands of visitors who started coming there.

"It was a total free-for-all," one longtime camp owner told me.

"Like trying to find a parking spot at a busy mall," said a third-generation local.

"A three-ring circus," recalled Rick Carlson, who served as the policy director for DCNR at the time.

With no official viewing areas and no public restrooms, people stopped on the roads where they shouldn't, peed where they shouldn't. Some tried to pet the wildlife. Others tried to feed the elk. Some didn't realize you might not be able to get fuel for vehicles. The situation, Carlson says, "was becoming a liability."

"Things really started to ramp up in the middle to late 90s," Rawley Cogan, who worked as a biologist for the PA Game Commission at the time, told me in an interview. "It was all word of mouth. You started to see small traffic jams. There was no destination point. We needed a destination."

Tom Ridge was governor of Pennsylvania at the time. He rode horseback with the Game Commission in Elk Country and heard the concerns.

The message that got back to policy people in Harrisburg, according to Mike Krempasky, the deputy policy director at DCNR at the time, was, "We got a lemon here. Can we make some lemonade?"

Krempasky was tasked with researching solutions. He flew to a wildlife conference in Wyoming, where he met Ted Eubanks, founder of Fermata Inc., a company that focused on sustainable nature and heritage tourism development. Eubanks impressed him, and he introduced him to others at DCNR, including his boss, Carlson.

Carlson, at first, wasn't sure what to make of Eubanks. He thought he might be a snake oil salesman, he told me, talking as he did about places like South Dakota being tourist destinations.

But Eubanks had an impressive list of clients and at the heart of his pitch was a belief that resonated with the Commonwealth's leading conservation agency: if you connect people in a meaningful way to special places, they will be better stewards of them.

In December 2000, DCNR, the Pennsylvania Game Commission, the federal Appalachian Regional Commission, and two nonprofits that serve rural PA, the Lumber Heritage Region and the North Central PA Regional Planning and Development Commission, issued a request for proposals titled, "Promoting Elk Watching and Other Nature Tourism: A Plan for North Central Pennsylvania."

Eubanks submitted a proposal and landed an interview. He flew to Pennsylvania and drove to Ridgway, a small historic town on the National Wild & Scenic Clarion River, about an hour and a half south of where I grew up, and an hour north of Benezette.

Like Warren, Ridgway was built on timber; in its heyday, it was home to many millionaires. Several of the old Victorian mansions, complete with ornate Hyde Murphy interior woodwork, still graced the town. Eubanks checked into one that had been converted into a bed and breakfast. The next day, he drove to North Central a few blocks away and met the interview team.

"I began to learn then that this was not just an elk watching project, but an elk public use conflict," Eubanks told me. "This was a contentious issue."

Eubanks won the contract. For the next eighteen months, he met with people in coffee shops, public meetings, churches, and their homes. He talked to township supervisors, county commissioners, local planners, people who work in tourism and economic development, business owners, and private citizens. He bought a pumpkin from a farmer who killed eight elk for damaging his crops and spent the morning talking to him.

"We would never have resolved the issues related to this complex of a project without being willing to talk it through with anyone who wanted to be heard," Eubanks told me. "It didn't mean that everyone walked away happy, but I do not believe that anyone can say that they were not listened to."

By the time the "Plan for Elk Watching and Nature Tourism in North Central Pennsylvania," was complete, Ridge was on his way out of office. DCNR held off publishing its recommendations until the new governor took office so the incoming administration could feel some ownership over it.

When Gov. Ed Rendell took office, in 2003, Eubanks was asked to brief his new DCNR Secretary, Mike DiBerardinis, on the elk study. "I spent twenty minutes with him," Eubanks told me. "And he said, 'Let's go talk to the governor.' The governor was in his office with a bunch of people . . . The Governor said to me, 'Let's talk.'"

On the campaign trail, Rendell, a Democrat, had visited the region's small conservative rural towns where he had little hope of winning votes, or even that there were many votes to win given the area's sparse population. So rare was it to see top gubernatorial candidates in these remote reaches during their campaigns that one town brought out the school marching band to welcome him. The region's natural beauty and small-town charm left an impression on Rendell.

"The trip blew me away," he told the *Philadelphia Inquirer*. "I came away thinking, it's amazing: Pennsylvanians will drive all the way down Skyline Drive in Virginia or fly out to the Rockies or the Pacific Coast Highway, and they can have the same experiences [here] at one-fifth of the cost and a fifth of the time it takes."

The trip sparked conversations about how the state had all this public land in north central PA that was surrounded by small communities that have seen decades of economic distress and population decline. Eubanks pressed the group to think bigger than the elk.

"That's where it started," Eubanks told me. "It quickly became this bigger thing."

After talking with Eubanks, the message coming down from above was that the elk plan wasn't big enough.

Ed McMahon, the national expert on sustainable community development, was part of some of those early conversations. Rendell, he told me, was "quite taken by the entire region."

"I sat with his advisors," McMahon said. "The discussion was, we need to have a rural initiative as well as an urban initiative. Out of that came the Pennsylvania Wilds."

This was not the first time a regional strategy involving public lands had been attempted. A 1980 effort is captured in the 98-page book, *The North Central Highlands: A Sketch Plan for a Special Place*, written by a former DCNR Secretary and published in partnership with the Western Pennsylvania Conservancy.

"Long and short of it—it never went anywhere," Krempasky said. "This area is not inclined to do those regional attempts . . . [it] generally does not like centralized government."

Leaders at DCNR saw the expansion of the elk plan as an opportunity to better connect with the distressed rural communities around the region's many state parks and forests.

"Sometimes the communities that are closest to the public lands don't always see the value of those lands," Krempasky told me. "This is true around the country. So, the thought was, this could be good for that."

McMahon, who has worked with dozens of communities across America that are gateways to public lands, explained, "Economic development anywhere—it's not so much about what you don't have, it's what you do have. It starts with inventorying your assets and building a plan around what you do have. Here northcentral PA had all this public land that a lot of people just sort of saw as a negative."

"The question became, how do you turn the region's public land legacy into something that local people would view as a positive? Out of those discussions came the idea that we need to give this place a branded identity," McMahon said.

The elk study touched on boundaries for a tourism initiative, but the lines were largely driven by where the state did not want elk. If the herd went too far east and jumped Pine Creek, they'd get into farm country and be a nuisance. If it went too far south, the 2000-pound animals could be walking down Interstate 80, causing a major safety hazard.

As the governor's team thought more broadly about the region as an outdoor recreation destination, they began to look beyond the elk range. But how big should this new tourism region be?

Some at DCNR pointed to the *North Central Highlands* book for the potential footprint. Major transportation corridors and county boundaries also factored into the conversation.

At DCED, the governor's new deputy secretary for tourism, Mickey Rowley, was adamant that Scenic Route 6, a state-designated heritage area that runs across the northern tier of Pennsylvania, be included. Rendell drove Route 6 and had taken in many of its popular sights, from Kinzua Dam near me, to the Pine Creek Gorge three hours east, to the many small towns with quaint '50s-style diners in between. Rowley had spent time driving the corridor, too.

"That Route 6 is just un-freaking-believable," Rowley said.[2]

The state pulls the region's local visitor bureaus into the boundary discussion.

"We went through a process," Krempasky told me. "Which ones wanted to be involved, which didn't. [The visitor bureaus] became important to drawing boundaries the first time around."

Top people from DCNR and DCED traveled to the region to meet with community leaders and hold public feedback sessions. At one point, Rowley said, DiBerardinis invited him on a trip north. I imagine they made an odd pair, DiBerardinis hailing from a community organizing background, and Rowley, a flamboyant former executive director of the Greater Philadelphia Hotel Association, who was already earning the nickname "Hollywood" at DCED.

Rowley recalled, "The whole way he was talking about nature tourism and the outdoor marketing and blah, blah, blah, and you could see he was really committed."

Eubanks was also there. "I learned a lot from him," Rowley told me. "He knows nature."

At one meeting in State College, home of Penn State's main campus, Rowley said a woman informed the state that she didn't like the idea of being labeled rural. "We have a Starbucks!" she told the group, annoyed.

At another meeting, in a more remote county, Eubanks got a positive reception to his presentation but then a woman raised her hand and told him she thought he was part of a United Nations plot. "She's very nice," Eubanks recalled. "I'm kind of taken aback. She launches off into this speech. She gets into black helicopters. I'm thinking I landed on another planet."

Terri Dennison, who lived in the region and at the time was executive director of the Pennsylvania Route 6 heritage area, said she heard the United Nations mentioned too. She told me she and others tried to convince the individuals there was no nefarious plot. "We said this is everybody coming together and working together," she said. "They did calm down. They were still people."

McMahon participated in some of the public meetings and discussions in the region, too. "This wasn't like someone opening a Tesla plant

---

2. Route 6 *is* amazing! The Bucktail Scenic Byway (Route 120) is also hugely popular with motorcyclists and others looking for a scenic drive. Find both, and others, at PAWilds.com/journey. Or visit PAroute6.com.

that employs 3000 people," he said. "It was lots of different things coming together to grow local businesses for a huge collective impact. We met with this one guy, a county commissioner, I think he was a truck driver," McMahon said. "He was a hunter and a fisherman. And he said, 'You know, some of these ideas you guys got aren't too bad.' That's when we realized we were making progress."

Eubanks drove the boundary discussion toward a sense of place: what thread holds the region together as an experience? It is the concentration of public lands, he said.

Eventually, twelve and a half counties are outlined on a map. Within them are twenty-nine state parks, eight state forests, fifty state game lands, and PA's only National Forest, the 500,000-acre Allegheny National Forest. It is the greatest concentration of public land in the Commonwealth. At the time, fifty million people lived within a day's drive of it. Few knew it was there or thought of it as an outdoor recreation destination.

Eubanks suggested the region be called "The Pennsylvania Wildwoods." He told me people in the tourism office laughed him out of the room because Wildwood is the name of a New Jersey beach town.

Rowley was serious about creating a brand that would have lasting power. "It has to roll off the tongue," he explained to me. "It has to be something the people who live there would say."

When Eubanks suggested "Pennsylvania Wilds," Rowley told him, "That might work."

"I'd like to be able to say this was a really high-tech, finely tuned process," Eubanks said of creating the name, "but it was seat-of-the-pants-let's-make-this-happen, and we did."

For Rowley, the work had just begun. He'd managed enough projects to know that a regional brand would be challenging, and his chief partner to roll it out in a region already skeptical of Harrisburg was the region's eight visitor bureaus, which did not have a history of working together as a collective group.

Rowley asked the visitor bureau directors to come to Harrisburg. His staff set up a meeting at a Department of Agriculture building near the Farm Show Complex, in a room with big windows. "My job is to corral them," Rowley told me.

David Brooks, then head of the Potter County Visitor Bureau, a one-person shop in Coudersport, population 2,600, told me he drove to Harrisburg with the executive directors of neighboring Clinton and Tioga County visitor bureaus.

"They called us all down to Harrisburg, put us all in the room and handed us all a map," Brooks told me. "It had the region outlined, highlighted, and at the top it said, 'Pennsylvania Wilds.' It was the first time anyone outside of the tourism office had heard it."

Eubanks and the state's creative firm at the time talked to the group about the number of state and federal parks, forests, and game lands the area had when viewed as a region. It was more public land than Yellowstone National Park.

"The emphasis was, that's a really powerful story when you put it all together like that," Brooks told me.

The other emphasis was how fragmented current marketing efforts were in the region. At the time, three counties were marketed as "Keystone Mountain Country," five as "Great Outdoors," one as "Susquehanna Riverlands," and two shared a star asset—PA's only national forest—but rarely did cooperative marketing because they didn't get along.

"There were all these competing regional interests basically promoting the same product, the outdoor product," Brooks told me. "[Rowley] was very blunt about how confusing it was. . . . It was very driven by him. Why not pool all of the resources and create this area of outdoor products?"

Rowley pushed the group to commit to the vision. "I'm a fast mover. Mike DeBerardinis is a fast mover. We only have four to eight years [before the governor is out of office]," Rowley told me. "I say (to the visitor bureaus), 'The State is about to pounce on your region with resources. Are you out or are you in? . . . They were accustomed to governors who didn't know where Potter County was. They didn't know what to do."

After the meeting, Brooks and his colleagues drove out of the city. "On the ride back, we had four hours to chew on it," he said. The reaction at first was skeptical. "We don't know about the term 'Wilds.' Does it make it sound like a free-for-all, like the Wild West? There was difficulty accepting the phraseology. But it was very exciting. Of course, we all got over it really quick when they offered us a regional grant."

Before joining Rendell's administration, Rowley helped establish the Greater Philadelphia Tourism Marketing Corporation and served as its director. He used that as a road map for rural PA, pushing the eight visitor bureaus to found a PA Wilds marketing corporation, so they could apply for regional marketing grants from the state. Such investments would allow them to leverage their local hotel tax dollars to do big things to promote the Pennsylvania Wilds as a travel destination. They complied, but Rowley's top-down approach did not sit well with some of them.

"The [visitor bureau] meetings were painful and long and not my idea of a good time," Rowley explained to me in an interview years later. "I definitely take everyone's opinion, but I also move at a pace that doesn't always allow time for a lot of collaboration."

A branding summit was set up with the visitor bureaus to add meat to the bones of the Pennsylvania Wilds brand. The purpose of getting together, according to the meeting documents, was to "imagine, in vivid detail, the ideal relationship between consumers and the PA Wilds brand;" to gather input from key stakeholders; and to develop a "brand promise"—"Literally, what will the PA Wilds brand mean to people five to ten years from now?" it asked on the agenda document.

The rules for the summit included, "No whining, no cell phones" and participants should "Commit to reckless creativity. The rational side of infrastructure development and marketing strategies are important, but those are issues for another day."

As the summit neared, tension built. An email between DCNR and DCED's creative firm, sent fifteen days before the summit, captured the heat of the moment:

"I've seen the flurry of e-mails over the past few days about the nature of the summit, the depth of people's parochial interests, the degree of distrust about objectives, agendas (personal and otherwise) and the likelihood of the meeting turning into a gripe fest," a woman from the creative firm wrote to the DCNR team. "That's all quite normal. I always walk into the room expecting that, and I'm seldom disappointed ☺ However, I'm not the least bit worried. What will make this summit work—and what will make it different than typical marketing strategy meetings—is that we're keeping the emphasis on high-level brand issues."

DCNR pushed for a second meeting to be held with the visitor bureaus to talk through concerns and build trust. It was held on the eve of the summit.

In an email to the president of the Marketing Corporation, DCNR outlined five main questions a facilitator would help the state work through with the visitor bureaus. Among them, "What does [the state] need to hear from you so that we are fully informed about both your hopes and concerns about PA Wilds?" and "How do we listen to different stakeholder perspectives and advice and yet not get trapped by personal agendas?"

The two meetings were productive but bruising. Emails sent in the months after give flavor for how they went. In one, Eubanks pushed on the State Tourism Office about marketing research.

"Please try and take your data wonk hat off for just a moment," their consultant wrote back to him. "Understand that we are trying to get so many disparate parties to agree on why they should put their pants on and go to work in their local marketing offices every day. Why they should embrace an idea like the Wilds, which is being forced down the throats of thirteen counties who have never collaborated before..."

"I've spent seventeen months now listening to the [visitor bureaus] complain about the mighty thumbprint of DCNR, Ted Eubanks and DCED," the email continued. "The charge of being treated like 'employees, rather than partners,' which was leveled on the Summit's Eve, is a very real and concrete barrier. This summit was for them. This mission is for them. Please don't get caught up in the finer points of data, research, and demography. Yes, we must be accurate and detailed and diligent in our scrutiny of the marketplace when we begin to invest our precious marketing dollars. But at this stage of the game, welcoming our [visitor bureaus] into the game with a clear message that says we respect your way of life, your sense of caution and your own personal passions will do more for us right now than all the data in the world."

"We had a hard time," Rowley told me in our interview. "I don't want to see the county boundaries. I don't market to county commissioners. I market to the visitors. I was maybe arrogant about that? But I don't care.... Who gives a shit about that stuff?"

Learning this backstory, I appreciated that Rowley had challenged an entrenched system to bring the regional brand to life. As one person who knew the region and the Commonwealth's tourism promotion apparatus put it, "Mickey was hugely creative. Fearless. I'm not sure it could have been pulled off without him."

But I could also see why the region's visitor bureau directors could feel slighted by how it all went down.

What I was most interested in and impressed by though was what the two sides had created. Out of this turbulent moment, the "Declaration of Principles for the Pennsylvania Wilds," the branding document that Piper found online, had been born. And literally weeks after it was published, it did what some probably would have thought impossible. It helped inspire two young women to move home to distressed rural PA.

And that was just the start.

CHAPTER 11

MORE SEATS AT THE TABLE

Another key group helping to shape the early Wilds work was the PA Wilds Planning Team, a regional network of county planners, economic developers, state partners DCNR and DCED, public lands managers, conservation organizations, and tourism and heritage professionals. The first Planning Team meeting I attended, with Meredith, I walked into the room and about two dozen people sitting around a table all turned to look at me. The group's chairman welcomed me and asked, "Are you a core member, a partner or a stakeholder?"

I smiled and looked at Meredith, feeling a little nervous, not quite understanding what those terms meant to this group or signed me up for. "I have no idea," I said. "But I'm glad to be here, and maybe we can figure that out as we go?"

People smiled, asked about my background, and then off we all went with the rest of the meeting. Despite being brand new, and hardly able at that point to track the team's sometimes esoteric planning discussions, I felt oddly welcome and at home, which would make a lot more sense when I learned their backstory, including that they had helped create the position that I now held.

After that first meeting, I set out, as I had with other aspects of the Wilds work, to try to understand how this part came to be.

What I discovered was that where the Marketing Corp was created top-down and some of its members seemed averse toward me or the initiative (it was hard to tell the difference sometimes), the PA Wilds Planning Team grew from the ground up, had a very different experience with the state, and a different relationship with me.

The Planning Team was founded shortly after the Wilds work launched in reaction to the state's marketing push. The seed for it germinated on the eastern side of the region, in the Pine Creek Valley, when people voiced fears at a local watershed meeting about the valley's special places being "loved to death" by this new state marketing initiative called the Pennsylvania Wilds.

The Valley was home to Pine Creek Gorge, a National Natural Landmark recognized for its superlative scenery and geological and ecological value. Pine Creek, a trout stream, snaked along the valley's floor, accompanied by a remote sixty-five-mile rail trail that ran through Tioga and Tiadaghton State Forests connecting the valley's small villages.

Pine Creek Valley stretched across two counties, Tioga and Lycoming. Tioga County Planning Director Jim Weaver was among those raising concerns. He'd attended a public meeting with people from the State Tourism Office and wasn't impressed. "We didn't get along at all," Weaver said. "City people parachuting in here telling us what to do, we were hicks . . . *that* didn't go over well."

At one public meeting after a thunderstorm, Weaver recalled, people from Harrisburg were talking about bringing bus tours to the Pine Creek Valley, and meanwhile, outside, there were much more pressing ecological issues to contend with, like erosion. "Pine Creek is running brown," Weaver told me. "Two thousand tons of soil is leaving this watershed."

Weaver and others found the state's intense focus on marketing unsettling. If the region wasn't intentional about the development, tourism could become another extraction industry, like lumber had been at the turn of the century, the area stripped of its trees. "Communities in Pine Creek had seen it all," Weaver told me. "There were no trees. They took 'em all. It was a barren landscape."

Weaver envisioned "people coming in with high expectations and attitudes . . . bus tours showing up, no cell phone service, no fancy motels, just who we are. We were not ready." Weaver said at one meeting he and others told the state that they were worried about the Valley getting overrun. "It was really a fun conversation. Everybody spilled their guts," Weaver said and left the meeting feeling like, "They've won. The flatlanders won. You are taking over this landscape."

Jerry Walls, then head of the Lycoming County Planning Department and a leader in his field, had read about the governor's plans in the news and wondered what the heck was happening. At one point, a friend and colleague, a man of prominence in the area who cared deeply about the environmental wellbeing of the Pine Creek Valley, poked Walls on the chest at a watershed meeting and asked, "What are you going to do about this Wilds thing, Walls?"

Walls returned home to Williamsport and started calling people he knew in state government. "All I could visualize is people coming in here in tour buses and overriding and overwhelming the special qualities of our special places," Walls told me.

A few days later, Walls got a call from someone in the policy office at DCNR, asking why he was raising concerns. Walls took his time to list his points with his calm, gravelly voice.

"Well, first of all," he started, "it is going to involve a lot of marketing to bring people here, and while that in itself may be good, what I'm concerned about is, we are not ready. And if they come here and we are not prepared to do a good job welcoming and accommodating their stay and their needs, and we don't have good, clear designation of routes, and our facilities are not where they need to be, then they are going to go back home and bad mouth us. We need to do some planning for infrastructure. We need to do some planning with our communities to receive these visitors."

DCNR encouraged Walls to organize a meeting with the region's county planners. Walls began calling his peers across the thirteen counties of the Pennsylvania Wilds region. Some counties had such small populations that they didn't have planning offices. Despite their common challenges, some of the planners had never met each other. Most had heard about this new "Wilds thing." The attention from Harrisburg was exciting, but it also caused trepidation.

"You had these very strong [state] personalities all trying to orchestrate something that was supposed to be organic," Deborah Pontzer, founder of a nonprofit, Grow Rural PA, told me. At the time, Pontzer worked as an economic and workforce specialist for the 5th US Congressional District, which covered most of the region.

"The name 'Pennsylvania Wilds' and the logo came from them," Pontzer said. "No matter how many times they tried to tell us this is all about us, we didn't have a say in that. People wanted to know, why are you coming to us now? You've always left us alone. What do you want from us? How are you going to change us?"

Walls told his peers, "Let's hear from the state about what they are going to do and then let's figure out what we need to do to get ready."

Rep. John Peterson's office, a Republican then serving the 5th Congressional District, helped organize a meeting. On July 26, 2005, planners from across the region arrived at the Moshannon State Forest District Office off Interstate 80 in Clearfield County. They met in a room with wood walls and exposed beams that highlighted the timber the region is known for. Animal mounts showcased the region's wildlife.

Walls and five other planners, from Tioga, McKean, Elk, and Clearfield counties, met for an hour. Dan Glotz, the county planner from Warren County who told my sister she was a firecracker, was also there. Walls shared a fifteen-point "Ideas for the Pennsylvania Wilds" list that touched on everything from the need for public restrooms and scenic vista pull-offs to concerns about emergency services, to potential models for regional planning collaboration. The planners agreed the list should be shared with the state. They passed around a copy of the brand principles that the Tourism Office and visitor bureaus had just completed.

The state entourage arrived just before lunch, DCNR Secretary DiBerardinis and Meredith Hill among them, outnumbering the planners. Denny Puko, a planner for DCED, walked in wearing a suit and sunglasses. He was tall, slender, tan, and uniquely calm.

"None of us knew each other," Weaver, the Tioga County planner, told me. "I was taken aback by Denny Puko. He looked like an FBI agent. I thought, what are we getting into? Within twenty minutes we were all laughing. The ice was broken really quickly."

Secretary DiBerardinis told the group that improving the economy through tourism and outdoor recreation development didn't have to come at the cost of deteriorating the region's special places and natural assets. His framing was different from the marketing-focused approach that many state and local partners had shared up to that point. He said his agency was in the process of identifying strategic investments to make at its state parks and forests in the region, and that local input was critical to helping to sustainably grow the region as an outdoor recreation destination.

Pennsylvania has more municipalities than most other states in America, and the state knew there was no practical way for it to interact directly with every township, borough, city, and town in the massive PA Wilds region. The counties were the natural partners.

"It was a true understanding from the beginning that this would have to be a cooperative effort by so many people," DCED's Neil Fowler, who was also at the meeting, told me. Fowler had worked for DCED for several years by then and remembered the first elk study coming across his desk for funding, under the Ridge Administration. He had to do a double take. Like a lot of people back then, he didn't even realize Pennsylvania had elk.

This was the first time Weaver recalled hearing the PA Wilds discussed as something other than a marketing effort. "The shift at DCNR from tourism to landscape initiative, that was huge to me staying involved," he told me.

Clearfield County Planning Director Jodi Brennan listened with interest. Brennan grew up playing in the woods around Benezette. Back then, many area creeks ran orange with acid mine drainage, scars from the coal industry. Some of the watersheds were being restored thanks to the efforts of many organizations and individuals, including DCNR and Brennan herself. By 2005, as the coal industry continued its decline nationally, tourist vehicles coming to see the area's rebounding elk herd had largely replaced the coal trucks that once ran through Bennett's Valley, irking some residents who had chosen to live in the area to get away from people. Brennan respected those views but also knew visitation would continue regardless of anyone's opinion about it. "This is happening whether you want it or not," she told concerned family and neighbors. "So, let's try to make it positive. Let's try to shape it."

Brennan brought that same approach to the July meeting. "There was a lot of good discussion," she told me. "We weren't against [the idea of the Pennsylvania Wilds]. We were more saying, 'Let's do this right so it is good for the people who visit and the people who live here.'"

At his seat, Puko scribbled notes from each speaker on a copy of Walls' fifteen points of "Ideas for PA Wilds." Number nine on Walls' list was a recommendation that DCED provide funding to help local communities "organize and sustain the partnerships needed to make PA Wilds successful."

Puko knew that DiBerardinis' presence in the room indicated a serious commitment by the state, and he was impressed by what the secretary and the others were saying.

"I love it," he told me. "This is a way to do resource protection and economic development. The county planners are a great go-between for the municipalities. I'm thinking that with the governor's commitment and DCNR believing they had a great new way of doing business, it brought out a lot of interest and commitment."

Meredith had worked on a number of projects at the intersection of conservation and economic development that required state and local collaboration across different agencies. Leading up to the meeting, she had sensed local distrust and a we-don't-want-government-telling-us-what-to-do attitude coming from parts of the region. But by the end, it was clear that local communities were interested in building a real partnership with the state.

"I remember thinking this is an important step. We can really do something here," Meredith told me. "I felt a lot of optimism."

Over the next two months, more meetings were held. Walls' list grew to twenty points.

"They listened to us," Brennan told me. "And then Gov. Rendell was very receptive."

DCED assigned Puko to help the group develop an Intergovernmental Cooperation Agreement, a legal instrument under state law that would pave the way for collaboration by the region's county governments around the PA Wilds' Initiative and give them a collective voice. A facilitator helped the group work through its purpose and function. Puko met with county commissioners across the region to explain the process and answer questions.

From his office near Pittsburgh, Puko began crafting a draft agreement. Pennsylvania law stipulates certain language, so he started with that, then wove in what the group discussed about purpose and function. Puko had drafted these types of agreements before, but never one covering such a large geographic footprint. His approach was to keep it simple, to give the participants "the ability to do the good and right things they need to do without binding them unnecessarily."

When he was done, the double-spaced document totaled three pages and included three signature lines on the last page for each county's set of commissioners to sign. He presented the draft to the Planning Team.

The agreement would not give the Planning Team a legal structure to do capital projects, but it would make them a force "to promote understanding and to develop consensus to foster the protection of our collective values in our region's communities," as Walls put it, creating an important buffer for the region to protect communities against potential downsides that amenity-rich destinations sometimes experience, such as unsustainable pressure on local systems and resources, low paying jobs, gentrification, and other inequitable outcomes.[1]

Cameron County, the least-populated county in the Commonwealth, was the first to sign.

"Every county enacted it," Puko told me. "Every county. I don't recall there being controversy in any one of them."

Geographically, it is the largest intergovernmental cooperation agreement in Pennsylvania history, a ground-breaking moment.

"It wasn't that we had to convince each other," Walls said. "We all felt it. We had something special in this area, and we had to come at it in a way that was respectful."[2]

Puko would go on to serve the team for more than a decade and reflect upon retiring that it was one of the most fulfilling things he'd done in his career. He was proud of the formal structure, he told me, but it went beyond that. "We facilitated this in a way that they really liked each other," he told me a decade after crafting the agreement. "To this day, they still do. There are occasional tensions. But there was a fraternity of appreciation. Everybody pitches in and fills a gap when it's needed."

It took about a year for the Planning Team to form. Once up and operating, they met monthly and began work on a regional planning study and on the *PA Wilds Design Guide for Community Character Stewardship*, a voluntary planning resource to help rural towns and cities protect their community character as they grow.[3] The *Design Guide* would become a cornerstone of the regional initiative, creating development guidance based in place, and a much-needed pathway to bring in investment to help small rural towns spruce up their main streets and entrances.

Before long, Farley Wright, an economic developer assigned to the team from sparsely populated Forest County, pushed a discussion about

---

1. Two excellent studies on this topic include Headwaters Economics *The Amenity Trap: How high-amenity communities can avoid being loved to death* (2023); and Aspen Institute's Community Strategies Group's 2023 report, *Mapping A New Terrain: Five Principles for Equitable Rural Outdoor Recreation Economies*.

2. Jerry's leadership was honored by his peers with a poem, "The Call of the Wilds" written by another Planning Team member, Farley Wright.

3. The *PA Wilds Design Guide* can be found at PAWildsCenter.org.

how there needed to be a focus on assisting rural entrepreneurs. He wrote a white paper on it and enlisted Deborah Pontzer to help him edit it.

Wright told me the concern he had at the start of the PA Wilds Initiative was that its main focus was on marketing to visitors and developing recreation infrastructure to better serve visitors. In his mind, there also needed to be a focus on supporting local entrepreneurs. Otherwise, tourism risked being extractive, leaving little behind for local communities.

Wright was asked to go to Harrisburg to present to Scott.

"You don't get asked to present to Scott to humor him," Wright said. The meeting went well and led to the development of the PA Wilds Small Business Ombudsman position.

"Secretary DiBerardinis and Scott Dunkelberger are two people that really got it, right off the bat," Wright told me. "And I always felt comfortable with them. Like we are finally going to get to something that will work for us."

It took me several months to piece this story together, and I was blown away when I finally understood. So often in economically distressed areas, communities desperate for investment will say yes to any development that comes along. But here these county planners, a group I'd never much thought about, had pushed back against the state when a tidal wave of potential investment was coming their way, essentially telling them: rural communities need a real seat at the table.

And then, the state listened.

It filled me with hope. Adding to the mix and moment, there was an effort underway to involve the region's artisans and makers to build the PA Wilds brand. A new study had shown that there were incredible jewelry makers, painters, woodworkers, fiber artists, blacksmiths, scratchboard artists, photographers, and other makers and artisans handcrafting products all across the region.[4] They were just difficult to see because many worked out of their houses or made their wares in a shop on a back-country road. Rural tourism didn't just have to be about heads in beds and the service sector. Those were important, of course, but we also had the opportunity to develop the supply chain that supported those businesses—including people and companies that made stuff.

---

4. Pennsylvania Wilds Artisan Development Plan, March 2007, PA Wilds Artisan Development Workgroup, Project Chair Robert Veilleux, Penn State Cooperative Extension, Potter County Education Council; Project Co-Chair Terri Dennison, Route 6 Heritage Corporation.

Sitting in my office in my trailer, reflecting on these breakthroughs, I thought about the brand principles, and the clever, humorous ads the tourism office and Marketing Corporation put out, and how *National Geographic* has just recently published a geo-tourism map of Northern Appalachia with the Pennsylvania Wilds identified. It dawned on me that this work was happening at one of those rare magic moments where the right mix of people intersected with the right ideas and the right market forces. I'd experienced something like it at the alternative weekly newspaper I worked at in Anchorage, but not at this scale and only as a periphery character. Such moments, I knew, had the potential to unlock incredible creativity and innovation, and with it, wealth. In this case, for a lot of locally-owned rural businesses and economically-distressed rural communities.

I gulped to realize that at the center of this potentially transformational moment, the thing that "communities were going to get that would work for them," as Farley put it, was me.

CHAPTER 12

INVESTMENT

As part of the initiative, DCNR completes several studies looking at outdoor recreation trends nationally, and at their lands and facilities in the region, to determine what they needed to build or upgrade in order to help the region establish itself as a premier outdoor recreation destination. A wave of investment, unlike anything I'd seen in rural PA in my generation, is underway in the form of upgraded land and water trails, new wayfinding and interpretive signage and access points, public restrooms with flush toilets, and new multi-million-dollar conservation visitor centers to help visitors and residents understand and connect to the region's tremendous natural assets.

Just as things began to move from concepts and designs on paper to real infrastructure in the physical world, the fallout from the 2008 recession starts to hit. The first casualty is DCNR's crown jewel, the Elk Country Visitor Center. The Rocky Mountain Elk Foundation pulls out of the project, leaving DCNR scrambling to find another partner to operate the facility when the construction is finished.

I am too new to be fully in the know, but there are whispers that a small group of die-hard Pennsylvania elk conservationists have decided to start their own conservation nonprofit and raise the $6 million it will take to match the state's investment and get the place up and operating. At that point in time, I couldn't imagine being able to raise that kind of money for a cause I care about.[1]

---

1. John Geissler, a retired school educator and administrator, went to Harrisburg and told a room of policy people that he'd line up "*legions* of volunteers," waiving his hand across the room for emphasis. At the time, it was just him and his best friend, Randy Kimmel, and their wives, Linda and Cathy. Still, with the help of Rawley Cogan and others, they eventually built those legions after founding the Keystone Elk Country Alliance. Today, this nonprofit operates the Elk Country Visitor Center through a public-private partnership with DCNR.

Despite the uncertainty, DCNR is pushing ahead, and today we are meeting in an old farmhouse on Winslow Hill called the Elk Mountain Homestead. It has a barn with a viewing deck that overlooks a large field where the elk often graze. Across the field, an area has been cleared and workers are starting construction on the visitor center.

About twenty of us gather inside the homestead to brainstorm about branding for the new facility. Many of the attendees are men and women who live and work in the region.

A creative firm has been brought in from West Chester, near Philadelphia, and they have a large blank notepad set up on an easel in the living room. People sit on couches and the floor and stand along the walls. A woman from the creative firm asks us to describe the people of the area. One by one, the group adds adjectives. Resourceful. Hard working. Friendly. Blue collar. Private. The consultant scribbles the words on the notepad.

"Real," one of the foresters, Tom, says, and it reminds me of what my sister told me about my husband, before he was my husband, when I'd come home to look him up after many years away in faster-paced places. I had a sense then that I would marry him and build something lasting, and I have a similar gut feeling now about the PA Wilds work. What I experienced helping Piper grow her business in Warren, what I saw happening in Benezette, this new brand, this fledgling, rocky state-local partnership, it was flawed and messy and fragile and *real*. Something that rural communities could develop into something lasting and powerful.

The more I came to understand the weight of it, the less sure of myself I became. Some days I felt like a complete fraud. I mean, who was I standing next to hardcore locals willing to raise six million dollars for the cause?

People thought I was more local than I was, and I let them think it. They thought I was smarter than I was, and I let them think that, too. Other times, I got so nervous I didn't take time to think before I spoke. At one of my first meetings with Rowley in Harrisburg, he asked me what I thought of the new PA Wilds logo.

"The one with the deer in the keystone?" I ask.

The room goes quiet. Rowley's eyes get huge. He has an exaggerated way about his mannerisms.

"You mean elk," he says, looking right at me, no doubt trying to make sense of how a person who came from the most rural part of Pennsylvania, a state with more hunters per capita than any other in America, could be working on the governor's big outdoors initiative and not know the difference between an elk and a deer.

I try to recover with a "that's what I meant," but at that moment, I feel like he'd looked right through me and saw me for what I am: a phony.

Rowley did not strike me as a hunter, and however brash he'd been with the visitor bureaus, he'd listened and observed and cared enough to get the brand right. On the way home, I listen to a song, "North of 80," (a reference to Interstate 80 that ran across the southern part of the region) that Meredith shared with me. It was released in 2002 by Van Wagner, a local school teacher and former coal miner.

> *When Armstrong stepped on the Moon*
> *America stepped with him, too*
> *A giant leap*
> *left some behind*
> *Buried in the foothills of time*
> *Not much has changed today*
> *Some say prosperity stayed away*
> *100 miles off of any map*
> *We all know exactly where we're at*
>
> *North of 80*
> *it ain't the same*
> *I don't know how else to put it, to explain*
> *There's a different tune in the air*
> *There a northern feel that makes it real everywhere.*[2]

The singer nailed it, I think. Real everywhere.

I think about my art and yearbook teacher from so long ago, and how much I grew when I tried to become the person she thought I could be. How I used to flip through vocabulary flash cards while hiking to become a better writer. I could become what this work needs me to be, I thought. In my heart, I knew I had value to add. I just didn't know exactly

---
2. "North of 80," by Van Wagner. Reprinted with permission.

what that meant yet. Quitting at this stage simply wasn't an option, I tell myself. Like my mom and her stethoscope-gas-station solutions, I must find a way. I turn up Van Wagner on the radio as I head north out of the Valley on Route 255.

> *So, the next time you're out on the road*
> *Feeling shaky in your soul*
> *Take off your watch, throw it away*
> *Come up north, just for the day*
> *Once your life learns to breathe*
> *You'll find it so hard to leave*
> *Don't be surprised if your tracks disappear*
> *And you're surrounded by a future up here*[3]

---
3. Reprinted with permission.

CHAPTER 13

SUBSISTENCE SEASON

"See that," Leonard says as we walk through the woods on his dad's land. He stops and points to a small tree where the bark has been scraped off. "That's a buck rub," he says. He looks around and points to another tree nearby. "There's another one."

Archery season for whitetail deer season is not far off, and rifle season after that, and we are looking for a spot to put up a tree stand. I have never hunted before and am excited to try.

I miss the confidence and perspective I got climbing mountains in Alaska and knowing a place intimately through my reporting. I want to feel those things here. Hunting, I think, will help me get there. A lot of people here hunt and sharing hunting stories is as much a part of the culture as people asking where I'm from and who my parents are. If I hunted, I might better connect with the rural communities I serve and also get more comfortable in the woods. I also like venison and knowing where the meat my family eats comes from.

When I was reporting in the Alaskan Bush, Alaska Natives I met often used harvest seasons to mark time. Events happened "before salmon season" or "after herring," or "during moose." I admired their subsistence lifestyle and longed to have more of my own life tied to the seasons of the natural world. With Leonard, that was becoming a reality.

I wasn't raised in a hunting family, so it was intimidating to start. There is a lot to learn about weapons and safety, fair chase ethics, scent control, the animal's seasons, habitat, patterns, and signs. Most boys learn how to hunt over years from their fathers, starting with small game like squirrels and graduating up to deer, elk, moose, or other big game. I have none of that prepping. Mom was deathly afraid of guns and loved animals. Dad liked to hunt, but we never connected on it.

I was drawn to archery. I bought a compound bow and set up big square foam targets behind my house to practice. I added an arm circuit with light weights to my exercise routine to build upper body strength so I could pull the bow back.

I don't think I will struggle taking the shot when the time comes. I learned that about myself when Sandoz and her husband took me dipnetting at the mouth of the Kenai River in Alaska. Only Alaska residents with personal use permits can dipnet. The number of fish you could harvest changed from year to year depending on the health of the fishery. The experience felt biblical, the way hundreds of local people gathered at the water's edge, waiting for the salmon to show up. When they finally did, people waded out with their nets, scooped up the fish, and brought them to shore.

Our group formed an assembly line. I was assigned to be the person who hit the fish over the head with a club when they were brought to shore. At first, I was not sure I could do it. One of Sandoz's friends saw my hesitation, reached down, grabbed a fish, and pushed it against the silty shore.

"Look, like this," he said and thwacked the salmon on the head. He moved on to the next one and then grabbed both salmon by the gills, one in each hand, and walked them up to our coolers where another person was set up with a filet knife. I reasoned that if I am okay eating salmon, I should be okay doing the dirty harvest work that gets it to my plate. Maybe now I'd appreciate the taste even more. I bent down and steadied the fish with my left hand. I lifted my club and brought it down with a thud, putting the creature out of its misery.

Whitetail season in rural Pennsylvania reminds me of salmon season in Alaska. The deer are plentiful and accessible, and the harvest season is the way many local families fill their freezers for the winter.

Nothing about hunting comes easy to me. I have to conquer my fear of heights just to climb into my treestand, a small bench seat platform fastened to a tree that sits about twenty feet in the air. Fortunately, I have a harness to catch me if I fall, which keeps me brave. I have a hard time sitting still. On warm days I move to swat the black flies away. When it is cold, I move my feet and hands to keep warm, giving away my position. One challenge of archery is that you have to get so much closer to the animal to take the shot, so a lot of the strategy comes down to minimizing the human scent that naturally comes off you so it doesn't signal the deer to run, and, for me, not losing my footing or my shot from shaky arms when my heart is racing as a giant buck walks in. Leonard spends hours trying to prepare me the best spots, helping me with my gear and scent control with specialized shampoos, lotions, deodorants and gear. Sometimes, I hesitate and miss the shot or don't shoot at all. One time, this happens with a giant eight-point buck standing broadside. I am thrilled to have seen it so close, and when I meet up with Leonard, I am smiling and excited to tell him about it. He looks at me like I just fried the engine of a 15-passenger van he told me not to drive. He grabs his hat off his head, frustrated. "How can you be happy about that," he says, "which way did he go?"

I point to the neighbor's land, embarrassed. "That way, I think?"

Leonard never gives up on me and over time, I get better. When I read the no-nonsense advice from legendary bow hunter Fred Bear, who died in 1988, that "The best camouflage pattern is called 'Sit down and be quiet!'"[1] it makes me think of the equally direct writing advice, "sit your ass in a chair and write."

The work of author and television personality Steve Rinella resonates with me because he seems approachable and explores the why alongside the how of hunting. "Maybe stalking the woods is as vital to the human condition as playing music or putting words to paper," he writes in *Meat Eater: Adventures from the Life of an American Hunter*. "Maybe hunting has as much a claim on our civilized selves as anything else. After all, the earliest forms of representational art reflect hunters and prey. While the arts were making us spiritually viable, hunting did the heavy lifting of not only keeping us alive but inspiring us."[2]

Scott Dunkelberger, who I've gotten to know a little better, is a passionate, lifelong hunter. He has a modest hunting camp in the PA Wilds that he bought as a young man, newly married, and spent a lot of time there with his wife and kids, colleagues, and friends. He shares with me that the first time he came up to the region, decades ago, "I had no idea

---

1. Bear's advice goes on, "Your grandpa hunted deer in a red plaid coat, think about that for a second!"
2. In Season 10, Episode 4 of his Meat Eater TV show, "Flash in a Pan," Rinella embarks on what he deems a "humbling, humiliating" hunt for deer during Pennsylvania's flintlock season. When I saw the episode with Leonard, I got so excited. "Oh my gosh!" I told him. "They're in the PA Wilds!!" We chuckle as Rinella begins the narration with his deadpan humor, "Outside of rural Pennsylvania it is not commonly held knowledge that certain 21st century people still choose to hunt with cutting edge 18th century technology."

something so vast and so rural existed in Pennsylvania," he said. "I was blown away."

Over lunch one day at the Driftwood Saloon in Driftwood, population sixty-seven, in Cameron County, he tells me about hunting in Alaska's remote Brooks Range, and how the experience helped give him perspective when he had to deal with angry politicians or similar situations at work. "Make a mistake out there and you might die," he said. "That's real pressure."

Hunting teaches me patience and decisiveness. It builds my confidence and also makes me more humble. Skills, I soon realize, I will need more than ever.

CHAPTER 14

CHANGING THE NARRATIVE

As DCNR begins building its major anchor attractions, I hear complaints in some communities about taxpayer dollars being wasted on Taj Mahals, in others about their county not getting enough investment, and in others still, there is a fear of outsiders coming in and changing the place for the worse, or a persistent belief that tourism can't work here. As Deborah Pontzer put it, "Most of the people who live here, early on would say, 'Why would anybody want to come here?' That was the mantra."

The traditional economic development focus of attracting and retaining existing companies, primarily large manufacturers, often dominates the local mindset. Manufacturing is hugely important to the region's economy, but I worry that focusing on it too narrowly overlooks the powerful role that entrepreneurship and small business can play in rural revitalization. In some communities, local politicians are stuck in "a very old way of thinking," as one county planner put it, lamenting why a big manufacturer doesn't plunk down a 200-job facility and save the town.

"That's gone," the planner told me. "Now it's entrepreneurship. It's quality of life. It's let's improve our housing stock so we can attract good teachers or fill some of these industry jobs. But the political leadership, they don't see the connection. And the county costs keep going up, like the jail. The kids are being taken away from their parents because the parents are all drugged up and in jail. But no one is saying let's utilize this program or this grant to try to get help. It is just cut, cut, cut. I've never been so blown down in my career. It's bad. It's really bad."

Some local leaders lament in the newspaper or in meetings that "the best and brightest" keep moving away, never mind how that mantra can undermine the confidence of people who have stayed or returned and are trying to make a go of it. Identifying a problem, like population decline, was critical to addressing it, of course, but in my mind little good came from dwelling on it. Keep saying negative things about yourself or the place you live and they can become self-fulfilling. One young cafe owner remarked that her town had a "curse of negativity" and then closed up shop and moved to Pittsburgh.

In my travels and my experience living in a rural area I see a pattern that sometimes when a small business opens, or a smart new idea is floated, some people sit on the sidelines and speculate about how long it will be before it flops. If it does fail, they are right there, telling friends and neighbors, they knew it would never work. The Wilds work itself faced this. A county planner I worked with described it as the "crab pot syndrome"—"one crab tries to climb out of the pot and the others pull it back down in."

Woven into this tapestry is the fact that many families have lived here for generations. There are good parts about that, but one challenging part is the baggage that can sometimes follow a last name in a small town. A Community Heart & Soul study conducted by one rural community revealed that some of its residents didn't think it was worth speaking up because no one would listen to them due to the family they came from.[1] Even among the more empowered, there is often insecurity. An outsider who made their home here described it to me as "this weird mix of shame and pride," and then demonstrated it by saying with a smiling face and good posture, "Yes, I've lived here all my life," and then repeating the same phrase with a frown and slumped shoulders while looking at the ground. "Yes, I've lived here all my life."

Many people speak as though it is just their town or county that suffers from these kinds of negative narratives but in my travels across the region, I have seen that is not the case. After so many years of economic contraction and underservice, rural PA suffered from a scarcity mindset that sometimes made it its own worst enemy.

I can relate to the insecurity from my own life experiences, a lack of resources and investment that left me feeling less than, but the negativity

---

1. Community Heart & Soul is "a resident-driven process that engages the entire population of a town in identifying what they love most about their community, what future they want for it, and how to achieve it," according to the program's website, communityheartandsoul.org. The program has been developed and field-tested in partnership with over 120 small cities and towns across America, including several in the PA Wilds region.

is like poison to me, and I protect myself against it in every way I can. I take walks in the woods with my son and husband to remind me what I'm grateful for. I run to release endorphins. I read books about people who have accomplished things against great odds to uplift me. I go to the racetrack and watch Leonard go door to door with hundred-thousand-dollar race teams on his laborer's budget. I spend as much time as possible with innovative thinkers and doers because they inspire the hell out of me.

Thankfully, I find a lot of these kinds of people in the PA Wilds. As the Aspen Institute notes, "Some rural areas grapple with limited financial resources and acute infrastructure needs. However, these constraints have also stimulated innovation and ingenuity in solving problems."[2]

I am especially drawn to the region's entrepreneurs. Starting a business is challenging anywhere, but it is even more so in a rural area given the dearth of capital and foot traffic. *War of Art* author Steven Pressfield writes, "Most of us have two lives. The life we live, and the unlived life within us. Between the two stands Resistance. . . . the most toxic force on the planet . . . the root of more unhappiness than poverty, disease, and erectile dysfunction. To yield to Resistance deforms our spirit. It stunts us and makes us less than we are and were born to be."

Most of the rural entrepreneurs I meet are at war with this resistance. They are the opposite of the armchair critics. They are Piper, "screw it, sometimes you just have to go for it." Or they are me, walking across the lobby in Harrisburg, having the gall to think I can make a difference in the place where I grew up.

Rural PA could not afford to be its own worst enemy, and I felt an urgency to help change this narrative. Making a comeback was difficult because there are fewer people and resources in rural areas. On top of that, an increasing number of anchor institutions in rural communities, from grocery stores to hospitals to newspapers to major employers, were no longer locally owned or controlled. There could certainly be upsides to consolidation and enlightened corporate owners, but this outside ownership, on the whole, sucked power, wealth, and agency out of rural communities like a giant vacuum, harming main streets, reducing philanthropic giving, affecting jobs and wages, and reducing community pride. Scott's big fear was that major rural employers that had been sold

---

2. Rural Development Hubs: Strengthening America's Rural Innovation Infrastructure, 2019.

to outside interests, now lacking the deep community connections upon which they were built, might not be willing to weather storms like they once had. If a major employer in a rural town can't find workers because people keep moving away or the population is aging, what's to say they won't move their company someplace else?

Start losing major employers in small communities already cut to the bone, and it would be far more difficult to turn things around. Place-based tourism and outdoor recreation development wasn't a panacea, but it was part of the solution because, in addition to being an economic force, if done intentionally, it supported the kind of amenities that improved rural quality of life and made a place feel vibrant and hopeful. And not just for tourists. For people who live here. Trails. Restaurants. Shops. Breweries. Galleries. Outfitters. It built on the assets a place had, strengthening other industries, like manufacturing, in the process, by making it easier for them to attract and retain the talent they need. Tourism focused on local entrepreneurs also strengthened a rural community's social safety net by creating more spaces where rural people could interact with their neighbors.

The reality really *was* changing. In a single community, people might see one or two businesses open, or a breakthrough conversation happening about how tourism and outdoor recreation development are important and dismiss it as a one-off. But zoom out and it was clear that all this investment by the state was instigating action by a lot of different kinds of actors—businesses, entrepreneurs, trail groups, nonprofits, local governments—in a lot of the region's communities. I was on the front lines watching it happen.

Just before the Elk Country Visitor Center opened, a man who worked for a top-five employer in Elk County, a paper mill, called me on the phone and told me that he drove up to the new visitor center to see for himself what all the local chatter was about and had been blown away. The facility will be a great place for industry to take clients when they come to town on business, he said, and he thanked me.

"Keep up the great work," he said. "This is going to help all of us."

I hung up the phone, elated. I needed to get more of these voices out there, and fast. If people didn't start to see this larger story, we'd dismiss every hard-earned micro-win as nothing special, ultimately losing momentum and the opportunity to unlock something truly transformative.

My gut told me I had to be the face of this thing. To be out there, every day, making a case for it, passionately. I was jumping from one rural entrepreneur to another, to the state's investments, to the marketing, to the stewardship efforts, to the planning, from county to county, as though hopping on well-placed stones to cross a crick. No one else had the same visibility on how it all came together to form a new path. *I* had to tell that story. Connecting entrepreneurs to resources might be my job, but this, I realize, is my duty. I must make it my mission to tell anyone in rural PA who will listen about the big picture of what is happening.

This is a stressful realization. There was a reason I'd been a print reporter, not a television reporter. I am not comfortable in front of cameras or crowds, and my second thought is often better than my first. I can think on my feet, but I appreciate the opportunity to revise. I tell myself that getting past that is what it means to be a professional.

I put close to 30,000 miles on my car that first year driving all over the PA Wilds and meeting with community groups, sometimes as small as four or five people. Public speaking drains my battery, intensely. Being gone so much also creates a hardship for my family. But there is no one else to do it.

In the beginning, many people are skeptical or downright cynical, arms crossed, asking me if I work for The State. I share how I left rural PA and did not think I'd ever return. I tell the story of helping my sister grow her business, pain points and all. I share what I know about the PA Wilds effort and why I think it matters.

In one small town, a young man who looks to be in his early 20s shouts at me during the question-and-answer period, "We don't need tourism. We need to bring back manufacturing!"

I try to explain that it isn't either-or, but I fail to get through to him, and he storms out. There are a lot of failures like this, and I have to keep getting back up, adjusting my approach, and doing it again.

Many people I meet are excited about the initiative's holistic approach and that I've taken the time to share it with them. Others, as Pontzer noted, wonder why anyone would want to come here or are skeptical that the state will make good on its promises. In a place built on manufacturing and resource extraction, some rural power brokers seem at first to eye tourism warily or pat it on the head.

Others, like in Pine Creek, fear tourism will forever change the special places they love or bring unsavory characters to their town. Others still get hung up on specific details, such as the elk in the middle of the PA Wilds logo when they don't have elk in their particular county. Wrapped inside most complaints, hostilities or gas-lighting are valid concerns, and I am convinced that these concerns hold the clues to how to make it all work, to win the trust and action of the people who live here, to accomplish a greater good.

In a region so big, with so much economic distress, there is no time to take the things people say to me personally or to try to manage every expectation. I just collect the clues and keep going. Some I use immediately to adjust my course. Others I carry in my mind, not fully understanding their significance until the work is in some hairy predicament, and I have to feverishly turn them over and plug them in like Indiana Jones trying to solve a cave puzzle before the ground falls from beneath him.

Among partners in the heady, well-funded early days, there is jockeying for position and power. I learn that like rural PA, DCNR and DCED are not monoliths. There are differing views about the PA Wilds effort inside the agencies. At DCNR, some feel the agency has no business building new visitor centers when it has millions of dollars in backlogged maintenance at existing facilities. Others are concerned that the marketing will create unrealistic expectations for visitors and that in such a distressed landscape, the private sector will not be able to respond fast enough, or at all, and state parks and forests will be left to deal with the ire of unsatisfied and unprepared visitors.

People on the Planning Team tell me not to even say the word "marketing" or the visitor bureaus will jump all over me. This seems accurate when I attend a Marketing Corporation meeting and one visitor bureau director yells at another about her county being underrepresented in a new visitor guide.

I am surprised by the infighting and ask Scott about it. We are standing in the doorway of a regional economic development organization, and there happens to be a stack of visitor guides by the door. He picks one up and thumbs through it, pointing to each picture from the county of the complaining visitor bureau.

"Looks pretty well represented to me," he says. He smiles and puts the visitor guide back in place. End of conversation. I appreciate how he doesn't get caught up in the dramas and personalities, and I try to model that in my own behavior.

At another point, I create a handout that highlights the different aspects of the PA Wilds' work—*Design Guide*, marketing ads, small business development, new visitor centers being built, etc.—and I am reprimanded by one of Scott's colleagues from the Tourism Office.

"This is not your job," she tells me. "The visitor bureaus have already done this."

Some of the visitor bureaus were helping spread the word, but it wasn't enough—may never be enough in such a large landscape where there is such limited media presence. I know this from my own presentations in communities and people's responses to them. I push back, and it is an uncomfortable conversation because I dislike confrontation, but the woman listens and changes her position, and I'm proud of myself for sticking up for what makes sense, versus letting someone at a desk hundreds of miles away in Harrisburg make that decision for me.

Some political operatives wonder if I'm trying to run for office; others think I'm trying to make a name for myself, which annoys me and hurts my feelings, because while I may at one time in my life have sought both of those things, this is different. My "second mountain," as the author David Brooks[3] so eloquently explores in his book by the same name. A job that pays the bills, yes. But more than that. A commitment to community, to family, to hope.

When I'm asked to join a deputy secretary in Harrisburg to brief a legislative committee, a staffer at a partner organization in the region calls to tell me I am overstepping my bounds, that it should be her executive director or the director of the Planning Team that does it. I know I am the better person for the job based on the topic and skill sets involved and am dismayed at the pettiness. I think of Eleanor Roosevelt's advice, which I read in a book my mom gave me, "Do what you feel in your

---

3. A different David Brooks than the one involved in the Wilds work. A conservative political and cultural commentator for the New York Times, Brooks has written several books, including *The Second Mountain: The Quest for a Moral Life*.

heart to be right—for you'll be criticized anyway," and politely disagree with the caller, knowing it probably only fuels what some people already think about me.

Some days, I am so spent, spinning on things said and left unsaid, that when I pick up my son from the babysitter, it is hard to let go of work. I try to fake it, but kids know when someone is there but not present. All I can do is recommit to being more present, and keep going. I run across a picture of Tina Fey in an American Express ad where the famous comedian and actress is sitting under a desk trying to get some work done, crumpled paper everywhere, her toddler at her computer, a knowing smile on her face that to me says, "Hey, this is what the working mom juggling act looks like, and it's okay." I admired Tina Fey as a creative ("Do your thing and don't care if they don't like it.") and as a mom ("Kids are definitely the boss of you. Anyone who will barge into the room while you are on the commode is the boss of you."). I tear the picture out of the magazine and hang it on my wall.

Leonard is always present in the moment. I love this about him and am grateful Max and I have his influence. As my work becomes more stressful, Leonard's dirt track racing becomes a welcome release, something we do as a family. Getting our motor back from being freshened, hearing it start for the first time, and the smell of race fuel becomes as much a sign of spring for me as Max spotting his first robin in the yard.

The Pennsylvania Wilds region had a dirt track scene. In addition to Stateline, which sat close to the state line of New York and PA (hence the name, and it was technically in New York), the Pennsylvania Wilds was home to Bradford Speedway, McKean County Speedway, Clinton County Speedway, Thunder Mountain Speedway, Hidden Valley Speedway, Hummingbird Speedway and a few others, as well as Close Racing Supply, a growing national distributor of circle track components.

Many race teams and racetracks were sponsored by local manufacturing or transportation companies, oil or natural gas or logging outfits, and it dawned on me one night at Stateline that dirt tracks are where industry meets tourism, a rich experience that attracted hundreds of locals, visitors, and race teams.

Before long, Leonard is racing across three states, a top five finisher many nights, and I look forward to seeing him and Snoopy setting up the car and then loading up our race trailer and heading to the track, Max in tow with his light-up sneakers and earmuffs to protect his hearing. At the track, my job is to walk up to the pit gate with Max and get the race lineup for the heats and features. One night, Leonard wins two features in a row. They give him the checkered flag, and we all gather at the flag stand for pictures. Leonard is always considerate of the next person in line and tries to hurry up. His dad, who had done so much for Leonard and me as we started our family, is almost in tears, and stops him. "Take your time," he says. "You earned this. Enjoy it. These moments go so fast." I know he is right, and I try to internalize his wisdom, knowing the pace I am keeping at home and professionally.

At work, I start incorporating more entrepreneurs' voices into my presentations. I tell people about Stephanie Distler, an artisan and huge champion for the PA Wilds work, who handcrafts jewelry that looks like bark, and then show a picture of how she stamped one of her bracelets with the PA Wilds logo and the words "charm not chain," a phrase from the PA Wilds brand principles that encourages visitors to support locally owned businesses.

I share the story of Joe and Andrea Lanich, a young couple who grew up in rural PA and moved away, who had recently returned to start a craft letterpress business, The Laughing Owl Press Company. Most letterpress businesses were located in major cities, but the Lanichs figured that with rural PA's lower cost of living and improved accessibility through the internet, they could leave their jobs in the city as a mechanical engineer and architect and build a letterpress business in the PA Wilds that could compete nationally.[4]

I share how Deb Adams doubled the size of her staff as she expanded the historic Gateway Lodge, and that her daughter and son-in-law joined her in the endeavor. Located among the old-growth pines of Cook Forest, the family appreciated being part of a regional movement. "I see us as pioneers blazing new territory and dusting off the hidden gems of this area," Adams' daughter told me for a story I wrote in an online magazine, *Keystone Edge*. "It's a brand that represents hope for our communities and natural assets. We're proud to be a part of such a positive force."

My second or so year on the job, I am joined by another full-time staffer, Sam MacDonald. Sam was my age, had worked as a journalist,

---

[4]. Andrea Lanich designed the cover for this book. Find the company at LaughingOwlPress.com.

and hailed from a big Catholic family that people liked to joke made up half the population of Ridgway (he and his wife would go on to have nine kids). Sam had written a serious book, *Agony of an American Wilderness: Loggers, Environmentalists and the Fight for a Forgotten Forest*, about one of the region's star assets, the Allegheny National Forest, and a hilarious memoir, *Urban Hermit*, about how he put himself on a "Financial Emergency Rotgut Poverty Plan" after he partied his way through Yale and became a "fat bastard" swimming in debt.

Sam was a shot in the arm, a boost of capacity helping me push this boulder up the hill. I loved co-presenting with him because he was super local and made audiences laugh, opening them up and making it easier to have a real conversation.

But more than anything, it was DCNR opening its new anchor facilities that helped the work turn a corner. In 2010, two years into my role as ombudsman, the Nature Inn at Bald Eagle State Park, the Tiadaghton Resource and Management Center in the Pine Creek Valley, and the Elk Country Visitor Center opened their doors. The following year, in 2011, the Wildlife Center at Sinnemahoning State Park and the Kinzua Skywalk at Kinzua Bridge State Park also opened. A final anchor investment, a visitor center to accompany the skywalk experience at Kinzua Bridge State Park, was under construction. The facilities, their interpretive exhibits and experiences, and the public lands they are connected to and help celebrate are world-class, and draw thousands of new visitors to the region, who spend dollars at local businesses in nearby gateway communities.

The Elk Country Visitor Center becomes the biggest juggernaut of all, going from 80,000 visitors in 2010 to more than 200,000 by 2013.[5] Doug and Sylvia Ruffo, longtime visitors to the area, retire and open Benezette Wines in a remodeled garage space. A few doors away, Brian Kunes and Matt Castle go through multiple expansions to transform the Benezette Hotel from a town bar into a family-friendly restaurant and event space. The restaurant had never broken 400 meals at dinner, but shortly after the elk center opened, it did—a month ahead of the peak tourism season. "We were like, 'Oh. My. Gosh,'" Kunes told me for a story I wrote about the growth for *Keystone Edge*.

Another man started a side business selling chocolate-covered candies at the center's gift shop under cheeky labels like "elk balls" and "dragonfly

---

5. By 2023, annual attendance hovered around 480,000.

droppings" when he sensed his manufacturing job wasn't going to be around a lot longer. When he started, he hoped to sell $1,500 worth of chocolates in a month and was stunned when they called to say he'd sold that much in a day and to bring more product.

"It was a life changer," he told me. "We're in the middle of nowhere up here. It gave you hope. The opportunities are everywhere."

At one point, in 2011, two faculty members at the University of Pittsburgh's Bradford campus ask if I can come tell freshmen at the college about the PA Wilds as a place and a movement, to help them feel more connected to the area and to help with retention. They encourage me to do something multimedia.

I was a slow adopter of new technology so despite YouTube's growing popularity, I had never before attempted to use the platform to tell a story. One night after putting my son to bed, as Leonard worked on his racecar in the garage, I started experimenting with the media player that came preloaded on my laptop. After an hour, I was totally into it, time passing without me noticing or caring, placing photos and writing captions, and then laying music over it.

I show the recreation infrastructure investments and the brand, people's fears and changing mindsets, and the business and community development the movement is sparking. For the finale, I create a slide that says the PA Wilds' work isn't really about the visitors—it is about us, and future generations of kids who grow up here. In a folder on my laptop, I find a picture of my son and his cousins carrying a long plastic orange pipe they'd pulled out of the Allegheny during the river cleanup and use it to illustrate this parting message. The video is super low-fi but from the heart, "quirky not slick," as the PA Wilds brand principles say, and I'm proud of it.

The next morning, I give the Planning Team and the small group of people I work with at the state a heads up about the video, and then jump in my Subaru and head to Bradford. I get an okay response from the students, but when I get off stage and check my email, it is blowing up with partners reacting to the video. There is one from a visitor bureau that is critical but constructive, and I appreciate it and make the suggested edit. The rest of the responses are overwhelmingly positive.

I am still reading through the emails, amazed by what is happening, when my phone rings. It is Meredith. She and I work so closely at this point that we can sometimes finish each other's sentences. She knows in intimate detail the daily challenges I face trying to grow support, and she is always trying to figure out where I am headed next so she can break trail around me or warn me about potential hazards.

Meredith is in as much shock as I am about the response to the video. There is not even a hello when I pick up the phone.

"That video," she says, and I can hear her smiling on the other end of the line.

"I know," I say, "Can you believe it?" I read her some of the messages, and she tells me how it is being shared inside and outside the Rachel Carson Building in Harrisburg.

The video quickly racks up more than four thousand views. For rural PA in 2011, where many communities still used dial up, or had no internet at all, it was the equivalent of going viral. I am excited about the reach, and to have this part of me, the creative storytelling part, be seen by my professional peers. It was such a big part of my life for so long, and I didn't realize how much I had missed it until now.[6]

After what seems like forever, with so many hands working to get the flywheel in motion, it finally starts turning and picks up speed faster than anticipated. The PA Wilds becomes one of the fastest growing tourism regions in the state. We go from $1.3 billion in tourism spending in 2009 to more than $1.7 billion by 2013. And not in some overrun theme park kind of way, but with growing local small businesses and inspiring stewardship at its core. More businesses and communities want to be involved, more stewards are eager to help, and more investors are interested in supporting the cause, which is fantastic because there is still so much need, opportunity, and work ahead.

But we do not have a good foundation for the flywheel. It starts to wobble, and all of us are trying like hell to hold it down and come up with a plan before it's too late.

---

6. Find my quaint retro video, "What is the PA Wilds Initiative," on the PA Wilds Center's YouTube page @PAwilds or directly at https://youtu.be/AulibWb8vsU.

CHAPTER 15

ON THE PRECIPICE

One of the reasons the PA Wilds Initiative got traction where other regional attempts had failed was that it tapped into "rural ideology and rural perspectives," as one regional economic developer in the Wilds put it. Namely, "generations of people used to working together and bootstrapping."

"The beauty about it is the way it's grown," David Brooks told me. "If somebody got way out in front, they had to stop and let everyone catch up. It was a series of pushes. It was DCED, DCNR, or something locally that pushed the envelope a little farther . . . a big facility, or a big campaign, or travel stories, or as you came on board, or Planning Team and the *Design Guide*. Big steps that someone said 'this is something new, but it is coming from a good place and it's something that's going to benefit everybody. Respect it. Use it. Take advantage of it. Those who do, great, those who don't, we'll move on without you.' It was a series of those."

Part of what all this meant in practice was that all these different moving parts of the initiative were incubated inside all these different organizations that had stepped up to help the cause. It *was* inspiring, and, we'd find, organizationally unsustainable. In an economically distressed region like ours, most organizations could only do the lift for so long. So each year, the suite of organizational homes for different aspects of the Wilds work changed based on leadership, staff capacity, funding, and other constraints.

As the Wilds' momentum increased, it became harder and harder to coordinate things. The PA Wilds Artisan Development Initiative, for example, which had systems for jurying in new members, dues, and more than 100 craftspeople participating, had bounced around to five organizational homes and was on the verge of collapse because of it. The Planning Team was on its fourth home, the ombudsman position its third.

Corporations, foundations, and grant funders showed interest in investing in the movement, but I was pretty sure if we pulled back the curtain and showed them the insane Rube Goldberg contraption holding it up, they'd run in the other direction. Our ingenuity and collaborative spirit had gotten us this far, but the back end of the work was quickly becoming an accounting and customer service nightmare.

"The folks who initiated this did the right thing by thinking big," Eric Bridges, then head of the North Central Regional Planning and Development Commission, the organization that helped fund the original elk study, told me in an interview. "But there were a lot of things that were stacked up against us. The scale of the vision, how are we going to manage this thing we've created? Do we have the skillsets, the capacity, the wherewithal, and stick-to-it-ness? That was the question."

Not helping matters, the very long tail of the 2008 recession had whipped around and smacked the PA Wilds effort hard, resulting in severe budget cuts to state grant programs that supported it, while tectonic changes in technology upended approaches as fast as anyone could get their minds and resources around them. Meanwhile, the region's rural communities were hit by some of the highest unemployment rates in the state. In one county, an educator friend told me, kindergarten attendance at the local Catholic school plummeted by more than half.

"People were broke," he said. "Or they just packed up and left."

It reminded me of my family's own story of packing up in the late 1980s and heading north on the Alaska-Canada Highway.

The Marketing Corp lost its funding and was now in "keep-the-lights-on" mode. One visitor bureau had resigned and said it no longer wanted to be involved. Rendell, the Democratic governor who launched the PA Wilds Initiative, was about to leave office, and a Republican was about to take his place. The work was nonpolitical, and supported by both Democrats and Republicans, but no one was sure what the administration change would mean for state support of the initiative.

These growing pains spilled over into the Planning Team's meetings, the one place where many of the partners came together, and for almost two years, it dominated their agenda. Large group conversations and decision making is often not an easy or fast process, especially when programs and projects are scattered across a variety of organizations, and nearly every person working on them is a volunteer, with whole other organizations to run.

At one point, I used my son's markers to illustrate all the different places the work had been housed, using a different color for each piece, and showed it to a group of partners. It looked like a scribbly mess. At another point, the Planning Team chair, frustrated with the bickering, stood up and said, "I can't do this anymore!"

DCNR and DCED started pushing us to have a single lead organization. We held retreats and kept talking. I could see where the work needed to go—a lot of us could—and I grew increasingly frustrated that no one would step up to do it. I worried about my job, of course, but also, didn't anyone care how much time and energy so many people had invested to get to this point? The whole thing was going to collapse if we didn't take some action!

I briefly thought that maybe I should do it, but quickly talked myself out of it. Who was I to take the lead? Would people even follow me if I did? I didn't know the first thing about running a nonprofit. All the systems that would have to be put in place. Raising money. Building and training a staff. I could never do it. And even if I could, I was pretty sure people would peg me as power-hungry or similar things I've heard said about women when they step up to lead.

I wasn't sure if I was more afraid of failing or succeeding. Either way, I abandoned the idea as quickly as it had arisen because it was easier to point fingers at others' lack of leadership than to look in the mirror and face up to my own. I let the *possibility* of others trying to pull me back down into the crab pot convince me to not even try. I let the resistance win.

CHAPTER 16

REDISCOVERING MY ROOTS

I'd been back in rural Pennsylvania for three years when my Grandma, Bernetta Brant, passed away at the age of eighty-seven in early May. Mom and her four brothers held a service in a church in downtown Warren, and then a caravan of us drove to a remote area of the Allegheny National Forest called Sugar Run. Kinzua, the village where they'd lived as kids, was not far off but had been underwater for five decades since the building of the Kinzua Dam. My uncles were giants in the landscape of my childhood. Like Grumpy, they were all funny characters who genuinely seemed to get a kick out of our company.

We parked along a road, hiked back to a brushy forested spot, and gathered around a shallow hole in the ground about the size of a coffee mug. Mom and my uncles poured Grandma's ashes and Grumpy's, who died of diabetes twenty-five years earlier, into the hole and covered them with dirt. I'd not heard of anyone burying their parents' ashes in a National Forest before, but it felt appropriate. They tamped a small wooden cross into the ground and set mementos nearby. A small American flag for Grumpy. A pair of clip-on earrings from Grandma's jewelry collection.

While I struggled to find my footing as a mom and rural change agent, I felt compelled to mine my past for wisdom, connection, understanding, or anything that could help me navigate the hundreds of daily decisions I now had to make. My family had lived here for at least four generations, probably longer. Who were they? What was their connection to this place? How did they handle life's challenges?

A few years after my Grandma passed, the uncle I felt closest to, Charlie Brant, got cancer. Like Grumpy, Charlie was a war veteran. He had served as a Marine in Vietnam and was exposed to Agent Orange, a chemical they used to spray the jungle during the war. Charlie's daughter, Michelle, who we all called Pugsa, was my closest cousin in age and friendship, so as a kid, I was a regular at their log cabin. To this day, it is the one house where I still know the telephone number by heart.

Uncle Charlie's cancer lent an urgency to the journey of rediscovering my roots. Very few family history records existed between my mom and her brothers. Even Grumpy's war medals, I'd soon learn, had been lost. But they all had stories. I set out to interview them before it was too late. Piper joined me and took pictures.

* * *

From what I could piece together, my grandparents had very difficult upbringings. Both of their dads were violent alcoholics, and Grandma was beaten and molested by her dad. Grumpy's dad also beat him, but his mom, Mary Brant, was by all accounts a saint who, through her kindness, left a huge impression on everyone.

My grandparents got married at a young age to escape their situations. According to news clippings Piper found, Grumpy, whose real name was Ashley Brant, enlisted in the military during World War II. He was sent to North Africa in 1943 and transferred to Italy in 1944, serving with the medical corps of the 85th Infantry Division, Fifth Army. He spent months in theater, and at one point, was a prisoner of war.

Grumpy's older brother, Charles Norman Brant, was also in the war. The brothers were stationed near each other but didn't realize it until one day they ran into each other on the ravished landscape. Charles wrote home to his mom about it, and the tale made it into Warren's local paper. Piper unearthed the article through an ancestry search site while helping Pugsa's daughter with a family history paper she was writing for school. Charles told his mother that on Valentine's Day, "a very dirty American soldier, with long beard and long hair," walked up to him and started teasing him. "The visitor turned out to be Cpl. Brant's brother," the news article said. "They both write how happy they were to meet and that they are stationed about fifty miles apart."

Piper and I couldn't believe it when she turned up this artifact. It felt so special to get this glimpse into Grumpy's life as a young man. I could just imagine their reunion. Before I had kids, I felt like I spent most of my time trying to reunite with my sisters. Our first careers kept each of us on the move to far-flung places. Sandoz a travel nurse, Piper in the Navy, me reporting. Money was always tight, so when we did manage to get in a room together, it was a joyous occasion that felt nothing short of a miracle.

Piper sent me the article about Grumpy via text. I reread it several times and then called her on the phone. Piper had been stationed in Italy, on the island of Sicily, when she was in the Navy, and I lived with her there for a few months, early in my journalism career, after I ran out of money in South Africa, trying to make it as a freelancer. Grumpy never talked to us about the war when we lived with him as kids, but he did tell us about the beautiful Sistine Chapel he'd seen while stationed overseas. Piper and I wanted to see it as a way to honor his memory. Both broke, Piper finagled us a free bus ride to Rome by signing up to run the Rome marathon under the team banner of her base, Naval Air Station Sigonella.

These experiences swirled with my memories of Grumpy and my own experiences of seeing my siblings after long stretches apart, and I began to cry.

It had been a long time since I'd thought about Grumpy in such detail. We had lived with him and Grandma for a while after my parents split. He had been a defining male figure in my life, influencing my creativity, my love of nature, and my sense of self-worth and belonging. He even inspired the creation of my name. My mom said he used to pat her lovingly on the head as a girl and say, "Ta Ta." I thought of the only picture I'd seen of Grumpy as a young man, smiling and playing near a crick in Warren, and envisioned him on foreign soil in a tattered war uniform giving his brother a huge hug.

"Can you imagine finding each other like that?" I said to Piper.

"I know," she said, "his big brother!"

Charles did not make it home from the war. He was buried at a cemetery in France. His mother, my great-grandmother, was notified by telegram. As for my grandfather, a newspaper clipping said he returned with "two bronze stars on his campaign ribbons for major engagements in which he participated, the Good Conduct Medal and the Bronze Star for meritorious performance in combat against the enemy." But inside, my uncles said, my grandfather struggled deeply with what he had experienced.

When he got back to Warren, my grandfather got a job with an oil company, and he and my grandma moved into a house the company owned on an oil lease in Sugar Run. My uncle Terry had been born shortly after his dad had shipped out for war and was now a young boy. Two more boys soon followed. The first was named Charles, after the brother my grandfather lost in the war, and the second, Frank.

Warren County was not far from where America's first oil well had been discovered, and drilling for oil was now a major industry. "Every place was loaded with oil wells back then," Terry said. "We called them 'the guns.' You'd hear them. Boom! Boom! Boom!"

Like a lot of young men working in extractive industries in those days, to keep a roof over their heads, my grandfather did dangerous, laborious work and didn't get paid much for it.

"We ate a lot of deer meat and a lot of groundhogs," my uncle Terry said.

Mom had a small framed black and white picture of my uncles when they were young displayed in her living room. Their stories fresh in my mind, I picked it up one day and looked at it anew. Charles and Frank look about seven or eight and are standing in front of what appears to be a sawmill, their dad working in the background. Their pants and coats are tattered and far too small, their faces dirty.

People in rural Pennsylvania didn't talk about being part of Appalachia very often, despite how the Appalachian Mountains shaped the physical and cultural landscape, creating economic hardships but also cultivating resilience and creativity in communities and often, a love for the outdoors. But looking at this picture now, all I could think was, *My family is from northern Appalachia.* And I was proud of that.

My grandfather worked long hours until one day his boss accused a friend of my grandfather's of stealing. The boss was a mean alcoholic who was probably the one doing the stealing, Terry said. My grandfather couldn't take it anymore and punched his boss in the face.

In need of a new place to live, the family moved about five miles down the valley to Kinzua. All three of my oldest uncles have fond memories of their time in the village, riding bikes, swimming, killing rattlesnakes, and putting the dead snakes in their mom's apple bag on the porch. My grandmother was "one yodeling lady," Terry said. "She had a beautiful voice."

After my mom was born, when she needed to take a nap, her brothers would put her in a baby buggy outside and "run like hell around the house." "If she fell out, we'd throw her back in and keep running," Uncle Charlie told me one afternoon sitting in his living room, where Pugsa and I used to have our slumber parties. "We called it bumper hugging."

"Pretty much every kid played on the baseball team," Frank told me as I interviewed him on another day in a classroom at Allegheny Outfitters. "We had the best ball diamond in Warren County, with dugouts. That's where our roots started to grow. We really found something."

But at home, there was little peace. My grandfather would hear a piece of drywall fall and jump up screaming as though he was back on the battlefield. "There was no post-traumatic stress disorder back then," Terry said. "He was in bad shape."

Terry described his dad the way I remembered him, as a "very generous and considerate person." But after the war, he struggled with an internal rage that he would sometimes turn on his oldest sons.

"When I was a kid, I didn't have to do anything to get hit," Frank said. "I think for a long time I was his favorite target. I resented him for a long time."

Bernetta could be cold, controlling, and manipulative. She and her husband fought bitterly with words, but Grumpy never raised a hand at her, no matter how awful she sometimes treated him. "I never met a man who had so much respect for women as my dad," Frank said.

Grandma cared a lot about how things looked and what people thought. "Dad, he didn't give a shit about that stuff," Uncle Charlie said. He'd rather make up songs or go on silly adventures. "He'd take us to go look for the dead horse in the road," Charlie said. "I just assumed every kid did that."[1]

There were no sit-down family dinners or games at the Brant house. Work and hunger were constants. At one point, my uncles said, things got so bad my grandmother suffered a nervous breakdown from the stress.

My uncles would disappear to the woods for days at a time. They'd hunt squirrels, peel bark off poplar trees, load it into boxes, and take it to

---

1. If you are looking for the meaning in this, don't. It was just a random mystery adventure Grumpy made up. He took me and my sisters to look for the dead horse, too.

a nearby tannery to make a buck. Charlie would spend days on a brook trout stream that ran through Sugar Run where he taught himself to fish.

"I never thought Dad was mean," Charlie told me. "I just thought that's the way it is. He was tough. He didn't raise you easily. It was a hard road. You were a man from the time you were old enough to walk to the time you die. It was a matter of survival. You weren't reliant on anybody. We were a different family."

Terry was the ringleader and the toughest of the Brant boys, and as soon as he was old enough, he joined the Army. There was a single bus stop in Kinzua and the day Charlie saw his big brother step off it in a crisp uniform and spit-shined shoes, he knew he wanted to join. "I just thought, 'Man, he is the toughest guy in the world.'"

There were no family conversations when my grandparents were told they had to leave Kinzua to make way for the building of the Kinzua Dam. As the Seneca Nation fought to stop the government from taking its lands, drawing national attention, people in the village wondered if it was really going to happen.

By then, a fourth boy, Ash, had been born. Terry said my grandparents didn't put up a fight and were compensated $5,500 for their house. Their oldest sons didn't go so easily, vandalizing construction equipment to try to hold up progress.

"I was always attached to Kinzua and Sugar Run," Charlie told me, recalling their near subsistence lifestyle in the woods. "I could do everything I needed to do right there. It was freedom."

Near the end, Charlie said, "They came to people's houses with weapons drawn and said get the hell out. It was horrible."

The woman who would eventually marry my uncle Terry, Diane, remembered government officials hurrying out of a beautiful home in the village and then watching it go up in flames. "It's excruciating to see all your friends and relatives' [property] destroyed," she told the *Warren Times Observer* decades later, the memory still fresh in her mind. "I could walk to my grandmother's, [to] six aunts and uncles, cousins. Everybody moved to a different place. Some friends I never saw again."

It made me think about the distrust some people in the region had of government. Listening to this story, I could see why.

After Kinzua, my grandparents moved fifteen or more times. My uncle Ash, who was two when the family left Kinzua, had no memories of the village, and, fortunate for him and my mom, they missed most of the period of Grumpy's life where he struggled with his rage. Ash was inseparable from his big brother, Charles, who taught him everything he knew about the outdoors.

As soon as he was old enough, Charlie enlisted with the Marines. The Vietnam War was just getting underway. When he told his dad, my grandfather ignored him and told him to take out the trash. Charlie refused. His dad pushed him and shouted, "You're nothing but cannon fodder!" no doubt thinking of the dead brother his son was named after.

"I hit the door," Charlie recalled. "Then I hit the back porch. Then I took the garbage out. I think a lot of that came from what Dad went through overseas. I think he was always tormented."

Charlie served fourteen months in Vietnam.

Ash, who looked up to his older brother, tried to follow his footsteps and join the Marines, but they wouldn't take him because he had a high risk of hernias. "I'd never really thought about it until then but we came from a military family. All my brothers, my dad, we even had aunts that were in World War II," Ash told me. "It really bothered me that I couldn't be a Marine. I got turned down twice. I wanted to be like Chuck. He had a lot of faults. But he was just an awesome dude."

Charlie told me growing up in Kinzua and Sugar Run is probably what kept him alive in Vietnam. He came home pretty messed up, suffering like his dad did from post-traumatic stress disorder.

"I resented the fact that I didn't die," Charlie told me. "I felt I let everybody down. So many of them had to die or get so screwed up and here I was, not dead. It just didn't seem fair to them. I still get stressed out over it."

The country was not kind to veterans at that time, and the military wasn't much better. But my uncle took his anger out on himself rather than others. He spent time in bars, rolled a truck with my dad, did crazy stunts like jumping off a tall bridge near Kinzua Dam into the water.

"For a while, we just lost him," my mom told me.

Charlie and Terry weren't close before the war, but grew close after, forging a bond that would last the rest of their lives. At one point, they got the idea to float the Allegheny River until it met the Ohio River, and eventually, the Mississippi, all the way to the Gulf of Mexico.

"We got all these maps and charts," Terry said. "It was like writing up a patrol in the military. Me and Chuck."

They made it all the way to Memphis, surviving on coffee, two cases of beer a day, cans of beans and sardines, and all the fish they could catch. "We were Huck Finn for a while," Terry said. "Every day was an adventure. We'd just laugh and laugh and laugh and see so much. And the driftwood. I'm a driftwood fanatic. I call them river bones."

Piper and I are stunned to learn that we had unknowingly followed in their footsteps, two sister siblings on our own river adventure writing a paddling guide, albeit with a lot less beer.

Charlie married my Aunt Carolyn, one of the most non-judgmental, devout Christians I've ever met. I don't think I've ever seen my Aunt Carolyn drink or curse. (Her go-to word is *garsh*.). I'm pretty sure her love and steadiness is a big part of what helped Uncle Charlie come out the other side of his war experiences with the grace he did.

Faith also played a role, and not just for Charlie. Terry said he went through some faith-based counseling, and when it helped him, he invited his dad to join him. "He completely collapsed over the idea because he had so much inside," Terry said. "He went, and it really softened things."

By the time my sisters and I moved in with my grandparents, they were living in a modest three-story house in Clarendon, outside of Warren. I thought they were rich. Grandma had a record player and a flowery couch in a sitting room that she kept covered with clear plastic unless it was a special occasion. Grandma's bedroom had a matching bed and dresser set, matching lamps, a pretty comforter, and a small TV where I could stay up late and watch this new channel called HBO.

Grumpy slept on a cot in a stark room in the basement. He had huge hands and was the gentlest person. During the day, he'd sit in a big wooden rocker with a cushion on it in the TV room, and we'd look at *National Geographic* magazines or watch the *Price is Right* or try to spy songbirds out the window, or I'd sit on his lap and write in my journals. After school, we sat down and ate dinner together. He taught us funny songs ("Peekin' through a knothole/in daddy's wooden leg/why'd they build the seashore near the ocean? . . .) and poems ('Will, Will, worked in a sawmill, tore his pants, lost his hat, got in jail and that's that.")

Grandma was a big woman. For many years, she cleaned banks and office buildings in downtown Warren. When she got home, she'd watch

TV or have my mom and Ash, her two youngest, walk to a nearby store to get her ice cream. "When she got home she was exhausted," Ash recalled. "She had nothing left. She was a good mom, but she was exhausted most of my life."

When I lived with her, Grandma would vacuum with an unlit cigarette hanging out of her mouth. If I asked, she'd yodel for me, and it always made both of us smile. Even in old age, her smile could light up a room. Her singing voice reminded me of Judy Garland's, and more than once as I got older, I wondered if Grandma had ever dreamed to be a singer.

Grandma was cold to my mom growing up, a situation that only grew worse when my parents split. When my mom said she was going to try to get a nursing degree, Grandma scoffed and told her she'd never make it. "Mom abused her," my uncle Frank said. "This woman has these kids, and she's busting her ass trying to do the right thing. Your mom struggled. She really, really struggled." Grumpy and my mom were a different story. They had a similar spirit and shared a tender closeness I'd recognize years later between Uncle Charlie and his daughter, Pugsa, and my other uncles and their daughters. Mom always spoke about her dad with great love and reverence, just as Pugsa spoke about hers. Charlie was the most like Grumpy to me.

After we moved out of my grandparent's attic, we continued our parade of apartments. When Grumpy died in 1984, we were living in Rembrandt Court in Virginia Beach. I still remember my mom sitting on the steps of our townhouse crying. I ran out the door, all sassy, self-centered pre-teen, biffing her on the back of the head as I passed by, thinking it was funny. Only later did I realize how inconsiderate I had been.

I'd learn decades later that a few weeks before Grumpy died, he was near Harrisburg helping Ash, who by then was married with two little girls and was building a house. Ash was working on the roof. As he moved to a new section, he intentionally dropped boards with nails sticking out of them to a sand pile below. Grumpy wanted to move the boards as a safety precaution, but his diabetes was so bad, he had to stick a hose with cold water in his boots regularly to try to bring feeling back to his extremities.

"If you fall on them, you are going to die," Grumpy told his son.

Exhausted, Ash climbed down and moved the boards. He returned to the roof one last time to button things up for the night, lost his footing, and fell on the sand pile right where the boards had been. "Dad worked on me until the ambulance got there," Ash said. "He got me breathing. He saved my life."

After Grumpy died, and we grew older, we saw less of my extended family. Grandma moved into a small house next to Uncle Terry. Sandoz and I moved to Alaska with Dad. Piper and my mom eventually moved back to Warren County, and Piper went to the high school my parents graduated from. On occasion, Piper said, she'd be out in the woods and come around a bend, and there would be Uncle Charlie, fishing. Sometimes, he'd be in his bare feet.

Like Grumpy, he was always so happy to see her; that's how he was with me, too.

By the time I moved home, Uncle Charlie had accomplished the rare and marvelous feat of successfully going pro, fishing for Zippo Outdoors and Case knives, which had their headquarters in nearby Bradford.[2] He fished in the Cabela's Masters Walleye Circuit with partner Doug Yohe, becoming the 2007 Team of the Year, six-time World Walleye Championship Qualifiers, nine-time Cabela's National Team Championship Qualifiers, and in 2012, he won the Cabela's Master Walleye Circuit Qualifier at Mile Lacs Lake, a big deal in fishing circles. It was a hell of an accomplishment for a country boy from Kinzua and Sugar Run who taught himself to fish with a tree branch, a piece of string, and a safety pin.

Success didn't change Charlie. He still lived in the same log cabin. He used his new platform to raise money and awareness for disabled veterans. I loved running into him at local events where he'd be dressed in his sponsor gear and his veteran's hat, greeting me with a huge grin. "Hey, kiddo! Whatcha been up to? How are those boys? Is Leonard racing this weekend? Did you get anything in archery? You gotta tell me about it!"

All my uncles were proud of Piper's military service and outfitting business, Leonard's racing, and my work as a reporter, and now with the PA Wilds, it meant so much to me. When I told them I wanted to

---

2. The free Zippo/Case Museum, in Bradford, is a must-see when visiting the PA Wilds. The fifteen-thousand-square-foot attraction includes the world-famous Zippo repair clinic, Zippo/Case flagship store, and some fantastic exhibits that showcase American craftsmanship and these two American icons in WWII, Hollywood, rock music, and the outdoors.

understand more about our family history, they were eager to help. All of them regretted not asking their parents more questions before they passed away.

"I don't know anything about my family," Charlie told me. "Anything."

CHAPTER 17

THE WAY YOU LIVE

It's hard to describe how grounding the conversations with my uncles were for me. At various points in different interviews, Piper and I would look at each other with exaggerated eyes, stunned. *Things make so much more sense now!*

I'd always seen my mom as an anomaly with her moving. Now I saw some of it was learned, and that the entire Brant clan was hardwired to seek new experiences, with a sense of adventure.

"I still want to go," Charlie told me while we talked in his living room one afternoon. His pro fishing days over, the cancer was visibly starting to take its toll. "You girls got so much Brant in you it's ridiculous."

Public service also ran deep in my family, I now saw. The military, nursing, journalism, even at Piper's outfitting business, service and stewardship defined the company's values. Other cousins were teachers or worked in corrections. Pugsa taught in Baltimore's inner city. Her daughter, who Uncle Charlie nicknamed Princess Elizabeth Spencer Fairchild the Second from Thomashire, was just out of college, and already you could see she was drawn to service, too, as were Piper's kids.

We all got some Mary Brant in us, I thought. My mom and Piper most of all.

Other congruencies struck me, too, like the deep connections different generations of our family had made to the Allegheny River and the national forest, without any sort of push in that direction or ever really talking out loud about it. Even me, the rolling stone gathering no moss, drawn back here after all these years.

"Where we live is truly a gem," Terry told us as we sat at his kitchen table. Like Piper, he lived on the bank of the Allegheny River. "My heritage is here. And that right there," he said, pointing out the window at the Allegheny. "*That* is something."

It was telling that my uncle, who in his prime as a union pipefitter had helped supervise the construction of the town's refinery and one of its largest employers, now spoke about the river as though it was a more defining force in his life. It made me think of the village of Kinzua, and how decades after people were forced from their homes, their property destroyed and foundations submerged under water, they still met every summer at a pavilion in the national forest to break bread together and share stories.

It was devastating to consider the larger story of what happened to the Seneca, and so many other Native Americans, whose special places had been ripped away. The Seneca Iroquois National Museum, just over the state border in Salamanca, New York, memorializes the Seneca Nation's fight to stop the construction of the Kinzua Dam. The Hall of American Indians at the Carnegie Museum of Natural History in Pittsburgh does, too.

I had listened to Ed McMahon talk about place several times in person since that day on the TV at Piper's. Learning about the history of Kinzua and talking to my uncles reminded me of something McMahon had said about the importance of community character stewardship. Trying to recall the exact wording, I looked online for a TEDx talk he did.

"All of us have a fundamental need for a sense of orientation, for a sense of roots, for a sense of place," McMahon said in his preacher's cadence, continuing later: "Why do you think people feel a sense of loss, like losing a loved one, when a grove of trees is cut down or a historic building demolished or a scenic view obliterated? It's not because we can't plant new trees or build new buildings. It's because our sense of identity and well-being is tied in a very profound way to special buildings and places and views. These places are invested with rich symbolic importance that contributes to our sense our identity and wellbeing in a way no less fundamental than religion or language or culture."[1]

I felt like I'd found a long-lost family treasure listening to this quote. There were things I'd come to appreciate about my constant moving growing up. It gave me a unique perspective, resiliency, and a healthy

---

1. *Where am I? The power of uniqueness.* TEDx Jacksonville, Florida, Jan., 2015. So recommend watching this! Find it at https://www.youtube.com/watch?v=qB5tH4rt-x8.

detachment from material things. It was adventurous and forged an unbreakable bond between me and my sisters. It also left a void.

By moving home, finding love, starting a family, learning about my family history, and getting involved in a movement that celebrated the many special and unique things about rural Pennsylvania, I was finding my place, and with it, an important part of my identity and the courage that goes with that.

It was validating to understand, too, that I wasn't the only one whose batteries got zapped by too much social interaction. Most of the Brants seemed to have a threshold and valued alone time. Charlie probably summed it up best. "All my life I'd rather fish than be around people," he told me. "People are a pain in the ass."

And then there were specific traits. Like the way Mary Brant walked around with her hands behind her back, picking up driftwood and rocks.

"That's in our bloodline," Terry told me. "We all do that."

Mary also never cussed, a trait I clearly did not inherit, but I'd seen my mom lock her hands behind her back like that, and I did, too. And the rocks and river bones, good grief. We all had fossilized wood in our houses as door stops or for decoration, driftwood and fossils, and primitive tools collected from fields and shores on our windowsills. Mom had been known to ship us rocks halfway across the country, completely unapologetic that it was so expensive and impractical. My sisters and I would call each other. What. Is. She. Doing? Now it was clear. It was in our DNA.

As a reporter, I'd read about how poverty and abuse can be handed down from generation to generation, and I took heart that I came from a line of good, flawed people who broke the worst of those chains with their ability to forgive, change, and grow. It was like the PA Wilds itself. Good and flawed and real. Even after how cold Grandma had been to my mom, she still kept a picture of her on an end table next to where she sat each day, as though she was there to keep her company as she watched her shows.

"There's a reason she was the way she was," my mom said when I asked her about it, and I was struck again by how strong and kind my mom is, for forgiving her mom and for not treating us the way she had been treated. Mom told me I could do anything I set my mind to, and I believed her.

Zooming out, I also saw there was great respect in my family for women and girls. I felt this growing up but had lost sight of it in storms I'd been through and as I'd experienced the way society treats women sometimes. To reflect on it now filled me up. To these people, I mattered. I was meant to take up space.

Charlie told me that the years we lived with his dad gave Grumpy something he'd missed with his own children and helped him heal. "You girls were something special to Dad," he said. "I'm really glad he got the chance to experience you kids. You meant the world to him."

"We are a different family," Uncle Charlie told me. "We're not a bunch of followers. Everyone's got their own mind and they do what they need to do and they don't quit. I really admire that. You guys know it as much as anybody. It's just the way you live. It's so important."

Uncle Charlie's wisdom reminded me of Piper's "you figure out what needs to change and you do it," and made me think, maybe I *can* lead the PA Wilds work.

CHAPTER 18

A CRUCIBLE MOMENT

In the spring of 2011, as local partners were trying to figure out how to fix the death wobble shaking the organizational foundation of the PA Wilds movement, four large storm systems dropped record rainfall on the Mississippi River drainage basin just as the snow began to melt, causing historic flooding along the Mississippi River that directly impacted seven states. For the first time in history, there was a national mandate to close all the dams whose water ran to the Mississippi, including the river my uncles had floated down and my sister operated her business on.

Instead of cranking out the area's big spring snowmelt through Kinzua Dam, the national mandate required the Army Corps of Engineers to hold everything back. By the time the flooding on the Mississippi receded, more than a month later, the Allegheny Reservoir was so far over its typical summer pool that officials had to open the gates at Kinzua Dam to the highest outflow in the dam's history: 24,600 cubic feet per second (cfs). My sister watches the dam's release plans the way farmers watch the weather and has a hard rule not to put paddlers out on the river if the release is over 5,000 cfs for safety reasons. The gigantic outflow continued for over two months, effectively shuttering her outfitting business in peak season.

This would have been an incredibly hard blow for a typical year, but Allegheny Outfitters was trying to recover from two previous soggy seasons. This same year, to bring some sanity to the highs and lows and better serve her customers, my sister had taken her business year-round by opening an outdoor gear store in downtown Warren.

"We have a five-hundred-thousand-acre National Forest with a National Wild and Scenic River running through it," Piper told me one day as she considered the expansion. "People shouldn't have to drive an hour or more to find quality outdoor gear."

Despite her success, lenders still saw my sister's service sector business in a distressed rural area as too risky. Piper didn't give up. She put everything she had on the line to make the expansion happen.

Piper and I ran to Walmart to buy supplies on the day of the grand opening. Both our lives at that point had an absurd pace, and our trip to the store reflected it. Piper and I were talking and walking so fast that we ended up at the back of the store, at the milk coolers, before we realized how off-course we were. The way out wasn't much better; again talking and walking fast, I tried to hand Piper some change as we approached a tall barrier with her on one side and me on the other. Instead of stopping and completing the handoff, we just pushed ahead, and coins flew everywhere. We both shook our heads, laughing, embarrassed.

"Oh my gosh! We have got to slow down!" Piper said, and I agreed, but we both knew we had way too many irons in the fire for that.

Once the store opened, I retreated into my own hot mess of trying to learn rural PA, grow the PA Wilds work, support Leonard in his racing, and figure out motherhood and domestic life. Leonard and I had finally bought the farmhouse next door to his garage and were living on the first floor while we gutted parts of the upstairs. Piper and I checked in from time to time, usually about touching or funny stories, or if a van broke and she needed Leonard to fix it, or when I needed an entrepreneur's view on an approach I was taking, or if either of us needed a fresh set of eyes on a creative project.

I didn't understand how bad the flooding situation was until a mutual friend called and told me he was worried about my sister. It didn't take long to understand that the thousands of hours Piper had invested in learning the river and woods and helping people plan their trips in the outdoors, all her creative projects capturing the story of the river, the trust she'd built with customers by making middle-of-the-night boat trips to check on Boy Scouts and families in thunderstorms, the many resources she'd put toward renovations and fixing equipment, all the business modeling and planning, the years of raising kids with little money, the enormous energy spent playing the chess game that growing a small business is when you don't have many financial options, all those years of stress and sacrifice and hope, trying to build a better tomorrow, was about to be for naught. Her business was on the brink of collapse.

We all pitched in to try to help her save her company. Mom, my older sister, my aunt, friends. My role was to help stabilize the company's finances amid a series of storms, both real and proverbial, that refused to let up.

Typically, I enjoyed finances. I was hooked after filling out my first Application for Federal Student Aid in high school to help pay for college. I took accounting classes and read books on organizing finances and saved. I came to see money as currency and currency as energy—powerful, neither good nor bad, but meant to flow and be exchanged. To be stewarded. I loved that numbers on a spreadsheet told a story that was blacker and whiter than the written word. Such clarity could take me multiple writing drafts to find, if I even did find it. I didn't have the patience to be exact with numbers (or a sewing pattern, for that matter), but I was good at ball-parking and enjoyed coming up with strategies. I'd helped more than one friend organize their finances and come up with a plan for action. I didn't see it as a situation to judge, but rather a puzzle to solve. But this journey was like a much scarier version of the right-of-passage hike I took in the Nushagak Hills. Like if the plane had left and I had to find my way 250 miles back to Anchorage on foot.

The gift of a crisis, so swift and absolute, is you either give up or find a way forward. I was determined to find a way forward, and not just for my sister. I'd shared the story of Allegheny Outfitters all across the region as part of my personal story to help me connect with rural communities and show them this can work. If the business failed, I'd lose a lot of credibility. I was convinced that the failure of one of the region's most visible outfitters would deliver a fatal blow to the Wild's efforts at its already fragile transition point.

I felt an incredible pressure to fix things, and to do it without drawing a lot of attention until Piper and I got things to a safer place. I knew that if I wanted to help transform this situation, for my sister and me, I couldn't just show up and work smart and hard. I had to take risks, too. I had to do what Piper had been doing. I had to have *courage*. I had to back her financially with everything I had.

Writing and publishing stories and shipping creative work into the public realm where it is likely to be criticized took guts, but over time, as my skills improved and my skin thickened, it took less courage. This risk was new and powerful, like a raging spring river, no telling where I'd end up once I'd entered its swift, murky, dangerous waters.

"Screw it," I say to myself one night, after dealing with angry vendors that were overdue payment. "We are going to save this thing."

It is like a major surgery, a race against the clock, meetings and calls and late nights and emergency tourniquets. I work as the ombudsman during the day and at Allegheny Outfitters in the evenings and on weekends. We close one location and sell the property, set up payment plans, and revamp all the company's systems and pricing structures. At one point, I picture a spaceship hurtling through the atmosphere, shaking uncontrollably, Piper and I in astronaut suits, feverishly trying every scenario, pushing buttons and pulling levers and yelling commands, praying that if we persevere just one more minute, we will blast out the other side and everything will go back to normal. For weeks a phrase runs through my mind.

The center must hold.

The center must hold.

The center must hold.

I am so stressed and overworked that one night in the middle of the night, unable to sleep, I walk to my kitchen to get a drink of water and break out in a sweat and start to see stars. I lower myself to the floor, relishing the cold tile against my hot skin, and pass out.

The next day, I go to the store and buy a pregnancy test, and it comes back positive. It might seem like stressful news in such a precarious time, but I take it as a sign that things are going to be okay. I'd always wanted Max to have a sibling; I couldn't imagine my life without my sisters. In nine months, I told myself, we will have transformed the dire situation we were in. There simply wasn't another option. In the meantime, being pregnant would force me to take better care of myself.

In addition to strengthening my resolve, the news also drew me closer to my sisters. Sandoz flew in from Alaska several times, and Piper started looking out for me in new ways, which meant a lot to me. One day, when an angry vendor the company had diligently repaid on schedule started to lay into me, Piper took the phone and headed for the door but not before I heard her tell the woman, "My sister is six months pregnant, you cannot talk to her that way!" Through the big store windows, I saw her pace back and forth, refusing to let up. My sister did not get mad often, but you would not want to be on the receiving end when she did. More than the heat, she had an incredible ability to humanize things, even for people who didn't particularly like her.

Inch by inch, day by day, vendor by vendor, as I grew bigger, we pulled the company back from the ledge. After months that feel like years, the day finally comes, and the company is in the black. A few weeks later, I start stepping away from the business. I move my office back to my home. I go from daily calls with Piper about the business to weekly and then monthly. I can see that before long the business won't need me at all, and it makes me feel proud and relieved.

I go into labor on Labor Day 2012. Leonard rushes around the house getting things ready. Leonard loved old cars, as did his dad, and they had a few parked at the garage. His big concern is which one we should take to the hospital to remember this moment. He pulls a 1966 Plymouth Fury that his dad picked up at an auction around the front of the house. My water has broken, and it is getting dark. It is a twenty-minute drive to the hospital, and I worry the car doesn't have any interior lights.

"What if you have to deliver the baby and you can't see?" I say as Leonard opens the door for me and I climb in.

"Don't worry, it has headlights," he says, laughing, and I chuckle too, imagining having a baby on the side of the road in the bright lights. Thankfully, we make it to the hospital on time, and at 3 a.m. the next morning, my second son, Cole, is born. He is perfect in every way. Leonard brings Max in and gets him set up in chair so he can hold his little brother. I take a picture of the two of them, later frame it, and hang it on the wall at our house.

Allegheny Outfitters remained a lifestyle business, inextricably tied to and impacted by the weather, yet refusing to give up in such a trying situation made every system and platform within the company stronger. Through the ordeal, Piper got divorced, and over the next year fell in love with a woman, Sue. They'd go on to expand Allegheny Outfitters' outfitting offerings and product lines, winning many new fans and customers and numerous community service and environmental awards in the process.

I'd come to learn that a lot of businesses experience a moment like Allegheny Outfitters did, when catastrophe strikes and everything is on the line. It reinforced a notion that I had read many times in entrepreneurial circles, "Failure isn't the opposite of success, it is part of success." Or as Appalachia icon Dolly Parton says, "Storms make trees take deeper roots."

The experience forever changed how I advocated for outfitters—lynchpin businesses to growing a region's outdoor recreation economy. I now understood, in intimate detail, the stacked challenges of being weather-dependent, seasonal, highly technical, and difficult to finance. Unique approaches would be needed to help them succeed.

Helping Piper save her business also showed me what I was capable of, honing skills that otherwise may have laid dormant.

As I let the responsibility of helping my sister with her company go, I spent the evenings reading Sheryl Sandburg's book, *Lean In*, and reflected on how many times I'd wanted to be taken more seriously in my professional life but had chosen to hang back, out of politeness or not wanting to step on toes or because I felt like I had to wait for someone's permission to sit at the decision-making table. I thought of recent meetings at work, where I had literally walked into a meeting and chosen to sit along the wall rather than at the table.

Good grief, I thought. *I'd been my own worst enemy!*

I thought about the difference the PA Wilds was making and how it needed a permanent organizational home if it had any hope of being passed on to future generations. About how unstable my job was, bouncing around to different organizations, and the uncertainty that caused for my family, especially now, with a second child. There was no one, outside of Meredith, who had the visibility I did on the many pieces and partnerships of the regional effort and how they worked together or how they could. And I'd just proven to myself that I could face the fiercest of organizational and financial storms and make it out the other side, stronger. What was I waiting for?

At home with my sons one evening in the spring of 2013, I went upstairs where I have my PA Wilds office set up in a four-by-five-foot closet. I wrote Meredith an email and told her I am not afraid anymore to start a nonprofit and lead the work. I reread the email once, took a deep breath, and hit send.

CHAPTER 19

TAKING THE LEAP

Meredith and I rope Scott into the conversation. My thought is to focus the nonprofit on the business development aspects of the PA Wilds effort, but to leave the organization's purpose broad enough that it can house the regional planning and marketing functions should it come to that. My ultimate vision was to have everything under one roof, and I thought that's what a lot of partners wanted too, but I was happy to let it be and see what happened. I was going to have my hands full trying to establish the nonprofit, secure funding, and shore up our business development programs. I also needed to build the right team to make it all go. People with an entrepreneurial mindset who were not afraid to work hard or challenge assumptions (including mine) who at the end of each day would get the job done. I envisioned a motley mission-driven crew with a little sass, a lot of humility, and a collaborative spirit like the kinds I'd found at the best newspapers, military units, and small businesses.

We talked through business models with Scott, and he assigned two of his analysts to help me work through financial projections and draft a set of bylaws. I'd read a few books and articles about starting and sustaining a nonprofit since emailing Meredith, my favorite of which was *Nonprofit Sustainability: Making Strategic Decisions for Financial Viability*, which helped me develop the broad startup approach that this new nonprofit should aggressively pursue grants to build out high-mission-impact, revenue-generating programs so that once a grant was gone, a revenue stream would be left in its place to support the nonprofit's mission long term. Rinse, repeat.

I needed three people to establish the nonprofit, myself included. I have two people in mind to join me. One is a banker, John Beard, who went to my church and was involved in a lot of community efforts. I didn't know him well, but he understood at a high level the lift I'd done to help Piper get Allegheny Outfitters into the black. I wasn't sure what kind of rockiness I'd encounter starting a nonprofit, but I thought John trusted my judgment enough at this stage to give me latitude to take calculated risks to get the Wilds' work to a more stable place. I thought it was important to have a private-sector person leading the board and that his finance background would instill confidence. John was new to the Wilds' work, a fresh set of eyes in a lot of ways. I approached Bob Veilluex to complement him. Bob helped found the artisan development program, served on the Planning Team for many years, and housed the ombudsman position at the nonprofit Potter County Education Council for a short time, where he was now the executive director. They both agreed to serve the cause and support my leadership.

Even though it would be several months before we started operations, I started thinking about the accounting system we'd need at the nonprofit. It had to be strong from day one.

Government and philanthropic grants, a common revenue source for nonprofits across the globe, would play a big role in our startup operations. Nonprofits did what was called "fund accounting," which from everything I could tell was a lot more complex than keeping the books for a small private-sector company. I immediately thought of Julie Iaquinto, a bookkeeper who lived in the region and worked with several nonprofits on a contractual basis, including some that managed grants related to the PA Wilds effort.

I didn't know the first thing about grants when I started as the ombudsman. I learned about them the same way Piper learned the river and woods, by becoming a student of them. I watched and listened to partners who were leading or wrestling with various stages of a given grant process. Grants do not have to be paid back (unless you really screw up), but they are in no way "free" money. In most cases, organizations have to compete for them. Each funding agency has different priorities they are trying to accomplish with their grant programs and different rules for how their monies must be applied, tracked, and accounted for at the end of the grant period.

I'd read some of the grants that funded my position, and helped write others. I'd met Julie at the Potter County Education Council, when we were closing out two such state grants. It was the first closeout I'd seen up close. One of the grants had changed its rules part way through, but Julie was determined not to let that trip us up.

For the closeout, we'd met in a small conference room at the Ed Council. Julie and her assistant, Carol Syzmanik, who ran the Susquehannock Lodge & Trail Center on the side, had all the paperwork laid out in meticulous piles. There were certain items they had questions about that were highlighted, and we talked through those until each item was resolved. Julie took pride in documenting how every penny had been spent. It reminded me of Sandoz, who had left nursing for a few years while her daughter was young to help with bookkeeping at her husband's restaurant and brewpub in downtown Anchorage. Just one cent off a reconciliation drove her nuts enough to spend hours scouring journal entries to locate the error.

I could see in the interactions that everyone in the room respected Julie—Bob, Carol, and the Ed Council's director at the time, Helene Nawrocki, who Bob and I called "Mama Bear" for the way she protected the PA Wilds' work from parochial forces. Helene was short and stout with black hair and glasses, older and funnier than the rest of us. Originally from Philadelphia, she was an accomplished nurse and teacher, had authored a book, *Nurse's Book of Courage*, and was madly in love with her husband, Stash, who did night sky programming at nearby Cherry Springs State Park. Helene was irreverent, spoke her mind, had a passion for gardening, and operated a side hustle business, Bear Mountain Herbs. After Cole was born, she sent me a package of oils and tinctures, including sex oils, which made me laugh and blush and wish I could be a little more like her in the way she unapologetically lived out loud.

Julie was more reserved, younger than Helene but older than me. She had raised six kids, all grown and on their own now, and was no nonsense when it came to her work—what some might call "old school." She had a great rapport with Helene and Bob, was a genuine listener, and could laugh at herself, but she had boundaries, and she'd let you know if you crossed them. Leonard worked as an oil rig hand when he was in his twenties, and back then, he had the mouth and quips to prove it. Julie struck me as someone who could go toe-to-toe with a group of young men like that, and with a look and a few choice words, make them smile *and* behave. I appreciated her professionalism, and her humility and directness.

Julie got both grants closed and accepted on the first try. I hadn't seen or talked to her since then. But now, with a new nonprofit on the horizon, I knew I needed to reach out to her.

When I call, she is at her home on a dirt road in a sparsely populated county of the Wilds known as "God's Country," for its natural beauty, working on another company's books.

Julie would later tell me that she stopped what she was doing and looked out the door at the woods and listened as I explained what I planned to do and why. She wondered if I was for real, or if this was one of those situations where someone had an idea but wanted other people to do the heavy lift to make it happen. She didn't know me or the Wilds' work well, but she remembered Helene had vouched for me some months back, saying, "She's going to do good things for the area."

I am picking up the house as we talk. I'd always thought of myself as productive, but the truth was I didn't fully understand what I was capable of getting done in ten minutes until I had kids as a career woman. I'd read about one mom who dressed her kids the night before school so she could make it to work on time. I was fortunate not to have to go to that extreme, but I still had to multitask to fit in everything that I cared about, and sometimes, I felt like I was failing as a parent, and often as a housekeeper. I thrived in a neat, organized space. Sandoz loved telling the story about how as a kid at one of our apartments, I spent hours cleaning and organizing my room, even tying thread on dozens of individual glow-in-the-dark blocks and taping them to the ceiling so I had stars at night. Then I locked my sisters out and just sat there on my bed, enjoying it. As a working mom, it often came down to choices: spend time with my husband and kids or clean? I usually chose the former, until I couldn't take the disarray any longer, and then I'd attack it like a news story on deadline.

Holding the phone to my ear, I look down at a pretend fish tank and wonder what to do with it. Max, who just started kindergarten, loved the reality show *Tanked*, about a family that builds custom fish tanks. After watching a few episodes, he dug through his toy boxes and collected every sea creature he could find and started laying them out across benches, chairs, windowsills, and stairs pretending that they were fish tanks. Cole, who is now one, likes to take a fish or octopus from his brother's creation and chew on it, carry it around the house, or push all the figures onto the floor, so his brother has countered by moving his tanks to higher ground. This one covers the dinner table.

As Julie and I talk, I weigh my options with the tank. If I break it down, Max will be crushed. If I leave it up, where do we eat dinner? Motherhood is filled with these types of choose-your-own-adventure kind of decisions. It strikes me that starting a nonprofit is similar. As *Grit* author Angela Duckworth put it, "Anyone who has started an organization from scratch can tell you, there are a million tasks, big and small, and no instruction manual for any of them."

I leave the tank for now, thinking maybe when my son gets off the school bus, I can talk him into memorializing it with a picture and then clearing the table so we can eat.

On the phone, I sense Julie's hesitation. I know I will be on an insanely sharp learning curve in the years ahead and will need people with her kind of grit and integrity to help me. I sit down on a bench next to Max's tank and look out the window at the barn across the road.

"I can't do this without you," I tell her. "The accounting is the backbone. We are going to be moving at a wicked pace. I have to know that piece is solid."

I know I've made headway when she tells me it is important for rural communities for the Wilds' work to succeed. "If I do this, I am bringing my people with me," she says, meaning Carol, and a certified public accountant she's worked with who is respected in his field.

She commits to ten hours a week, but stresses she has other clients. She says we can put a contract in place when we are ready to start. I am excited when we get off the phone. Before long, I see the yellow school bus pull up out front and hear the hissing TSSSS of its air brakes and go to meet Max at the end of our driveway. He runs across the road, his book bag flopping on his back, gives me a hug and starts rattling off exciting things about his day. Inside, we take a picture of the fish tank and then sweep the small plastic creatures into his toy buckets and set the table.

* * *

Racing season has ended, the leaves are turning, and Leonard has set archery targets behind the barn to start practicing. I download the IRS Form 1023, the application to request tax exempt status, and start to slog through it with Bob and John. John reserves us a room at the bank for our organizing meeting to officially found the nonprofit. I ask my pastor to meet us ahead of time to give us a blessing. The nonprofit isn't a religious organization, but I figure I can use all the help I can get.

On October 28, 2013, we hold the meeting, officially establishing the organization. We elect officers. I am president, Bob is vice president and treasurer, and John is secretary. We pass our bylaws, set the nonprofit's fiscal year, approve whistleblower and conflict of interest policies, and give me permission to file the 1023 and our articles of incorporation, and to apply for a federal tax ID number. At home, I tuck the paperwork into envelopes and get ready to drive them to the post office so they can be weighed for postage. I am terrible at memorializing things but realize this is a big moment. To me, it is more important than hearing back from the IRS or earning our first dollar to support our mission. By sending this off, I'm betting on myself and rural PA. I think of my father-in-law's advice when my husband got that first double feature win, to slow down and enjoy it because life goes fast.

When Max gets off the bus, our border collie, Lox, and I are there waiting for him. I ask him to take a picture of me holding the 1023. Lox gets in the picture with me. As I look through the pictures on my phone, I smile, proud of myself for taking the time to do it, and grateful to have Max there to be part of it.

The ombudsman contract—the funding for my job—ends in eight months, so I start applying for grants to expand my work under the new nonprofit with the understanding that the following July, I will stop being the ombudsman, step down as president of the board, and become the new executive director of the nonprofit, which we've decided to call the PA Wilds Center for Entrepreneurship. Before any of that can happen, the IRS needs to approve our tax-exempt status, and I have to secure, at minimum, $150,000 to cover a starting budget for our programs, administrative and fiscal support, travel, and my salary. The budget feels ridiculously small to do something meaningful across a place the size of the Pennsylvania Wilds, and, at the same time, intimidatingly large for someone like me, who has never secured that kind of money before. Knowing I have a verbal commitment from Julie to manage the fiscal administration of any grants we land, I apply for double what we need to give us better odds and trust I'll figure out the rest as I go.

As part of the grant writing process, I turn to our programs to lay out what we hope to accomplish. Over the years as the ombudsman, a few small businesses asked me about using the PA Wilds logo on items they want to sell. They were willing to pay a royalty to use it, but every time I asked the DCED about it, I hit a wall because the Commonwealth did not have mechanisms to fulfill such requests. Now that we are founding a nonprofit focused in part on helping rural businesses leverage the brand, the conversation is much more straightforward. We ask for a long-term, exclusive contract to develop the trademark for the public good, which will allow us to set up a licensing program. To inspire confidence in our ability to manage the trademark, I take a months-long licensing course. Scott starts working our request up the chain.

From what I can tell, it will take many years of investment before licensing royalties will fully cover the cost of running a licensing program, but we have to start somewhere, and investing in the brand and small businesses is a natural place to start.

A few months go by. That winter, the Planning Team holds a retreat and I share our plans to establish the new nonprofit.

As I finish my slides, economic development people and some planners in the room seem impressed and ask questions. I hear quiet chatter and then one of the visitor bureau directors says something about a "few people in Harrisburg making all the decisions." I feel my throat catch, and my cheeks get red. I didn't expect the news to go over well with the Marketing Corporation, but I didn't expect people to think I was some kind of pawn.

The Marketing Corporation had accomplished some important things, bringing the regional brand to life with promotional materials that included PAWilds.com, videos, and print guides for everything from fishing to motorcycling. It had also helped fund the ombudsman position in the early years. But over time it had proven to be another example of an urban model not really working for a rural place. Created top-down, hindered by structural challenges that included a lack of capacity, high turnover in leadership, and territorialism baked into some of its underlying frameworks, it struggled to survive.

I knew from reporting that when there is a lot at stake, the messenger in the middle sometimes takes the heat meant for the other side. For years I tried not to take the tension with Marketing Corp personally, but at times, it got personal. Once, the corporation stopped sending my paycheck and didn't even tell me. Another time, some of its members joked that I must be sleeping with someone to keep the Wilds' work funded. After a while, I gave up. I started to go around the corporation, focusing instead on building relationships with individual visitor bureau directors who seemed open to collaborating.

At the retreat, I was prepared to argue that the Marketing Corp had a decade to make the case for the trademark and come up with a plan for building capacity and sustainability, but for whatever reasons, it had not done so. And so we were.

But instead of getting that satisfaction, I was treated as though starting the nonprofit was the state's plan and they had just *handed* it to me. The visitor bureau director said it out loud, in front of everyone.

I wondered: *Did all these people who had inspired me with their own dedication to our collective work think I was some kind of puppet?*

Even if it was just the person who said it, it hurt my feelings. He was from a small town in the Wilds, and I knew him to be a fair person who believed in the power of working together.

I considered for a minute that it might be because I'm a woman. I'd dealt with plenty of mansplaining by that point, and in some situations, had even asked male colleagues I trusted to triangulate around me with key messages to certain decision makers because I was pretty sure they wouldn't hear or accept the same message coming from me. Such is life as a professional woman.

But this visitor bureau head didn't strike me as that kind of person. Which meant that part of this was on me. Here I was five years into my work on the Wilds and key partners—ones I trusted—still didn't understand much about me. And in my gut I knew why. I was a chameleon. It was a skill of mine, rooted in my chaotic childhood of moving all the time, and refined through my reporting career, that I could fit in pretty much anywhere. There was value, of course, in helping others feel comfortable in a situation, and to having footing in multiple worlds to help translate and build bridges between them, but I also knew I used this skill as a defense mechanism. If I didn't let people see or hear the real me, I didn't have to worry about being rejected.

I was driven, which society often seemed to spurn in women, so I sometimes played small. I was positive and optimistic and believed in the power of collaboration, which some people in power patted me on the head for while calling it naïve, so at times I second-guessed that intuition, too. I believed people's stories were important, and that good ideas could come from the left and right, from the top and bottom. One of my favorite biographies was *Team of Rivals*, about President Lincoln, because it showed the remarkable things that can happen when you invite competing views into your circle in a constructive way. I was pretty sure nothing magical had ever happened from having a bunch of yes-men in a room together.

So, why did I feel I needed to apologize for these things? To hide them? To make others feel comfortable at my own expense? To not be myself, or trust myself?

I was going to have to let my guard down more, to risk being vulnerable. If partners didn't understand some basic things about me, there was no way they were going to trust me, and if they couldn't trust me, there was no way I could lead this work.

* * *

In late May, with one month to go before I lose my job as the ombudsman, and the Wilds movement loses its only local staff capacity, I walk across the country road I live on, open the mailbox and find a letter from the IRS addressed to the PA Wilds Center for Entrepreneurship. I rip it open as a tractor from the dairy farm next door rolls by with a spreader full of manure.

> "*Dear Applicant, We are pleased to inform you that upon review of your application for tax exempt status . . .*"

We did it! I hustle inside and email John and Bob and my former colleague, Sam, who by then had moved on to another job but stayed involved with the Wilds by accepting our invitation to join the board. I also shared the news with Scott and Meredith.

Astonishingly, one by one, every grant we applied for comes through. I write up a contract scope for Julie and Carol's services. They become the Center's first contractors when we start operations on July 1, 2014.

I am hugely relieved that I will continue to have a job, slightly stressed about the intense workload now ahead of me, and momentarily disoriented by the financial success of our funding pitches. I am so stunned at one point about the grant announcements, I ask Scott over lunch at the Texas Hot diner in Kane, "What do we do?"

He doesn't answer right away. I am more used to his pregnant pauses by now. He takes a bite of hot dog. Finishes chewing. Takes a sip of his drink. Wipes his face with a napkin. Takes a deep breath and lets it out. Smiles and looks at me.

"You do more," he says.

I repeat the phrase back, quietly, forcing it to register. Then I smile back at him. For once I appreciate that he is a man of few words. He didn't try to tell me what to do, or how to do it. That was up to me to figure out.[1]

"That's right," I say. "We do more."

Over the next few weeks, I work with the funding agencies to retool our approach to do more. When one of the checks, for $86,000, arrives at my home office, I hold it up and look at it. Founding a nonprofit is an odd thing. The minute you do it, it is no longer yours. It is not like a business, where you get to call all the shots. It's a group effort for a public good.

But still, I think, flipping the check over and back again. I did this. Had I not made a powerful case for this investment in rural PA, this money would not be here, and the work we are about to accomplish would not exist.

---

[1]. I'd learn I wasn't the only one who had once been intimidated by Scott. At Scott's retirement party in 2020, then DCED Secretary Dennis Davin, a seasoned former county economic development director for the greater Pittsburgh area, told the crowd that he'd seen Scott's name on documents for many years before taking the helm at DCED and finally meeting him in person. "When I did that was pretty scary because he's pretty intimidating," he said, doing a spot-on rendition of Scott's stoic visage, long sighs after someone explained a complex situation where a decision needed to be made, and how, in Davin's case, Scott's tea leaves advice was, "Do the right thing."

I tear the check off its stub and set it on the kitchen counter with the other checks and bills that I need to mail or deposit. I make sure it is on top, hoping Leonard will see it and ask me about it. It is an odd feeling, after so much hardship growing up, to discover I have this skillset. Somewhere at the nexus of being a reporter, my interest in budgets and financials, and my sheer pissed-off-ness at systems that had failed rural places like ours and families like mine, my grit had created this pearl. After six years working on the PA Wilds, I *was* the kind of person who could raise $6 million for the cause. And now, like peering through the peep on my bow, I had a line of site on how to begin and a target to aim for.

CHAPTER 20

NETWORKING A REGION OF RUGGED INDIVIDUALISTS

The first time Abbi Peters and I met was in 2008, shortly after I was hired as the ombudsman. I was giving a presentation, "Small business development in the PA Wilds," at the Elk County Courthouse Annex in Ridgway that she attended.

"The majority of the workshop was just you trying to convince people that it was important to have a website," Abbi explained to me in an interview. "You were very professional and committed to helping the businesses and sharing the big picture of what was happening with the PA Wilds. But mostly I remember thinking, 'Oh my goodness, where did I move, that a retailer doesn't understand why it is beneficial to have a website?'"

Abbi had lived in the region for about a year and, like me, was still coming to understand the ripple effect of what happens when a rural region is left behind from basic infrastructure like broadband.

Abbi grew up in a small town in New Jersey, studied arts in college, and moved to Los Angeles in her twenties, vowing never to return to small town life. She got a job in the music accessories industry, met an artist, Charles Wish, fell in love, and got married. After five years in LA, in 2006, the couple visited a family friend in Ridgway. While walking back from the Fireman's Festival parade, they passed a 10,000-square-foot historic Georgian Schoolhouse-turned-apartment-building with a For Sale sign in the yard. Like a lot of rural PA's building stock, it was in rough shape. The property piqued their interest, and when they got back to LA, they had their friends back in Ridgway tour it and send them pictures. Previous owners had gutted half the building to the studs, and the other half needed to be gutted. There was about five miles of coax cable inside for no apparent reason. "It basically looked like a war zone," Abbi said.

By then, city life was starting to wear on the couple. A one-bedroom, 750-square-foot condo in Compton cost upwards of $350,000 at the time. They did the math and realized they could have seven and half times more space in Ridgway at eleven percent of the cost. Charles knew a little about plumbing and electrical and construction, and Abbi was a do-it-yourselfer. They took the leap.

Shortly after moving to Ridgway, Abbi joined the board of a small nonprofit, the Elk County Council on the Arts, called ECCOTA locally. She was hired as its executive director about the same time I became the ombudsman.

By then, Bob Veilluex had completed a study showing the region's potential to grow its cottage industry of artisans and craftspeople and had secured a small slug of funding to seed an artisan development initiative. Bob assembled a volunteer workgroup to inform the effort, including ECCOTA. When Abbi took the helm at ECCOTA, her predecessor encouraged her to stay involved. The regional artisan effort was still fuzzy and moving slow, she told Abbi; it had to go through a lot of channels because it was tied to the state's new PA Wilds brand, but it was a great group of people and worth investing in.[1]

Abbi gravitated toward the PA Wilds' movement's "pioneer spirit."

"Many things at the local level in a rural place feel capped, either naturally or through self-limitations," she'd explain to me years later. "The PA Wilds was never like that. It was grounded but dreamy. The opportunity was everywhere. It was gray and you didn't always know what the opportunities were. Some people really struggle with that kind of uncertainty, and I understand that. But to me it always felt like, we can make this what we want it to be. It was filled with possibility."

Interesting models had been developed across the thirteen state Appalachian Region to lift up rural craftspeople and grow place-based tourism, such as the multi-million-dollar Tamarak marketplace and visitor center off Interstate 77 in West Virginia, and the Crooked Road Music Heritage Trail in Virginia.

---

1. This kind of vouching for people and projects behind the scenes (like Helene had done for me with Julie) is one of the most important kinds of capital in rural areas. Fail to earn it and your project is most likely plagued, even if you bring money to the table.

"Artisan trails" were a popular model at the time in Pennsylvania, and a practical way to start with a small budget and zero organizational capacity, so the workgroup started there. Bob led the charge, organizing a "trail" of galleries, like the one ECCOTA operated, in each county, and then developing jury processes to bring skilled local woodworkers, blacksmiths, painters, jewelry makers, photographers, and other craftspeople into the program. Once juried in, the makers could put "Proudly Made in the Pennsylvania Wilds," hang tags on their wares, and the galleries would be encouraged to carry their handmade goods on consignment. This experience could then be marketed to visitors.

The effort had some energizing early wins, publishing a brochure to promote the trail, developing hang tags and flags to brand the locations and products, and getting local handcrafted products incorporated into the construction of DCNR's new anchor attractions. The most visible was a large stained-glass mural of a soaring eagle by local artist Dave Haring, installed above the Great Room at the Nature Inn at Bald Eagle State Park.

Like the Planning Team, the artisan effort grew from the ground up, led by locals, and had a lot of heart. When it looked like the most remote and least populated county in the Wilds might be left off the trail map because it had no galleries, the local chamber stepped up and started one.[2] Abbi recalled at one point the workgroup passed a hat to collect donations so they could start a Flickr account to share photos with each other to promote the artisan trail.

"There was a fun sense of comradery," Abbi recalled. "It was a very dynamic group."

I loved the focus on local makers. Despite my constant moving growing up and lack of financial resources, Mom always kept art displayed, inspiring a lifelong love of handcrafted things. As a writer, I also identified with the region's artisans on a creative level, even if most of them didn't know that about me. Like Bob and several others, I believed they were key to helping establish the region as a destination.

Like the region's public lands and outdoor experiences, local artisans could infuse the PA Wilds brand with meaning and value. They could be part of *our* region's competitive advantage.

---

2. The Cameron County Chamber and Artisan Center in Emporium. A lovely place to visit and find authentic local wares, from John Sidelinger paintings and Brian Reid night sky photos, to Ted Horner pens, to Matt Zoschg wood bowls.

I worked with Bob to launch a website to augment the program's printed marketing materials and worked one-on-one with artisans who were trying to connect to resources to grow their businesses. With our limited budget and vast territory, things grew in fits and spurts.

"It sort of felt like a rollercoaster," Abbi told me. "There would be this momentum that would build to get these smaller projects done. The first trail map. The initial flags. Then that thing would happen. And then it would go quiet for a while."

Before long, one hundred rural craftspeople and two dozen trail sites were participating. By the time I really started to dig in, the program was out of the honeymoon stage and Bob and the workgroup were trying to figure out how to sustain it beyond its seed funding. We incorporated a $25 membership fee that came nowhere near underwriting the cost of the program, but it was a start. A handful of artists and businesses dropped out, but most stuck with us.

As Bob switched jobs and the ombudsman position bounced around to different organizations, the artisan trail got moved from one organizational home and contracted manager to another, bleeding hard-earned institutional knowledge each time. I almost killed the program completely when, out of desperation for help, I placed the management contract with a skilled graphic designer I was working with at the time, a terrible fit for all involved. The program had champions, and skilled managers at different points, but that didn't make up for its wobbly foundation. At one point, we tried to do a three-year membership to cut down on paperwork, and at another time, we stopped charging altogether because the records of who had paid weren't reliable.

Complicating things, time had shown that the trail model was not the right one for us. Galleries that were located hours apart did not really constitute a trail experience, consignment didn't work for some vendors and retailers, and many place-based businesses in the region like breweries, bed and breakfasts, and outfitters wanted to be part of the program but had no path to do so.

"It started to be clear what a logistical nightmare this kind of program can be," Abbi said. "The geography of it, it felt like herding cats."

By the time I founded the PA Wilds Center, I had come to understand a harsh rural development reality: launching something is a lot easier than sustaining it. It was true of the artisan trail, the regional brand and marketing, the small business development aspects of the regional movement—pretty much everything. There was no plan for how to sustain any of it.

But Bob's work had uncovered core truths that were hard for me and others to ignore or let go. Rural PA had a skilled, vibrant maker culture that wanted to collaborate, and there was growing market demand for their locally made, handcrafted goods. We just needed to find a way to evolve our model.

As the program struggled, Abbi watched from the sidelines, frustrated. Why didn't someone reach out to ECCOTA to help manage the program? It was a nonprofit arts organization, after all, and had been a partner since the start.

"I could feel the growing pains of what the artisan trail wanted to do and where it was at," Abbi told me. "Part of it was me not knowing how to be properly active in it. I was still in the mindset that an opportunity would have to come to us versus reaching out for it."

Deborah Pontzer knew both Abbi and me and understood from separate conversations with each of us that I needed help and Abbi had ideas about how to help. Working as she did for so many years for federal congressmen, Deborah was always careful with how she presented things, so much so that I often had to read between the lines, which drove me nuts. She had the opposite of what Leonard called my "karate chop" style of getting right to the point. (In my defense, I can be way more tactful when properly resourced.)

Creating a permanent organizational home for the artisan effort was the first step to turning things around. We checked that box by founding the Center. The next step was actually fixing and evolving the program. And for that, with Deborah's careful prodding, I turned to Abbi via a short-term contract with ECCOTA, one of my first moves as the Center's new executive director.

I once asked Meredith, after years of working together, what she thought of me at that first interview for the ombudsman job. "I thought you were bright and capable," she said and then pushed her hands out flat as though introducing me on stage, "but I didn't know you were all *this*!" It made sense to me because I didn't know what I was capable of back then, either. The work we'd done together had helped me discover and achieve it.

I had a similar experience with Abbi. She seemed smart and capable, and yet I underestimated where she would take things. Maybe, like me, the constellation of star contributors moving the Wilds work forward gave her the opportunity to understand and value her own power, lean into it, and shine more brightly. Whatever the case, Abbi took the hot mess I handed her. She considered the vision that Bob and I and several others—including Abbi herself and dozens of rural artisans and businesses in the program—had for where things needed to go. And then she pivoted the artisan trail into what ultimately became a "value chain network," a remarkable economic development framework that speaks to self-interest while also serving a greater good.[3]

Abbi didn't have a road map from me or others when she started retooling what would become one of our largest and most impactful networks across rural PA, and she still remembers the day she was at a workshop at a Rural Rise conference in Canaan Valley, West Virginia as she described what we were building, and everyone in the room was like, you're building a rural value chain![4]

I loved the intentionality of involving more kinds of businesses, and that the new model spoke to the very need—to grow local and regional wealth through entrepreneurship—that the Planning Team had identified way back when. And I was thrilled that it addressed self-interest. Even the most giving people needed to make a living, and if our program couldn't first answer the question, "what's in it for me?" it was not likely to last very long, no matter how well-intentioned.

Of course, seeing or reading about a model or having an idea is one thing. Putting that model into action—building the technology and community to make it all go—in a giant, economically distressed rural landscape with unreliable funding, limited broadband, and minuscule staff capacity, while battling systemic underinvestment and a scarcity mindset was another. Abbi, I came to understand, was many things.

---

3. The Aspen Institute's Community Strategies Group's WealthWorks value chain model is probably one of the best known nationally. It is described as a "a network of people, businesses, organizations, and agencies addressing a market opportunity to meet demand for specific products or services—advancing self-interest while building rooted local and regional wealth."

4. Recognizing that innovation and entrepreneurship are blind to location, RuralRISE seeks to increase the opportunities, increase accessibility, and spotlight innovation, entrepreneurial, and startup activities that work in a rural context. Find them at ruralrise.org.

A big picture thinker, a tactical go-getter, tech-savvy, hugely creative, a great manager, and a rock-solid individual. "You look out for people even when you don't even like them," one of her colleagues said during a toast on Abbi's birthday. But the thing that really set Abbi apart was that she was a master *implementer*.

Abbi did not evolve the artisan trail in one fell swoop. That was not her way. She did it in iterations, just starting and then building or reforming processes and systems as needed along the way.

I once asked Abbi, after years of working together, to describe Meredith's contributions to the PA Wilds, and she told me, "She is like water over rocks in a stream, a constant pressure shaping things over time." I thought it was a lovely and suitable analogy for Meredith, but that it also described Abbi herself. If partnerships and navigating and needling government bureaucracies for the greater good were part of Meredith's superpowers, Abbi's was the ability to see things in terms of processes and systems and feedback loops and iterations. And not in some cold, overly engineered way, but in a human way that made people want to be a part of it. How could we arrange things to make a system really *go*, while building in appropriate feedback loops to hold all the people participating (herself included), accountable for the results, and able to learn from those results to make the system even better?

As we were wrapping up one major iteration of the artisan trail, I drove to Harrisburg to meet with a new deputy secretary at DCED, a meeting Scott had arranged. He and Meredith intentionally kept the PA Wilds' work in front of their departments' leaders, which I was grateful for, especially now that Rendell had left office. Scott sat next to the deputy secretary with what I now understood to be his "CFA face," a serious visage that gives away nothing, which he'd learned to wear in his post as executive director of the politically charged Commonwealth Financing Authority. The deputy secretary asked me about our growth strategies and then told me, "We don't want you doing the work. We want you managing the work."

I felt validated that they saw me as capable of managing the work, but they offered no promise of future funding or details on how I was supposed to step into more of a management role when I had no staff. I'd love to grow the Center's capacity, and my family would love it, too, gone as I so often was. But how? I could write a grant to fund a position, but like the artisan trail, that seed funding would one day be gone. And then what? Hire a person and lay them off? I'd watched other rural nonprofits go through that. I wanted nothing to do with that approach. The Center needed real, lasting staff capacity if it had any hope of building impactful programs to serve such a giant landscape.

Licensing had become an actual revenue stream, but few businesses could be convinced to bring PA Wilds-branded products to market with the brand so new and regional marketing unfunded. A few artisans had signed licensing contracts with us to support the cause, and I was proud and inspired by the products they brought to market. But at this rate, it would be many years before royalties could support a staff position, let alone marketing efforts. The first royalty check was for $86.99. It was from my sister's company, for logo use on the cover of the *Paddling Guide*. Like the artisans, she did it to support the cause.

All this was on my mind, when one day over lunch at Jordan's Bar and Grill in Ridgway, as we were wrapping up a contract and sharing stories, Abbi told me about how she dropped out of college to go to LA to try stand-up comedy, and about her adventure fixing up the Georgian Schoolhouse.

I set my fork down. I thought of the tattered Tina Fey Amex ad that had been hanging on my wall for years, my own winding professional path, and the chances I took and how they helped me grow. I had actually quit college to go to South Africa to work as a freelancer, which led to my first reporting job. It wasn't until a journalism colleague and mentor of mine, who had taken a job teaching at the University of Alaska Anchorage, looked at my transcript several years later and saw how close I was to getting my bachelor's degree and called me about it, that I decided to go back. She told me I was too close to graduating not to finish, and that as a woman, my degree would help me compete.

I listened to her advice and years later, when I landed the ombudsman position, I found her on Facebook and thanked her. I'm not sure I would have gotten the job without that piece of paper.[5]

---

5. But times may be changing. When Pennsylvania Gov. Josh Shapiro took office in 2023, his first executive order announced that 92 percent of state government jobs would no longer require a four-year degree, but would instead be competitive based on skills, relevant experience, and merit. Similar actions have been taken by Republican governors in other states.

I valued college, especially for certain fields, but I did not subscribe to the idea that college was for everyone, or the only path to success. I wasn't sure if Abbi had finished college or not, but I didn't care. She was clearly a lifelong learner, disciplined, and civic-minded. Now, I understood she was also willing to challenge herself and convention and take risks. She was exactly the kind of innovative thinker and doer I needed to help grow the PA Wilds Center.

I come right out with the karate chop, tell her I am working on grants to grow capacity, that I'm committed to figuring out how to sustain the positions even if that map is fuzzy right now, and ask her what it would take to get her to join the nonprofit.

Abbi gives me a figure, which is super modest given her skills, and then tells me that while she is flattered, she is not interested right now. She's a partner in a side-hustle, a tech startup, she explains. It might be a long shot, but to her, it's worth a try.

"I don't like to live with what-ifs," she says.

I smile. I need to hire this person! I ask about her tech venture; it sounds interesting. I tell her about a few resources I know about for tech startups. I also thank her for being direct with me and let her know that if the tech thing doesn't work out, I am still interested. I figure if her startup succeeds, Abbi is already endeared to the PA Wilds cause and could be courted as a donor. If it fails, she'd take away huge lessons and industry knowledge that could be put to work to help grow the Center.

I drive home, glad to have left the door open.

***

The visitor bureau chief I locked horns with at the retreat tells me that the reason he was upset about my founding a nonprofit was because, "Now we have four entities that are trying to do the same work, and nobody is talking to each other. We can't keep doing our own separate things and it needs to be under one umbrella."

Basically, we were on the same page. When we figure that out, we make progress. Things accelerate quickly. There is talk of moving the marketing and planning under one roof with the business development. The Planning Team sets up another retreat for everyone to talk things through. Members of my board join me, and we share with the group that we'd like the Center to be the new organizational home.

Another visitor bureau suggests another organization to lead the work, which takes us down a rabbit hole. She has worked hard for her county and has a record of accomplishments that I admire. But in my view, she is obstructionist about the regional brand, and there is little trust between us. I suspect she just wants to kick the beehive. I'm also annoyed because we'd already asked the leadership at the suggested non-profit about it, prior to founding the Center, and they weren't interested. Some of the people who had been part of that conversation were in the room, but no one was volunteering that bit of backstory. I push back, maybe too hard but the moment feels personal. Things get quiet, and I think, *is no one going to stick up for me? After all the sacrifices and hard work of the last few years?*

After what feels like an eternity of silence, one of the Planning Team's founding members, Jodi Brennan, one of the quietest people in the room, speaks up.

"If the Center wants to take this on, we should let them," she says. "This is a lot of work. And Ta has a great track record."

Brennan carried weight with the Planning Team and state partners. She had worked tirelessly behind the scenes to advance the *PA Wilds Design Guide for Community Character Stewardship* and build mini grant programs to help communities and small businesses put it to use on new welcome signage and sprucing up building facades. Others chime in with similar thoughts. Their comments turn the tide of the conversation.

The meeting ends in a positive way, but as we all pack up to leave, Scott can tell I am upset. "Try not to take it personally," he says. "The state was prepared to step in and say the Center is the lead. But it's good we didn't have to. Now you have buy-in."

CHAPTER 21

BREAKTHROUGHS

With the help of several visitor bureaus, I am making progress with the Marketing Corporation about transferring the marketing functions, including the PAWilds.com domain, to the Center. The stakes are high. There is no way we can unlock the economic power of the regional brand without the platform where the brand's story is told. The story *is* the brand.

We do one-on-one calls with the visitor bureau directors, but the transfer is not without challenges. The Marketing Corporation invites me to a conference call where they plan to vote on the transfer. I am on a two-day road trip, tired, and missing Leonard and the boys. I drop my bags at a hotel room and dial into the meeting.

One visitor bureau chief tells me ahead of the meeting that there are concerns our nonprofit will try to come after hotel tax dollars, the lifeblood of the visitor bureaus, if we get the PAWilds.com domain. That is nowhere in my plans, and I make sure to tell the group this when I join the call.

The visitor bureau director who suggested at the retreat that another organization lead the Wilds work starts grilling me on how I plan to manage the domain with no staff, and where my funding will come from. She lectures me about grants, how they require matching funds, and asks where I plan to get that match.

With the Marketing Corporation almost out of money, she is pushing to make PAWilds.com a landing page that redirects digital visitors who stumble upon it to the visitor bureaus' websites. I start pacing in my hotel room. I think about the power of a place-based brand. With the right investment and frameworks, ours could help us increase visitation to support local businesses, be a tool to develop new product lines, help rural PA retain its workforce, and attract new residents. Rural PA *needed* this brand to work!

I start to spin. I feel like she is positioning things as though giving the brand to the Center will put it in jeopardy, and that her plan to downsize it to the point of insignificance is the responsible path. I start to panic. *How is this happening? How am I getting so outmaneuvered? Are others buying this?*

If the Marketing Corporation doesn't transfer the domain, the best-case scenario I can see is that it takes decades to get done what could be accomplished in a few years, because so many decisions would involve an insipid fight like this one, and the whole situation would be an anathema that drives talented people away. The worst-case scenario is people would give up, and the brand would die.

My heart is beating fast, and I am about to completely lose my cool when I am saved from myself by Holly Komonczi, who at the time ran the visitor bureau for Clearfield County. I didn't know Holly well, but she seemed to play fair and work hard. I knew she had Multiple Sclerosis, and I admired from afar how she was open about that and didn't let it slow her down, at one point even serving as mayor of her hometown. I wasn't sure what Holly thought of me, so I am surprised when she speaks up.

"I'm so sick of this," Holly says. "I don't even care about the brand. I mean, I do. I try to do my part. But I have my own organization to run. We all do. None of us has time for this. We should give it to the organization that cares the most about it, and that's Ta and the Center."[1]

I say thank you and sit back down on the bed.

I tell the group I don't have all the answers about how to fund regional marketing, but that money follows good ideas and there is huge power in getting the business development and marketing functions under one roof. We gave the artisan trail and small business development components of the work new life, we can evolve the marketing, too.

The president of the Marketing Corp thanks me for joining the call, and I hang up so they can vote and finish their meeting. I replay the

---

1. Holly would share years later that her comments were less about being supportive of me, and more about being frustrated with the PA Wilds Marketing Corporation and just wanting the fighting to end. "I was ultimately as mad as everyone else about the whole process," she said. "At that point I was totally done with the stress the PA Wilds was bringing me. I just wanted to put it on the back burner and continue doing work to better the place we live in."

conversation in my mind a dozen times and wish I'd brought better data to make my case. But when was there time? And the reality is, there isn't a clear path forward. I'm confident I can find it, but the question is, are they?

About a half hour later, the messages start to come in. All but one of the visitor bureaus voted in favor of transferring the domain to the Center for short-term management of one year while we worked through any thorny issues around the permanent transfer.

I celebrate by myself with a giant burger at Denny's Beer Barrel Pub. I skip the beer. Most people don't know yet, but I'm pregnant with boy number three. I shared the news with Abbi when we were at lunch one day when I ordered two giant plates of food and she gave me a curious look. I smile when I see that this menu includes a reference to the Pennsylvania Wilds and nearby attractions. It reminds me of the time Piper called me about seeing the kayaks strapped to the roof of a car in Warren County where paddling never used to be a thing.

"It's happening!" I say to myself and smile.

A few weeks later, Cathy Lenze, the Vice President of Sales, Marketing, and Public Relations for Straub Brewery, an iconic business in the region, invites me to talk with her about co-branding ideas the company is considering. Abbi, who is still working as a contractor for the Center, joins me.

Located about 35 minutes from the Elk Country Visitor Center in the "powdered metal capital of the world,"[2] a city of 13,000 called St. Marys, Straub was one of the country's oldest and most historic American Legacy Breweries, family-owned and operated since before prohibition. Visitors could tour the brewery, which still operated with a gravity-fed system as it did more than a hundred years ago. The tours ended at the Eternal Tap, a keg in the wall that never ran out.[3]

Straub's marketing and core brand values aligned with the PA Wilds brand. The company supported a number of hunting, fishing,

---

2. The powdered metal industry supplies component parts to a wide variety of industries including lawn and garden, automotive, biomedical, aerospace, appliances, and others. Nearly 40 percent of the world's powdered metal parts are produced in the PA Wilds region. St. Marys, one of the largest communities in the Wilds, is the epicenter.

3. "Eternal Tap" is trademarked and . . . worth experiencing! Straub has expanded its operation to include a taproom, restaurant, and retail area and won numerous awards in the process, including the 2016 "Leadership in Reusable Packaging" Award from the Pennsylvania Resource Council for its 16-ounce Straub American Lager returnable package. Fodor's Travel named Straub Brewery one of the "5 Best Places in America to Drink American Beer."

conservation, and outdoors causes, including the Lower Pine Creek Brown Trout Club in Slate Run, on the eastern side of the region. Their "Fiercely Independent," tagline[4] resonated with a lot of people, including me, and I was excited to finally meet the people behind the curtain. Lenze had heard about me from mutual acquaintances who encouraged her to reach out. Little did I know she'd been circling around the Wilds brand for months. She talked fast and was high energy. When I got to her office, she pulled out a white board with a dozen or more sticky notes on it; smack in the middle it said "PA Wilds."

Straub had all sorts of plans. For PA Wilds-branded pint glasses. An adventure series of new craft beers, each named after a special asset in the region with GPS locations. An Adventure Series map of the region that could be given to all their distribution partners across the state to encourage visitation. Boxes that said, "Proudly Brewed in the PA Wilds." Most of the items didn't carry the PA Wilds logo, so there would be no royalties, but the marketing boost alone would be significant—for us and for them.

As Straub's CEO would later share in a panel discussion at one of our rural entrepreneur conferences, "The PA Wilds brand helped us expand our home market by a factor of 12. That was huge for us."

Back in the parking lot, the sun shining bright, I look at Abbi, wide-eyed over what has just happened. It feels like the turning of a tide. She informs me that her tech venture didn't work out and that she is still really interested in joining the Center. I smile.

"We have to find a way to get you on staff, fast," I say.

---

4. A Registered Trademark.

CHAPTER 22

LIGHTBULB

That winter, Abbi and I drive two hours through the woods to the Wildlife Center at Sinnemahoning State Park, the most remote of DCNR's new signature anchor attractions. We've added several new people to our board of directors, but growing staff capacity is a slower process. Abbi and Julie are still contractors.

Long and narrow, Sinnemahoning State Park stretches across Potter and Cameron counties in an area of the PA Wilds known for its steep valleys. The park is nestled between the green-shouldered ridges of Elk State Forest and Susquehannock State Forest. The First Fork Sinnemahoning Creek, a major tributary of the West Branch Susquehanna, runs through the park. At the southern end is a 145-acre reservoir created by the George B. Stevenson Dam. Visitors come to the park to fish, paddle, camp, bike, see wildlife, and to take in the park's epic scenery. Bald eagles, elk, bobcats and other wildlife call the area home.

DCNR opened the park's new Wildlife Center in 2011, with a gallery of interactive, interpretive exhibits that highlight the history and ecology of the First Fork Valley. The park manager at the time, Lisa Bainey, was a huge champion of the local area and of the PA Wilds Initiative, telling me once as we sat in front of the stone fireplace in the lobby, with local artwork hanging above it, about how many locals came out to share stories and contribute artifacts as DCNR was putting together interpretive exhibits at the new visitor center. "The PA Wilds has really helped give this region an identity," she said.

The Wildlife Center had been laid out with a space to incubate a nature-based business, ideally a guide service. But with no public Internet or cell coverage at the park, and very few people living nearby, it was one of those things that sounded great on paper but proved hard to pull off in real life. Five years after opening, the incubator space still sat empty.

The nearest major town, Emporium, population 1,900, was forty-five minutes away, so any retailer or guide service that occupied the space would have to pay their people enough to make it worth the drive. And the Internet situation was a showstopper, impacting a businesses' ability to market, operate point-of-sale and reservation systems, and do basic communications.

If we could figure out the connectivity issue, and provide some seed funding and marketing support to help de-risk the venture, we might be able to find an outfitter who could build on the park's opportunities. Given the park's remoteness, it would take a highly skilled operator to make the business model work.

I'd heard of innovative approaches being taken to get the Internet to unserved locations in the PA Wilds. From what I could tell, they required special equipment and getting permission from different agencies to use their towers to bounce signals from one spot to another, with the hope that after all that, one or two bars would light up on your phone. These stories always impressed me with their backwoods ingenuity while also irking me because here it was 2016 in a state with the sixth-largest economy in the country, and we were still trying to figure out how to make a basic utility available in the most rural part of the state.

DCNR's facilities had hardline Internet, but for security reasons, the public, including nonprofits like ours, were not allowed to use them. Sometimes these lines were abandoned through upgrades, leaving an option on the table. An IT team from DCNR's Harrisburg office drove up to the park to meet with me and DCNR's field staff to explore options.

Pennsylvania had an incredible, award-winning state park system, and a lot of mission-driven people worked for the agency. There was never enough money to do all the things that needed to be done, and dealing with the inertia of bureaucracy was sometimes maddening (for me and them), but there was incredible talent, heart, and creativity within DCNR that I was eternally grateful for. I once asked Ed McMahon if all state conservation departments were like Pennsylvania's, and he said that in many states, public land management agencies mainly focus on managing what they have. In Pennsylvania, he said, DCNR also looks at enhancing the value of the lands they manage through partnerships and economic development.

"That is pretty special," he said. "They are way more entrepreneurial than most Departments of Natural Resources."

Lisa Bainey walked the walk. To better serve visitors, she had started a small retail area in the new visitor center with sweatshirts and hats and also put "Proudly Made in the Pennsylvania Wilds" artisan products on display, encouraging visitors to stop in at the Cameron County Chamber and Artisan Center in nearby Emporium.

But even to Bainey, it was a Band-Aid. Retail wasn't the wheelhouse of public lands managers. What would be ideal, it came out in the meeting, would be to have a partner with shared goals to operate the gift shop. And it wasn't just at Sinnemahoning. An hour's drive north, a new visitor center was about to open at Kinzua Bridge State Park, where the Skywalk had opened two years prior, and it also had retail space.

"Maybe the Center would be interested in partnering with us," said DCNR's Region 1 Park Director, Alan Lichtenwalner, who oversaw most of the twenty-nine state parks in the PA Wilds. "I mean, you work with all these local artisans," Alan said. "You are in charge of the regional brand, and these are signature PA Wilds' sites. You are our lead external partner in the Conservation Landscape. Maybe we could try it as a pilot. Maybe there's even a way to weave in some of the work you are doing with youth."

I am caught off guard. I had never once considered the Center doing mission-driven retail.

I knew from our experience with the artisan trail that there was demand for locally made products and PA Wilds-branded merchandise, but more often than not, when we approached local businesses about the opportunity, whether on the supplier or retailer side, most didn't act or played it so safe with the action they did take that it didn't really move the dial in the marketplace. I didn't blame them. Why should they shoulder the risk on this unproven idea? Running a business in rural PA was hard enough.

Someone had to go first and do it in a big enough way to help de-risk things and instigate more action in the marketplace. Who could do that better than a nonprofit charged with helping rural entrepreneurs and growing the regional brand? We could show what was possible. Help define and set standards. Share real sales data and lessons learned.

Developing a mission-driven retail arm of the nonprofit, focused on selling locally made products, would improve market access for rural makers and producers, giving them a straightforward way to plug in and leverage the region's growing visitation to sell their products. It could also be a learning lab. It was not uncommon to find an artisan in our network who made an incredible product but didn't know how to price it, or create an invoice, or tell the story of their craftsmanship. A mission-driven retail operation would create a way for newer businesses to learn by doing.

At the same time, we'd take some of the burden off DCNR and help better serve visitors at highly rural state parks with growing foot traffic.

And create a new sustainable revenue stream to help support the PA Wilds effort.

And have a way to build a staff presence in more of the counties we serve.

And grow the brand. And licensing.

It is like a dam has been removed in my mind. How did I not see this before? We *had* to find a way to do this.

* * *

Early that spring, a path presents itself.

Seeing how we've retooled the artisan trail into a more inclusive network, Meredith encourages us to do a presentation for the Governor's Green Ribbon Task Force on Forest Products, Conservation, and Jobs, a cross-sector group that is looking at challenges to Pennsylvania's seventeen million acres of forestland and forest-dependent industries.

Timber and outdoor recreation are inextricably linked in the PA Wilds, two industries dependent on the same forest resource to thrive. Most of the two million-plus acres of public land in the region is forested. The bulk of these lands, forests owned by the Commonwealth and the US Forest Service, are what's called "multiple use" forests, managed for resource extraction, watershed protection, and recreation. These public lands are then surrounded by even more privately held forest lands,[1]

---

1. Forest management on all state forest land and approximately 500,000 acres of private forest land within PA are certified under the Forest Stewardship Council or the Sustainable Forestry Initiative programs.

creating a giant block of collective green that is critical to Pennsylvania's economy, climate resiliency, wildlife, and water quality and protection. As Matt Marusiak from the Western Pennsylvania Conservancy, a long-time member of the Planning Team, put it to me, "Forests are the earth's natural water filters," improving water quality and storage, reducing flood damages and storm water runoff, restoring groundwater, and other benefits for communities nearby and downriver. Forests in the PA Wilds supported seventy percent of the state's finest headwaters and helped to filter the region's 16,000 miles of streams and rivers.

Few things shape the health of a forest more than logging. When done sustainably, logging benefits the overall health of a forest, its watersheds, and wildlife while supplying a steady supply of renewable wood for lumber, energy, paper, packaging, and many other items that consumers use every day.

Some of the largest private timber landowners in the region, such as Collins Pine/Kane Hardwoods Division, left their lands open to most forms of public recreation, which supported the work we did. The region's rich lumber history was part of the experience of visiting the PA Wilds.

Given that the timber industry was such a heavyweight in shaping the forest and the culture and political landscape of the region, and the experience of visiting the region, I felt it was important to stay connected and to share what we were building and how and why it mattered.

The Green Ribbon task force adds me to one of their meeting agendas. I am six months pregnant with boy number three when I show up to present. I know this baby will be my last and I am mindfully trying to appreciate each moment, even the getting winded mid-presentation. The crowd includes mainly timber or forestry-related agencies and businesses. Most are familiar enough with the Wilds work, or me, at this point to know I'm not there to advocate against logging. The vibe feels respectful and curious.

I share the big picture of the PA Wilds work, how it is helping to revitalize rural communities, and how the forest and public lands are the foundational resource it is built upon. Without the forest, we would not have our famous wild elk herd, incredible trout fisheries, or internationally known dark night skies. I describe the rural value chain we are building, and how many of the small businesses and craftspeople in our network draw inspiration from the region's natural landscape for their products and services; several used forest resources to make them. In some cases, local timber companies or loggers donated tree knots and other scrap lumber to artisans, raw material they turned into stunning bowls or furniture or other creations. I underscore that the region's rich lumber heritage was part of the experience of visiting the PA Wilds.[2]

After I finish, I answer a few questions and then head for the door so I can get home in time for dinner with Leonard and the boys.

The building we're meeting in is a former grade school. With so much population decline, empty or repurposed elementary schools are a common sight in the region. As I walk down the hall to leave, the executive director for the North Central Pennsylvania Regional Planning and Development Commission at the time, Eric Bridges, asks me to wait up.

Eric is an ally, an economic development professional with a regional and statewide platform, who advocates for the PA Wilds as a comprehensive economic development strategy when others try to pigeonhole it as just a minor tourism initiative.

He tells me the Appalachian Regional Commission, a federal funding agency, has just announced a major new funding program, Partnerships for Opportunity and Workforce and Economic Revitalization, or "POWER" for short. He thinks the Wilds' work could compete for funding. The program helps communities and regions affected by the decline in the coal industry transition to grow new industries.

"We have communities with coal impacts," he said. "And the approaches you just shared seem like exactly what they are looking for."

I didn't follow other industries too closely, but I knew enough to know that Eric was right about the Wilds having coal impacts. One of my first joint presentations with Sam was in a town called Coalport. Remediation of historic mining scars in the elk range is part of what enabled elk tourism. The Kinzua Viaduct, in McKean County, once the tallest railroad bridge in the world, was originally built to carry coal, timber, oil, and gas across the deep Kinzua Valley. Through the PA Wilds Initiative, it had been revamped into a Skywalk, attracting hundreds of thousands of visitors a year to experience its dizzying heights and glass floor.

---

2. The PA Lumber Museum, located on Route 6 in Potter County and operated by the Pennsylvania Historical and Museum Commission, is a must-see when visiting. The Lumber Heritage Region also offers great land and water trail experiences that showcase the region's lumber heritage.

If we weren't an example of an Appalachian economy in transition, I didn't know what was. The funding was huge, up to $1.5 million per application. Even if we went in for a third of that, it would be transformational. I could build a staff. With three years to implement the grant, I'd have the runway to figure out how to sustain the new positions.

On the drive home, I envision what we can accomplish and how we can line up matching funds. Finding a way to reboot regional marketing, and launch a commerce platform, is at the top of my list.

CHAPTER 23

SHUCKING AWAY THE BULLSHIT

I have my work cut out for me making a case about our coal impacts. The Wilds is not the deep coal country of Southwest Pennsylvania or Kentucky or West Virginia. Parts of the region had heavy impacts, I learned, and we had a compounding effect as such a rural region that had lost so much other industry and population. By 2016, every job and every industry mattered, including the hundreds of coal jobs we'd lost since 2000.

I am working on our POWER grant proposal when I hear my cell phone vibrating with a call. A weak morning light shines through the windows. I am at my desk, a garage workbench Leonard has converted into a standing desk for me. I lift a few papers, looking for the phone.

I turn and survey my office, an alcove off the dining room that is about the size of a diner booth. Leonard had finished the space with rock, hand-hewed beams, and weathered boards he'd salvaged from a barn a mile up the road that had been in his family since before he was born.

I check the filing cabinet, then the shelf. Both are covered with big leafy ferns and sprawling vines. Their leaf tips are brown.

I look up at a picture that my oldest son drew me a few years ago that is stapled to the old barn boards behind my desk.

"Step away frum the computr mom" it says in a child's handwriting. Next to it is a picture he drew of his dad's racecar, colored with crayons. To make it all work with our growing family and my increasingly demanding schedule, Leonard had given up his racing just as he was really coming into his own as a driver. The sport possessed him the same way writing and advocating for rural PA did me, and it was painful to watch him sell off each piece of his equipment. I refused to let go of the idea of him getting back into it one day.

The phone vibrates again. So pregnant and forgetful. I follow the sound to a notebook that I take to meetings and find the device sandwiched between a few handouts and my mileage report. I hit the green answer button. It's Piper. She's gotten one of those calls that so many small businesses fear. While busting her butt running her business, she apparently missed filing an important document with the state. They are threatening late penalties, all the things. My sister's company is not my responsibility, but I appreciate the situation she's in and the call takes me back to our ordeal together after the floods.

I take a deep breath and back away from my computer, cell to my ear. I put a hand on my hip and take a wide stance. I'd watched Amy Cuddy's TED Talk about how physical stances can give you confidence and presence in stressful situations, and had devoured her follow-up book, *Presence*. Now, I regularly did the Wonder Woman pose.

I can feel the tension in my neck and back and in the way my vision for the future starts to constrict, like a dark cloud has moved in around it, and I can't see as far. I take a deep breath. As we talk through the situation, I learn that she has actually made no mistake at all—the state has. She just wanted a sounding board for how she planned to respond.

I am proud of my sister, and relieved. But when I get off the phone, I reflect that dealing with stressful situations is the new normal for me as CEO of a startup nonprofit. Sometimes, I spend time worrying about things I have no control over.

I bundle up and walk a few laps around the field behind my barn. How many hours had I spent worrying in the last week? Five? I multiply that by fifty-two weeks. Think of all the things I could do with 260 hours. I could be more present with my boys. Have a date night with my husband. Write a kick-butt grant application that brings half a million dollars back to rural PA to accelerate our work with local entrepreneurs.

I remind myself that there are so many things in the world I cannot control. I tell myself that whenever I start worrying about them, I should change my perspective. Zoom way out and think of the big picture or zoom way in and focus on a tactical project I do have some control over. And however small, take some kind of action. The universe rewards action.

I'd recently heard from a state forester that Teddy Roosevelt had traveled through the region when he was president. I had been down a rabbit hole reading about him in the evenings, and in the course of that, I had come across his famous "Man in the Arena" speech, where he rallied against cynics who looked down on people who were trying to make the world a better place.

"It is not the critic who counts," Roosevelt said. *"Not the man who points out how the strong man stumbles, or where the doer of deeds could have done them better. The credit belongs to the man who is actually in the arena, whose face is marred by dust and sweat and blood; who strives valiantly; who errs, who comes short again and again, because there is no effort without error and shortcoming; but who does actually strive to do the deeds; who knows great enthusiasms, the great devotions; who spends himself in a worthy cause; who at the best knows in the end the triumph of high achievement, and who at the worst, if he fails, at least fails while daring greatly . . ."*

I walk one more lap and then go inside and sit down at my computer and order a poster of this quote to hang on my wall.

Meredith had shared with me over the years how inspiring she found DeBerardinis as a leader in the early PA Wilds work. I was moved by his passion and big thinking, too, but it was something that his wife, Joan, had said to me one year, on a walk at Forty Maples at Sinnemahoning State Park, that stuck with me. The DeBerardinises had raised a family while both being involved in work they cared deeply about. "How do you balance it?" I asked Joan.

"There will always be people who came before you and people who will come after," she told me. "You have to figure out what you can do with the period of time you have and do it to the very best of your ability. But don't miss your kids' art shows or sports games to do it."

I took her wisdom to heart and was proud that I rarely missed my kids' activities. But my role at work had been in a state of constant evolution. Now I understood. Growing and stewarding the region's outdoor recreation sector to help revitalize rural communities was generational work that would never be done. But building and sustaining the core systems and capacity, the backbone hub organization to support it, was much more contained, and achievable, and it was what I as the Center's founding CEO, needed to do, God willing, with the period of time I had. Despite obstacles, or my own stupid mistakes, or tomatoes others might throw at me. This was my worthy cause. Maybe I'd succeed, maybe I wouldn't, but if I failed, at least I'd know I gave it my all.

For the next few months, I am deep in spreadsheets and conversations with my board and DCNR. We hammer out a four-year pilot lease agreement to operate a gift shop at Kinzua Bridge State Park. Like so many things with the Wilds' work, it is an experiment.

We have no money and very little time before the visitor center's grand opening. Abbi and I tour the visitor center at Kinzua Bridge State Park to check out our new space and get a flavor for its design themes so we can create a seamless experience for visitors with our new gift shop. Exhibits at the visitor center explain how a crew of forty men built the Kinzua Viaduct, the "Eighth Wonder of the World," back in 1882 in a mere ninety-four days. The bridge eventually stopped operating and became a state park. Then in 2003, a tornado ripped through the valley, toppling many of the bridge's iron girders. As part of the PA Wilds strategy, and with a lot of community support, the bridge was reinvented as a viewing platform with a glass floor, offering the tens of thousands of people who trekked there each year stunning views of the valley and the twisted wreckage below.

Learning the history, Abbi decides that if crews could build the Viaduct in ninety-four days, she could certainly get us a retail operation set up and operating in the same amount of time.

I reach out to a number of organizations I think might have mission alignment to the project and ask them to pitch in and help us. Several do, including the West Penn Energy Fund and the Stackpole-Hall Foundation.[1] We purchase locally made products for our startup inventory and with the help of our creative firm, name the store the PA Wilds Conservation Shop and develop a brand and interpretive signage that incorporates buy-local and conservation messages.

---

1. The West Penn Energy Fund would go one to be a hugely impactful investor in the PA Wilds movement, funding a number of energy-related projects across the region, including helping us establish a Media Lab in Kane, PA, a town of 3,500 that was leveraging the regional work in its own inspired ways. The Fund then built on this momentum, taking some of its money off Wall Street and putting it on Main Street by buying the building next door to our Media Lab, which had pigeons living in it at the time, and investing $6M to make it the first commercial retrofit of a Main Street building to Passive House energy standards in America. The demonstration project, named Six&Kane, drew international attention, and benefitted us in a number of ways, including that it had a shared elevator that improved accessibility to our second floor space. But more than the scale of the investment, it was the Fund's approach that stood out to a lot of locals. They used the *PA Wilds Design Guide for Community Character Stewardship* to help guide the renovations so they fit the landscape, engaged the community to learn about their history, and the building's, so it could be incorporated in the designs, and sourced huge parts of the project and supplies locally and regionally. Watch a video on the project, "New Energy Ideas Helping to Revitalize Rural Communities," at https://www.youtube.com/watch?v=OiAt_oViyro.

The activity is exciting, but as the opening draws closer, a voice inside me nags, *what if it doesn't work? What if we don't have the foot traffic to support the operation? What if we can't find workers? What if 'buy local' is just another theory that sounds good on paper but in reality, people just want cheap tchotchkes from China to commemorate their trip to the PA Wilds?*

Straub's investment is on my mind, too.

What if it falls flat? What if consumers don't value the PA Wilds brand?

I felt like I'd been debating some of these questions for years. And here, finally, was a moment of truth. The market, I knew, does not mess around. Like a storm that leaves no question that Mother Nature is in charge, markets are a force to reckon with. Within days, sometimes minutes, you know if your ideas are valid.

This is what it is like to be an entrepreneur, I think. So much uncertainty. So much risk. And it dawns on me that I'm proud to be building an organization that stays close to that experience, however painful it is sometimes. It is like spending a night in the woods. It shucks away the bullshit. It keeps us real, keeps us true.

It's *our* differentiator.

CHAPTER 24

HITTING OUR STRIDE

On a beautiful summer day in June 2016, Leonard takes me to Warren General Hospital, and I check into a room that overlooks the Allegheny River. My grandparents, parents, sisters, husband, and both of my sons had been born in this town, some maybe even in this room. My oldest son was now eight, his brother, four, their heights etched by year into the door trim at Leonard's race shop. My last baby, Dash, arrives just before 5 p.m., a healthy eight pounds, nine point six ounces.

Our chariot this time is a 1977 Chrysler Newport two-door hardtop with bench seats, emerald green inside and out. My two older sons each take a window and we buckle the baby in his car seat in between them. The sun is shining. We are all smiles. Leonard has worked for a construction company for the last six years and the next day he is back at work. I take the boys and our dog to a nearby crick to play while I sit and watch in the shade and hold the baby. Three days old, he is already spending time in nature, and it dawns on me, I am living the life I once dreamed.

A few days later, I learn the Center has just been awarded Pennsylvania's first POWER grant. I am sitting on the edge of my bed, nursing, when a colleague at DCED calls and shares the news. I am not sure who is more shocked, him or me. A month later, we open our first PA Wilds Conservation Shop at Kinzua Bridge State Park.

These two things, combined with the reorganization we'd done with partners, lead to a total breakthrough for the PA Wilds work. The next few years remind me of running down Flattop, the mountain I used to climb in Alaska before my shift started in the newsroom. The up was a slog but the down was equally as challenging, my eyes darting from rock to rock, my body trying desperately to balance the pitch and pace of my feet as they covered a huge distance in record time.

Abbi becomes our second full time staffer. For the first season at the Conservation Shop she carries much of the management herself while helping build the Center's other programs. It is a long twelve months. By the second season we post a job for a store manager. A spunky, seasoned retail manager, Libby Bloomquist, applies. Libby had a degree in psychology with a focus on youth and families but enjoyed retail so much that after college she spent the next two decades working for major retailers across the country. She had recently moved home to rural PA, where she and her husband grew up, when she saw our opening.

By then I had come to realize that the PA Wilds' work had an almost magnetic force about it, often bringing the right person into its sphere at the exact right time. I saw Libby as another example of that. Abbi and I desperately wanted her to want the job.

We interviewed her in an unfinished space at the new visitor center. The interview started normally, but as soon as it was clear Libby was the person in real life that she appeared to be on paper, Abbi and I came unleashed, energetically explaining what the PA Wilds is all about, what it's taken to get to this point, how critical it is for this store to work, the good it could do, and why we think she's the perfect fit. I fed off Abbi's energy, and she off mine. We talked faster and faster until the motion-sensor lights shut off and then one of us got up and did a little dance to turn them back on.

After a few minutes of this, Libby gets quiet. She says she wants to think about it. After she leaves, I think, *Shit!* I am disappointed in myself for not showing more restraint. Abbi is worried we scared her off, too, but concludes that if someone can't handle the energy of us in an interview, they will struggle to handle the energy flying off the nonprofit's work.

Turns out, Libby was just stunned by what she was hearing—in a really good way. She accepted the job the next day.

With the Conservation Shop, we create a whole new market for locally made products, and for PA Wilds-branded products. Annual gross sales climb from $116,000 the first year to nearly $400,000 by 2019. New businesses sign up to create PA Wilds-branded t-shirts and hats and coffee mugs and the licensing program that started with that $86 royalty check grows to more than $10,000 annually, a tiny fraction of what local businesses are now making off the brand.

Stephanie Distler, the jewelry artisan from Elk County who championed the work for so many years, develops a product line just for the Conservation Shop. The improved market access allows her to buy new equipment and expand her production studio to four times its original size. A t-shirt company we start working with in Clearfield County brings on three new workers to keep up with the demand.

Behind the scenes, Julie, our accountant and a soap-maker herself, is shocked as she does the books. "I just cannot believe what we are building," she said. "It's incredible."

Developing and expanding our high-mission-impact revenue-generating programs enabled us to have a far more aggressive grants strategy, too, because now we had the elusive match dollars to compete. Before long, Julie and her assistant, Carol, come on full time, too.

"I never wanted to do nonprofits," Julie would explain to me years later. "I just kind of fell in love with it. When I came with you, we just kept growing by leaps and bounds. We learned together and grew together. It was such an adventure. It didn't even feel like work. I quickly learned that if you said we are going to do a project, it was going to get done, even if it took a few tries to get it funded. We truly could make a difference in the community."

With the visitor bureaus' help, and the POWER funding in hand, we reframe and reboot regional marketing. All of the visitor bureaus save for one support the permanent transfer of the PAWilds.com domain to our nonprofit. I try to win over the final visitor bureau but fail miserably. At one point, she demands that we promise never to sell ads on the site and tells me over the phone, "No one is going to tell me how to market my county!" I am sitting in my car on Fraley Street in Kane when she says it, and I shake my head and look at the heavens for patience. No matter how frustrated I got, I still had to try to keep partners at the table. "I am not trying to tell you how to market your county," I say. "I'm telling you how *we're* going to *help* market your county."

With the Marketing Corp's funding cuts, the PAWilds.com domain is in rough shape when we get it, running on expensive, outdated technology, its listings out of date, and operating at one-tenth of its capacity, according to a consultant we hired to help us reposition it. Using the brand principles as our guide, and fresh insights from the visitor bureaus, heritage areas, public land managers, key attractions, and other organizations serving the traveling public, we scrap all the old content and rebuilt the site from scratch.

We stopped marketing the region by county and instead packaged it by major experiences. Dark Skies. Elk Country. The Allegheny National Forest and Surrounds landscape. Pine Creek Valley. The I-80 Frontier. Cook Forest and the Ancients.

We make an intentional decision to not use stock photography and instead to hire local photographers to capture the images we needed to market the region, leaning on public lands agencies for images we might be missing. In a world where marketing and advertising had grown increasingly slick, it helped differentiate us while putting local creatives to work.

A new communications director we've hired helps lead the charge, writing content and launching a photo contest to involve more volunteers in telling the region's story. We bring on a young former reporter from Clinton County, LaKeshia Knarr, as a contractor to help us build connections with the business community on the eastern side of the region, eventually so impressed with her work and dedication to the cause and her community that we bring her on full time. She helps us build a stable of writers and other contributors. I knew from my own storytelling days that readers and communities appreciated authentic local content by skilled contributors, and I was proud to be building a platform to enable more of that.

Contracting with local creatives and creative services firms, from graphic designers to website developers to photographers to writers, becomes another robust lane of the rural value chain we are building, a way we take the money we raise and intentionally push it out into rural communities to create new work opportunities for local small businesses.

Since my ombudsman days, I'd wanted to build a photo library that better documented the region's maker culture so we could use them to market the region in a more authentic way and encourage visitors to buy local. The few pictures we had of locally handcrafted items, shared across that early Flickr account, seemed so powerful to me, a push-back on the culture of throw-away consumerism.

Abbi took this idea and ran with it, securing funding from the Pennsylvania Council on the Arts to hire local photographers to drive all over the region documenting artisans making their crafts in their unique workspaces. We gave the participants copies of the images so they could use them on their own websites and at shows and turned the collection into a traveling public art exhibit that hung at galleries across the region and at the East Wing of the Capitol Complex in Harrisburg. We also used the photos at our new Conservation Shop to show customers who made the items they were purchasing and for marketing the region on PAWilds.com. This became our way: to make every project, every dollar, do the work of five.

Visitation to PAWilds.com climbs from 40,000 a year to more than 300,000. We launch a blog and an Instagram feed and steadily grow our Facebook page.[1]

With the marketing reorganized, the visitor bureau that had resigned from the Marketing Corp, who had helped launch the Wilds brand, gets back involved and becomes a huge champion for our work and is invited to join our board of directors. Out of the gate he helps us accomplish some fun wins, including a licensing partnership with New Trail Brewing that saw seventeen breweries from across the region collaborate on an innovative "Wilds Are Calling" brew, with royalties from every can sold going back to support our mission.

At the Conservation Shop, much of what our nonprofit brings in is pushed right back out to purchase inventory from local businesses or to contract with local firms for creative services or to accomplish other parts of our mission, like telling the region's story.

As participation in our free rural value chain network soars past three hundred members, we realize we have taken all these once disparate parts of the PA Wilds' work and reorganized and evolved them into a high-functioning, sustainable, entrepreneurial ecosystem tied to the region's outdoors brand. Even the smallest, most remote, hardest-to-reach rural makers and artisans and service sector businesses could enter the ecosystem through the Wilds Cooperative and then have access to all this stuff to help them thrive: new markets, workshops to grow professionally, referrals to lenders and technical service providers, opportunities to license the brand and develop new products, marketing and branding support, access to business-to-business sales opportunities.

---

1. Follow the PA Wilds Center on Facebook and Instagram @ThePAwilds.

Essentially, we had taken the need the Planning Team had identified so many years back, and organically, piece by piece, built a new regional system to address it. And not just on paper. But tied to the actual market. And it was *working*.

Now we had to find a way to scale it.

CHAPTER 25

BUILDING ON A LEGACY

Prior to working on the PA Wilds, I had never identified as a conservationist or an environmentalist. Growing up, Mom had instilled in us that we should do our part: don't litter, don't let the water run while you are brushing your teeth, turn off the lights as you leave the room, etc. But our struggle for basic necessities didn't leave much room for worrying about the larger environment.

Even as late as my sophomore year in college, working on a campus grounds crew to help pay my tuition, I remembered talking with a co-worker and fellow student about an environmental concern he had and being completely annoyed with him. What a luxury to have to worry about *issues*, I thought, and dug my trowel into the dirt.

I valued the outdoors and nature and was quietly horrified by the super-size-it, make-it-as-cheaply-as-possible, throw-away culture that was polluting the oceans with plastic and the Earth with garbage and tried to do my part by reducing, reusing, and recycling. But even as I worried more and more about the planet, I eyed environmental causes warily. Watching them unfold in local and national news over the years, it sometimes felt like the people and communities most connected to the threatened resource were left out of the discussion of how to design a solution, or even recognized for the work they had done, fueling anger and distrust.

Like politics, I viewed environmentalism as polarizing, something to steer clear of.

Time and maturity, having kids, watching the glaciers melt and Alaska villages fall into the ocean, and living through the largest mass extinction event in human history, helped change my thinking. So did working and living in the PA Wilds.

My edification in the PA Wilds came in three distinct waves.

First was watching DCNR launch its Conservation Landscape program. At its heart it was an approach that said, in order for the Commonwealth's leading conservation agency to better care for the state's special natural places, it had to care more about the communities around them. In the PA Wilds, rural park managers and foresters who were already doing a lot with a little, were now instructed to look beyond their borders and build deeper and wider relationships with the struggling gateway communities around them.

This was a new way of thinking back in the early 2000s, and like any big change, it was not always easy. Seeing some of those struggles and conversations up close, the agency's commitment to working through them, and to making investments in rural communities in new ways, went a long way toward building trust, with me and a lot of others.

Alongside this, I started learning about the region's conservation legacy. I read about "The Big Cut," an era in American history when places like the Pennsylvania Wilds had been nearly completely clear-cut to fuel the country's rapid expansion during the Industrial Revolution. The excess led to wildfires and floods and the extinction of animals.

Ted Eubanks had written about the Big Cut in some of his early studies about the PA Wilds, so I asked him about it. In his line of work, he was familiar with the history, but that wasn't the same as experiencing it, he said.

"I never had it made real for me until I worked in the Wilds," Eubanks told me. "That literally everything I was looking at had been totally destroyed at one time. A war-scape. That's what it would have looked like."

Eubanks said that as he spent more time in the region, he started reflecting on how the PA Wilds fit into the country's larger conservation narrative. He said he was especially drawn to Joseph Rothrock, the "Father of Forestry," who died in 1922.

"Here's the guy who really started it. He went out there in a wagon and started documenting what happened and took that information back to Philadelphia. That Penn's Woods had been raped and that the

Commonwealth had to take measures to start restoring it," Eubanks said. "He goes to the Clarion River and writes back, only two words come to mind in this landscape: 'Abomination and desolation.' That's now in a place that's designated Wild and Scenic."

It made me think of the Clarion River Clarion Partnership, one of the first PA Wilds projects I learned about as the ombudsman. Meredith of course took me on a tour of it. Ten municipalities that bordered the river came together with public lands and waterway managers through the partnership to successfully attract public and private investment to improve roads, public restrooms, access points, and signage along the Clarion River. By then, the Clarion had been voted Pennsylvania's River of the Year multiple times. Learning the history, it was hard to imagine it as once so ravaged.

Our landscape wasn't the only one laid barren. When Franklin D. Roosevelt dedicated the Great Smokey Mountain National Park in Central Appalachia in 1940, he told the country, "We realize now that we committed excesses which we are today seeking to atone for." He put young men to work in the Civilian Conservation Corps, or CCC, during the Great Depression, fighting fires, building trails, and planting trees in many of these devastated areas.[1] The Pennsylvania Wilds region has more Civilian Conservation Corps camps than most states.

"I started to realize, this is the cradle of conservation in our country," Eubanks told me. "Not the birthplace of the philosophy of conservation, more the *practice* of conservation. What do you have to do to restore these lands? That was born in Pennsylvania. You see the results; you live in it."

After talking to Eubanks, I read about one of Rothrock's speeches where he recalled how devastated the forests of his youth had become. "Sixty years ago, I walked from Clearfield to St. Marys to Smethport, sixty miles," he said in 1915, "most of the way through glorious white pine and hemlock forests. Now, those forests are gone."

It made me think of the dozens of times I had driven to Clearfield, St. Marys, and Smethport to do presentations, meet with businesses, or hold a board meeting. It was more than an hour's drive to each of them

---

1. The CCC program was based on work camps that Gifford Pinchot, Roosevelt's first chief of the U.S. Division of Forestry (the pre-cursor to the U.S. Forest Service), who had set up similar work camps throughout Pennsylvania when he was governor of the state. The camps became the model for the CCC program.

from Warren, most of it through the woods. It was stunning to imagine it was all once barren.

By the early 1900s, the region was once so depleted of its trees and wildlife that people abandoned the land. They made jokes when the government started to buy it up to create state and national forests and game lands. Our elk went extinct. Whitetail deer nearly suffered the same fate. "The Pennsylvania Desert," they called us. The first PA game lands ever purchased are here. The first PA state forest lands ever purchased are here. It is here, decades later, that local Howard Zahniser drew inspiration to pen the nation's still standing Wilderness Act of 1964.

It was an incredible story and legacy that, oddly, I never heard about growing up here. I don't think I'm the only one.

When I start learning about something new and fascinating, I let it spill into other conversations. At one point, I mentioned to the CEO of a manufacturing company that the Allegheny National Forest was once so cut over that they called it the Allegheny Brush Pile.

"*Here?*" he said. "Really?"

Another time I had my aunts and some family friends over for lunch, and one pointed to a large picture on my wall, an aerial landscape shot taken by a local photographer that we used on the back cover of the PA Wilds Outdoor Discovery Atlas.[2] The entire image is filled with mountains and trees, and very small in the middle is a car driving down one of the mountains. I loved the picture because it captured the experience of exploring the region's vast public lands and big woods. Abbi made it into a wall hanging and gave it to me as a gift for my birthday one year.

"It's hard to imagine at one point all that was clear-cut, isn't it?" I said, and she was as stunned as I had once been.

It was a remarkable story, how we got from point A to point B. Out of the devastation grew one of the world's most valuable hardwood forests, and a sustainable timber industry that to me told a powerful story about redemption, balance, and resilience. The ultimate public-private partnership, long before that was a buzz term. Some people had a knee-jerk reaction to logging the same way they did to hunting, feeling it was wrong, but the reality was, both were critical modern-day management tools, to say nothing of their economic or cultural impacts.

---

2. Before disbanding, the Marketing Corp used some of its last funds to help us create the Atlas. From the photography to the layout and design to the paper it is printed on, the Atlas was proudly and intentionally made 100 percent in-region, putting locals to work. Find it at ShopThePAwilds.com.

Today, the PA Wilds is home to America's largest block of Forest Stewardship Council-certified public forestland, and many people who still make their living from the woods. Log trucks are as ubiquitous a sight on the region's winding roads as tourists or wildlife or the sound of cricks.

Rob Fallon, a district manager for the Allegheny National Forest, in 2023 shared parts of this history as a guest speaker at the annual meeting of the Allegheny Hardwoods Utilization Group (AHUG). It was the 100-year anniversary of the national forest. AHUG was a timber industry trade group that worked closely with the state's Hardwoods Development Council, public lands managers like Fallon, and others to expand and diversify the forest products industry and maintain a sustainable, high-yield forest within a fourteen-county region that covered all of the ANF and most of the PA Wilds.

"This group knows more than anyone the importance of sustainability," Fallon told the timber industry crowd, reflecting on how far the national forest had come. "One hundred years ago it was about purchase and protect. In 2023, it is all about how do we partner? How do we collaborate to address landscape-level challenges, like invasive species?"

We were fortunate in rural PA to have the Lumber Heritage Region (LHR), the nonprofit that helped launch the Wilds work by partnering on the early elk watching study, and housing aspects of the initiative as it grew. Beyond partnerships, LHR's specialty was documenting in different mediums the "struggles of the pioneers to the cut-and-run practices of the early lumber industry to the conservation efforts that led to the managed forests of today."

Holly, the person who saved me from myself that day on the conference call where we were discussing the future of PAWilds.com, had left her post in Clearfield County and was now LHR's director. Under her leadership, the nonprofit created new staff capacity, overhauled the organization's websites, and completed new projects, including a study documenting women and Black people in the early lumbering industry. My boys loved visiting the state-run PA Lumber Museum, which was established in 1972 but went through a major expansion and reopening in 2015, just before the Kinzua Skywalk opened. The Lumber Museum's exhibits included a train room, a twentieth-century lumber camp, a seventy-ton Shay geared-locomotive, a Barnhart log-loader, two historic log cabins, and interpretive panels designed to help visitors "discover the courageous yet reckless spirit of Pennsylvania's lumbering past while learning to care for the forests of the future." I smiled the day they came home from school excited to tell me all about the WoodMobile, a thirty-four-foot trailer that provides an interactive experience educating visitors about the forest, the sustainable forest products industry, how products are made, and threats to the forest, like invasive insects and plants. Operated by the state through a partnership with the timber industry, the traveling exhibit has participated in hundreds of events reaching more than 232,000 students and teachers.

Most of these things didn't exist when I was a kid. To think of how the region went from war-scape to the forest it is today gave me hope that humans could tackle other complex environmental challenges. The PA Wilds, with its consumer-facing brand, platforms like PAWilds.com, and focus on connecting people with outdoor recreation experiences on the region's now-restored public lands, created new opportunities to continue to lift up this tremendous conservation legacy.

The third thing that really deepened my thinking about the environment were the people.

People like George Durrwachter, who way back when, helped light the fire under Jerry Walls to push back on the state's intense marketing approach with the PA Wilds, poking Jerry on the chest at a watershed meeting and asking him point blank, "What are you going to do about this Wilds thing, Walls?" which helped lead to the creation of the Planning Team and a robust focus on stewardship in tourism development.

I was curious to learn the backstory when I first heard about this. I reached out to George, introduced myself, and asked if I could interview him.

George grew up on the eastern side of the region, in the Pine Creek Valley, a forty-seven-mile north-south canyon in Tioga State Forest that had been carved over the centuries into the Allegheny Plateau by Pine Creek. Thousands of people came to the Valley annually to visit the Pine Creek Gorge, a National Natural Landmark, to trout fish, and to bike the Pine Creek Rail Trail, which tracts alongside much of Pine Creek on the valley floor.

The sixty-five-mile rail trail is punctuated by Wellsboro, population 3,200, in the north, Jersey Shore, pop. 4,200, in the south, and a handful of small villages in between.

George, a retired orthodontist, grew up in Cammal, a tiny village that sits about midway along the trail. When he was a boy, the rail trail was still a rail, trains ran through the valley, and Cammal had about seventy-five residents. George's dad was a forester, and his mom took in hunters at the family home.

Young George loved to hunt, trap, fish, and read *Field & Stream*. More than a few times he slept on a raft on Pine Creek "like Huck Finn." Sometimes he'd skip school and turkey hunt all the way down to Waterville, nine miles away, and pick up the school bus there in the afternoon for a lift back home. The bus driver didn't mind him climbing aboard with his harvests or gun, he recalls; it was a different time. At home, with no TV, George would listen to the stories of travelers who came through. One was a dentist who regaled him with hunting stories from around the globe. Young George thought that sounded like a pretty good gig and eventually followed in his footsteps.

George's parents never went on a vacation, but they lived a rich life in Pennsylvania's big woods that inspired in their son a deep love for Pine Creek and other wild places.

George went on to become a man of local prominence, practicing orthodontics in Williamsport for thirty years and eventually inducted into nearby Lock Haven University's Business Hall of Fame, with the Alumni Conference Center named after him. He worked over many years with Jerry and others on local planning and zoning efforts to help protect the Valley from unplanned development. His main concern, he said, was always carrying capacity of the landscape. Too many visitors can fundamentally change a place, and often not for the better.

His story reminded me of so many of the things I loved about the PA Wilds: the rich family histories, the independent spirit, and the care and connection many residents here have to the outdoors and the region's special wild places.

"Every beat of my heart really is about Pine Creek," George told me.

He'd been opposed to the development of the Pine Creek Rail Trail when it started but had come to think of it as one of the best things that had ever happened to the Valley.

"It's hard to say you're wrong. But I was wrong," George told me. "I read all the negative stuff." But from home property values to health and wellness, to the safety of not having to bike or walk on the road anymore, he said, "The Pine Creek Rail Trail has improved the quality of life of the people who live in the Valley one hundred percent."

Surrounded as it is by so much public land, there are not many amenities along the trail. "It kind of takes you back in time," George said. "As I'm sitting here talking to you, I can see an eagle and a junior eagle flying over the trail. People see that sort of thing. That makes your whole day."

He was still cautious about the PA Wilds.

"My greatest threat is people coming here and loving this place to death," he said. "People are the ruination of special places."

When Leonard gets home from work, I tell him about my conversation with George.

"He's right you know," he says as Cole tugs at his sleeve to go look at a Lego creation he built upstairs. "You should listen to George. Smart guy."

There are so many people like this in the PA Wilds, across so many industries and walks of life, that are doing conservation and stewardship work, planting riparian buffers to keep streams from eroding, cleaning up acid mine drainage to bring cricks back to life, restoring elk habitat, trying to protect special places through wise land use planning, hunters and sportsman's clubs raising funds for conservation, artists drawing pictures on sidewalks near the sewers to remind people that what goes down this hole eventually flows out into our cricks.

People like Jan Hampton, the first woman to lead the Planning Team, who worked for her county conservation district for many years. When the Wilds' work first started, she convinced others to give it a chance by describing it as "a gentle sharing of the things we hold most dear."

People like Tom Kase, who for many years worked for Collins Pine/Kane Hardwoods, who, the first time I met him, brought me books about the company's long history in sustainable logging and explained to me that when you talk about sustainable forestry, you are not looking five or ten years down the road. You work from a 150-year plan, the life of a tree.

People like my husband, who built parts of entire buildings out of reused materials, intentionally saving and organizing them because, "Where do people think all this stuff goes when they throw it away?"

People like Piper, so irked by the trash she saw that she launched a river cleanup that brought out thousands of volunteers over the years.

Or like Jerry, who marshaled a whole region of planners together to create planning resources for rural communities to help them get development right because, "We have something special here, and we have to come at it in a way that is respectful."

It took me some time to uncover this conservation apparatus and stewardship ethic because people here don't really talk about it, I suspect for some of the same reasons I never did. In rural places where there is a lot of public land, or resource extraction occurring (even sustainable extraction), or both, certain words—*conservation, easements, extraction, climate change,* etc.—can feel loaded, politicized, even if you don't mean them to be. So best not to say anything at all and just keep working.

Others were just too humble. Seriously. We once tried to give an award to a man who had spent decades restoring a creek that had been devastated by coal mining. He thanked us but declined the awards dinner, saying that seeing the stream cleaned up was award enough.

Abbi gave me a hardcover of Hellen Keller's essay, "Optimism," one year for Christmas, and in it, I read a quote that immediately reminded me of this tribe and the region's stewardship ethic. "I long to accomplish a great and noble task, but it is my chief duty to accomplish small tasks as if they were great and noble."

Meredith had a huge influence on me, too, in the way she quietly lived her stewardship values, diverting every leftover pamphlet at events from the trash so they could be reused (even when she had nothing to do with organizing the event), shopping at second-hand stores for many of her clothes, showing up to every meeting, year after year, encouraging people to stay at it, driven by her own love for the region and its people and a deeply-held belief that projects can have good economic outcomes and good conservation outcomes. "It isn't always easy," she told me, "but it can be done."

Jodi Brennan, the Clearfield County Planning Director, probably captured it best when she told me, "Meredith has inspired me not to take our region for granted. There has been so much progress over this last decade and a half. When I was a child living in Benezette the Bennett Branch of the Sinnemahoning was orange and slimy with acid-mine drainage, used as a dumping ground for trash. There were no kayaks on the stream, no fishing, no bald eagles. The stream was not viewed as an asset. I never thought I would see the stream improve in my lifetime but happily, that has not been the case. Just this summer my son caught and released twelve trout from that very same stream. Today, folks flock to our streams to swim, fish, kayak, and view wildlife. Now, our streams are valued as the precious recreational assets they were always meant to be."

Sam, my former co-worker who wrote *Agony of an American Wilderness*, had a memory of Meredith, too. He said he, Meredith, and some others were meeting with a creative firm about an interpretive exhibit. The vendors weren't from rural PA. A sidebar conversation came up about the installation of a "wood hick" statue in nearby Williamsport, along a trail adjacent to the river. Wood hicks were like early lumberjacks.[3] The Lumber Heritage Region was helping communities erect the statues to tell the story of the region's lumbering past. Hearing the conversation, one of the outsiders gasped, Sam recalled, and said something along the line of, "Why would they want to honor people who devastated their environment like that?" Sam explained to me in an email:

> As you might imagine, I cringed a bit and prepared to launch a stinging rebuttal. And the rebuttal was launched! People in the PA Wilds aren't ashamed of their history. They recognize that it's complicated. They live with the consequences of those excesses. In fact, they were instrumental in CORRECTING those excesses and building the forests and rivers that are here today. They have an intense sense of pride in what we built, how we built it, and what it has become. In a certain sense the wood hick is a great example of how this place came to be. He had a hard life. He did his job. It was an incredibly important job, insofar as he helped build this country but was never really recognized for it. Much like the Wilds region itself. It was a great rebuttal, I thought, especially since I wasn't the one being bothered to deliver it. Meredith was! I thought man, this [PA Wilds thing] just might work. She gets it. She totally gets it. She's not "from" here, but she can eloquently and passionately make the case for this place. She wasn't combative or abrupt or political. She made a rock solid case for the

---

3. Learn more in the beautiful coffee table book, *Wood Hicks and Bark Peelers*, by Ronald E. Ostman and Harry Littell. https://lumberheritage.org/product/wood-hicks-and-bark-peelers/

wood hick, and in doing so made a rock solid case for the Wilds. And the vendor totally saw it. Totally understood. It was like a lightbulb went off. It was just a really great moment for me.[4]

Through all this, I started to see, like many others did, that the Wilds' work was part of a continuum that had been going on for more than a century. And so, from the earliest days and increasingly more as visitation to the region grew, we worked stewardship into every program and way of being at our nonprofit.

We gave out conservation awards to people and companies each year. We launched a permanent charity checkout campaign on our commerce platform and donated one hundred percent of the dollars raised to the PA Parks and Forests Foundation to reinvest in state parks and forests in the region.

We launched a stewardship section on PAWilds.com. Inspired by the region's CCC heritage, LaKeshia helped us launch WildSPEAK: Civilian Storytellers Corps, encouraging visitors and residents with "Stories of Personal Experience And Knowledge" to help us tell the story of the PA Wilds in a passionate way, in many stories, mirroring back the region's stewardship ethic and weaving in its conservation legacy.

We worked with partners to better understand peak seasons and strategies for dispersing visitors to tailor our marketing so places didn't get loved to death.

We signed a tourism licensing partnership with the Leave No Trace Center for Outdoor Ethics, a national leader in stewardship in the outdoors, to create tailored stewardship, safety, and preparedness messaging for the region and make it available for free to the hundreds of businesses and other organizations we work with.[5]

Our region's conservation story was complex and beautiful. We'd reclaimed coal strip mines and turned them into elk habitat. The Clarion River got cleaned up to a point that it now had trophy trout, and it did it with a major paper mill still operating on its banks, employing hundreds of local people. Not only did the Allegheny get Wild and Scenic designation status, it did it with a major refinery, one of Warren's largest employers, just upriver from where that designation begins. Our

---
4. Meredith doesn't recall this moment, but it sounded very Meredith to me, so I include it here.
5. Learn more at PAWilds.com/lnt/

restored forested landscape supported not just tourism, but timber, oil, gas. This daily striving for balance—which included, sometimes, tension or conflicts—was not something to hide from visitors, but to interpret. We weren't Yellowstone. Or Denali. We were the PA Wilds.

CHAPTER 26

RURAL DEVELOPMENT

The PA Wilds' movement couldn't address all of the challenges facing its rural communities. But one thing my team and I could do is scale our ecosystem to drive wealth back into rural communities through locally-owned small businesses.

If one Conservation Shop with forty rural vendors could do almost half a million in sales of local products, what could a network of the mission-driven shops do over five, ten, twenty years?

Selling wholesale wasn't for every kind of local business. But what if alongside the brick-and-mortar shops we created an online marketplace for rural makers and small businesses to sell directly to consumers with the added marketing power of the regional brand? They, too, would have an easy way to plug in and benefit.

If we could convince even a quarter of the tens of thousands of unique visitors coming to PAWilds.com to buy a locally-designed or handcrafted item from a local business online, or to book an outdoors adventure here, or to patronize a local brewery or restaurant, or stay overnight in a locally-owned lodge or bed and breakfast when they got here, imagine how many rural small businesses it would support. If we could make it easier for more rural businesses to do business with each other, including tapping into the creative services type businesses in our network, it would have a huge ripple effect.

We had some heavy hitters in our network, but for the most part, most were not big and powerful enough to be making political contributions, to have capital systems designed just for their sector to help it grow. They were the little guys. Yet they were critical to the future of rural communities.

I knew from my work with Piper and working with other businesses as the ombudsman that it was a fine line between success and failure in small business. One steady, reliable revenue stream could make all the difference in a tough year. We could build the mechanisms at the regional level that enabled that opportunity for more rural businesses.

If all the locally owned lodges and breweries and shops and restaurants and craftspeople we worked with could actually be successful, how much more vibrant would our communities be? More vibrant communities would make it easier for bigger rural employers to attract and retain the talent they need, and communities to attract other investments. It might even help stop our population exodus, as more young people felt more pride in growing up here, and saw more pathways to fulfilling careers, including in small business.

A mission-driven commerce platform like this could also be sustainable. It had revenues attached to it that could underwrite its operation and stewardship over the long haul. A virtuous cycle of good, operating in perpetuity. That's what I wanted to build and hand off, and now, finally, after so many years of test, fail, correct, I saw the way to do it.

The clarity of vision is galvanizing. But it was a massive system to try to stand up with no dedicated funding. I had an engaged board, and a skilled and passionate staff, but we were still vastly under-resourced and up against a lot of challenges.

Much has been written about "food deserts," where residents in economically distressed areas do not have access to retailers that sell fruits, vegetables, and other fresh foods. The PA Wilds had food deserts. We also had broadband deserts, news deserts, maternity deserts, pretty much all kinds of deserts except the actual dry, arid kind. High-speed Internet at our gift shop at Kinzua Bridge State Park cost our nonprofit nearly $1,200 a month, almost $15,000 a year. For basic Internet. At Leonard Harrison State Park, where we opened a mobile unit, the Internet wasn't available at all. We had to build an entirely offline system, relying on a telephone line to run credit cards.

Access to capital was another issue, for nonprofits, governments, and businesses. The new communications director that had joined our team came from the private-sector franchising world. She only stayed at the nonprofit a few years, but in that time, she opened my eyes to different types of capital that could advance the Wilds work. Venture capital funds were near non-existent in the region, and investments by major foundations, an important source of funds for public needs in America, were also rare. One study showed eight of the region's counties saw zero to ten dollars per capita in this type of philanthropic giving. Another study showed this was common in rural landscapes.[1] Not one of the eighteen Community Development Financial Institutions (CDFIs) based in Pennsylvania were located in the quarter of the state that made up the PA Wilds region. CDFIs are like banks that have a mission to invest in higher-risk areas; they can provide loans and help build credit in underserved areas. A few of the CDFIs based outside the PA Wilds region did loans here, but we frequently heard from businesses that had been turned down (including some that would go on to be some of the region's biggest names in tourism). One study, published in 2023, showed eight of the region's thirteen counties saw zero CDFI lending.[2]

Doing systems development in such a landscape is a slow process, like rehabbing an old farmhouse in the country on a budget. You go to change a lightbulb and realize all the wiring needs to be redone, there's no electrician for miles, and not enough money to hire them even if you can get their attention. So, you enlist the help of friends who have been there, try to teach yourself what you need to know, and then several weeks or months later, the lightbulb finally gets changed while people cluck from the sidelines, "took them a month to get the lightbulb changed."

Internally, we are still constructing the nonprofit, so there is a whole layer of development work happening that no one but the board and staff can see. Every situation is new and only goes to highlight something we are missing that we then have to stop and do first. A policy or manual or piece of tech or system. It reminds me of Piper teaching herself design software as she was laying out the paddling guide. At least we have heat in the rooms we are working in.

Our work is pushing the envelope at DCNR, too. As we look to open more Conservation Shops at other state parks, DCNR realizes it has no

---

1. A December 2021 report, *Rural America: Philanthropy's Misunderstood Opportunity for Impact*, funded by the Bill and Melinda Gates Foundation and developed by FSG, a mission-driven consulting firm supporting leaders in creating large-scale lasting social change, found that 20 percent of Americans live in rural areas, which are among the most disadvantage areas of the country overall, with 91 of the 100 most disadvantaged communities in the United States being rural. Only 7 percent of funds from the top 1,200 major philanthropies go to rural areas, the study found.

2. *Community Development Financial Institutions in Pennsylvania*, January 2024, Center for Rural Pennsylvania.

model for multi-site leases and will have to figure that out before we can move forward.

In every direction, there is never enough. We are so busy internally trying to build the systems we need to enable growth that we don't have much time to spend in our actual communities and partners think we are ignoring them or get weird notions about why we are building what we are building. Some cynical small business owners dismiss the idea as an effort to make money off them.

Abbi found this maddening. "So, they are willing to pay these ginormous corporate-owned platforms a cut of each sale, but if we set up a similar model, with a better rate and any revenues the nonprofit receives will actually be reinvested back in their communities for a public good, they are against that? It makes no sense."

In other cases, businesses join the ecosystem but don't put in work and then complain publicly that it did nothing for them. At different meetings, I share news of what we are building and the results. I am so excited because it is really a "we" moment of so many hands helping get the work to this point after so many years, but some take it as bragging or can't see past the silo they are working in, and I leave questioning why I try so hard.

And then there is the funding. Imagine going to work tomorrow and you are given a massive, critical, complex project under a deadline that will impact your community. You like your job, appreciate a challenge, and care deeply about your community, so your mind is racing to organize the best approach, back up plans, all the things. Then you are told that on top of this difficult quest, in order to keep your position and everyone else's going, you also have to raise all the money—salary, payroll taxes, health insurance, money for gas, ink, paper, etc.

This is what it's like at a lot of nonprofits that don't have dedicated funding, and definitely is reflected at the one we're building. It doesn't help that our nonprofit is a complete anomaly. Attempting to carry out a long-term regional strategy across a quarter of the Commonwealth yet operating outside the state's existing economic development frameworks and funding mechanisms. We do regional marketing, but we aren't a designated visitor bureau supported by hotel tax dollars. We work with businesses, but we aren't a small business development center. We have a regional footprint and do economic development, but we aren't a local development district. All these organizations are our partners, and important ones.

DCNR had institutionalized support for the PA Wilds through its Conservation Landscape program, which translated to roughly $300,000 a year in direct financial support for us as the lead nonprofit. We still had to compete for it, but it was the closest thing to dedicated funding that we had. Had they not, we never would have gotten liftoff. For the scale of what we were building, it didn't go far, but it was predictable, our ember. From there we did what any scrappy rural nonprofit would and leveraged it to the hilt. We used it as a match to secure other state, federal, and philanthropic grants, and then we'd use that combined money to build out high-mission impact, revenue-generating programs, so when the grants ended, there'd be a revenue stream left in their place. Rinse, repeat. Until the work was more sustained. That was my start-up plan.

This sounds really straightforward; "just develop, implement, and manage," as Abbi and I would come to joke. But in reality, it was anything but. It was so exhausting that on more than one occasion, I thought of quitting.

Any single program was like a mini business model we had to figure out and pitch to investors. Some could involve a years-long digital or physical construction project, dozens of partners, and legal consulting to ensure we stayed within our charitable mission.

Grants themselves were highly technical and specific in how they must be applied for, implemented, tracked, and audited. And each one was different. Piece by piece, Julie and I built a finance department to handle that and all the intense compliance requirements that went with it. Each funding stream was like a new nut to crack. At times, the task felt overwhelming.

"We just do it the way we've done everything since day one," Julie would mentor me. "We take it one step at a time and do our best. That is all we can do."

It reminded me of Maya Angelou's sage advice: "Do the best you can until you know better. Then when you know better, do better."

We work at a maniacal pace, trying to move the work to a more stable place. One day I pick up Abbi at her house for a meeting. I start backing up my car before her door is closed. She stops me, and I apologize, suddenly realizing that I do this a lot, actually. For years after, as we are working on a big pitch or partnership, Abbi reminds me, "You're a great storyteller. You just need to give yourself the time and space to tell the story. And of course, wait until everyone is in the car before you start moving."

What this meant in the short term was that we lived grant-to-grant. My initial reaction to this reality was to pay staff less and have them give more, me included. There is no faster way to burnout. Thankfully, several people from the board and staff helped me come to my senses. Here I'd been trying to convince rural communities to shed their scarcity mindset, and I was guilty of it myself!

With the help of my colleagues and mentors, I came to understand that unlike in the private sector, there would be no liquidity moment for me or Abbi or Julie or anyone else at our nonprofit that was doing the hard, highly technical, systems development and partnership work needed to unleash the brand's economic potential for rural communities. We weren't going to build this multi-million-dollar platform and complex value chain network and sell it. We were going to relentlessly pursue investment to build it with an inspiring company culture and sustainable revenues and all the appropriate checks and balances and then hand it off to the nonprofit's next set of leaders to steward so it could go on driving wealth back into rural communities through small businesses, hopefully for generations. To help make rural PA's economy a little more inclusive, as well as more resilient.

That was our goal. My staff knew it and took a lot of pride in it. For many of us, it would be our life's work. At least for the pioneering founding team, there would be no pension, no retirement, for this public service. The pay, mission, and company culture, that's what we had to offer. No one was going to get rich working at the PA Wilds Center. But we had to be competitive, or we'd never be able to attract and retain the talent we needed to make the thing sustainable. We had to make the Center a place people *wanted* to work for.

My executive team walked through it the way we did everything else, step by step. We pulled the tax forms of similar organizations in the region, Pennsylvania, Appalachia, and the nation, and looked at what their executives were making. We looked at national studies on nonprofit pay scales. We looked at our own business and growth models. We developed a tier of positions, from our front-line store people on up to the CEO. Then, we set baseline wages for each and took that to the finance and executive committees and then to the board. We made a strong case, and they supported us.

POWER was ending, and we'd applied for a second slug from the program to get our next shops open and got turned down. We entered a national philanthropic grant competition and lost there, too. I thought of the mallards and other ducks I saw while kayaking on the Allegheny, and how the water rolled off their backs as they dabbled or dove for food and tried to envision every "no" rolling off me in the same way.

CHAPTER 27

LEARNING TO LEAD

Change does not come easy here, in this most conservative, independent, and remote part of Pennsylvania. You must earn it, inch by inch.

On hard days, my job feels like a war for the future of our rural way of life, and my role is to recruit troops from villages near and far, guide us into battle, and yell "Charge!" One morning I climbed on my stationary bike in the living room and imagined this very scene. I raised my imaginary sword as the Kongos' "Come with Me Now" blasted through my earbuds while my kids and husband slept upstairs. Me and my team dressed in full battle regalia like some scene out of *Wonder Woman*, lined up beside us brave souls from every walk of life—men, women, young, old, Black, white.

I can never see the faces of the enemy when I visualize these scenes. To me, it isn't people with whom we're at war, it's a belief. A belief that this place is not worth investing in, that amid so much loss for so many decades, our best bet is to lower our standards and take what we can get, to fight over scraps, or leave. To defeat this belief, we must go to war every day and prove there is a better way.

I do everything I can think of to deal with the stress of starting a nonprofit in positive ways. I read countless self-help books, exercise, meditate for ten minutes each day, spend hours hunting for turkey and deer, and in one proud moment, become the twenty-sixth woman on record in Pennsylvania to harvest a black bear with a compound bow.

"If you lived closer, I would take the bear fat and make you soap with it," Julie says when I text her a picture. She texts me back to ask if she can share the picture with a few friends. "I just want to brag about my cool friend who killed a bear with her bare hands!"

Our board of directors was growing in size and experience, and their feedback and direction was helping shape not just our organization, but my leadership of it. Julie and Abbi are my day-to-day sounding board, and I am grateful that I am not alone when trying to work through the complexities of what we are building.

I screw up as I learn to lead. Sometimes I move too fast, don't listen closely enough, assume too much, or fail to set or hold the right boundaries for me or my team. I bring biases to the table, don't ask for help and support when I need it, or get my messaging or timing wrong. I miss important opportunities to connect, interrupt when I should stay quiet, and stay quiet when I should speak up. I forget people's names, get too in the weeds when a moment calls for high-level strategy, and second-guess my own intuition and understanding.

Instead of beating myself up or spinning on how I might have done things differently, I dedicate myself to a service and growth mindset and try not to waste time on guilt or shame. The work wasn't about me. It was about a worthy cause bigger than me, and my job and privilege was to learn from whatever stupid mistakes I made and grow to help lead it. I often thought about what one policymaker told me when I interviewed him about the early rocky years of the initiative: "We all make mistakes, and we all have to make those right and keep going."

The more I leaned in, the more it paid off. "You changed the dynamic of who we were and what we were doing and how we were going to do it," Jim Weaver, who had led the Planning Team during the reorganization of the Wilds work, told me at one point. "When you started talking about entrepreneurship, I thought, okay, whatever Ta says I should do, and I will do. Because you have been able to build trust with all of us."

Fortunately, my hardscrabble upbringing and my time as a reporter gave me a high tolerance for not taking things personally when people threw shade at me. But even I had my moments. I read somewhere that when you encounter a tense professional situation, such as with a manipulative person, instead of focusing on why you don't trust the other person, a tactic is to ask yourself: Why don't I trust *myself* in this situation? And then try to solve *that*. It was a hugely useful and sometimes painful exercise, given how much I undervalued myself and my contributions most of my life. As author James Victore wrote in *Feck Perfunction:*

Dangerous Ideas on the Business of Life, "Trust is a hard issue. Trusting others is a test of your faith in humanity, but trusting in yourself is a total revaluation of your worth and personal authority."

Safe to say the Wilds work forced me to do a lot of reevaluating of my own self-worth.

Other times, when I felt overwhelmed by a giant complex obstacle, I'd turn to the Jersey girl voice of one of my favorite podcasters, Marie Forleo, to remind me that "everything is figureoutable!" Other times, when an investment pitch would fail or I'd come up against intense parochialism, I'd try to channel the spirit of those ultimate badasses, former US Navy Seals.

"Ignore and outperform," says Jocko Willink in *Discipline Equals Freedom*.

"I don't stop when I'm tired. I stop when I'm done," says David Goggins in *Can't Hurt Me*.

I read about the potential health benefits of cold water immersion. It reminds me of what my dad once told me as a young girl—that the best way to start the day was to jump in a cold crick. "It's good for your soul!" he said. "Makes you tough!"

I started giving two-minute cold showers a try. I'm not sure it helped make me more courageous, but it definitely got me out of my head for a while. My middle boy, Cole, was 10 by now, a competitive soccer player, and my buddy in all things self-improvement. We had an above-ground pool at our house with no heater and it was freezing cold at dawn. I'd tell him when he came down for breakfast. "Let's go jump in the pool! We'll own the day!"

A few times, out of the blue, I'd get a call from a movie producer who was looking to dredge up one of the past crimes I covered and make a true crime documentary about it. It was one of the downfalls to having a weird name in the age of the internet. Everyone could find you. I always declined and saw the calls as a reminder that even on the hardest days, the Wilds was incredibly inspiring, joyful, hopeful work.

Over time we build a staff, and they are incredible. A creative, passionate team of doers and problem solvers. Dash's favorite bedtime story around this time was *Mighty, Mighty Construction Site*, written by Sherri Duskey Rinker and illustrated by Tom Lichtenheld, a book we got from

Leonard's boss after Cole was born, and one night as I read to him, it reminded me of my staff, how dedicated they all are to the mission we are trying to accomplish, each bringing a different skillset and approach to the job. Dash loved the end when I'd read about the crew driving away for the night, "feeling tired, but strong and proud."

Dash repeated the last phrase, "strong and proud," as we completed different projects around the house, adding a little fist pump for emphasis when he said it, melting my heart. So, one year I told my staff about my son and the book and gave them each a copy and read it to them. I felt a little goofy doing it, but for years after, when we hit a particularly high or low spot, they'd text me, #strongandproud, and it would mean so much to me.

Another year, I sent my entire team Jen Scerio's humorously inspiring *You Are A Badass* calendars (which they later dissected and framed to make wall hangings for our Media Lab offices in Kane. "Badassery Doesn't Happen Overnight" it now reminds us above the sink in the breakroom kitchen.) Most years, just trying to keep up with the insane thing we are building and three boys at home, I send nothing at all.

In the most trying times, Abbi and Julie would thoughtfully reach out with a personal card or gift. One year, from Julie, it was a wooden sign with a tree in the middle. "In the PA Wilds" it says above the tree, and then all around it, different things: "We believe in community. We trust and treat others with honesty and respect. We work hard and stand for creativity and innovation. We are inspired by each other. We are not afraid to be great."

I put it on the windowsill above my desk next to a cactus that is almost dead from lack of water.

Over time, I started to feel more comfortable leading. After Dash tries to shred some important documents at my home office, I realized I need a space with a locking door and Leonard built me a she-shed behind the house out of reused materials. He put a hand-hewn barn beam on one wall to hold my books and I intentionally dug through old boxes to find things to hang on the wall to remind me of the journey I've been on and keep me inspired.

I finally framed and hung my bachelor's degree from the University of Alaska and used two old iron nails to pin a stack of my writing awards to the barn beam. I dusted off an inscribed gold pan I got when I left the

Anchorage Daily News. "Thank you for your extraordinary efforts in telling our story," it says, and is signed, "Your friends in US Army Alaska."

The Allegheny Reservoir was low that year, and Piper went out exploring as she often did with her camera, taking pictures that she'd later use in calendars or books or make into posters. There in the middle of a big mud flat, she found a crack that revealed below it the double yellow line of the old road to the village of Kinzua. The picture got hundreds of shares on social media, and when she finally got it made into a poster, I bought one and hung it above my desk. On another wall, I hung the sashes from the ribbon cuttings at the Elk Country Visitor Center, Sinnemahoning Wildlife Center, the Kinzua Bridge State Park Skywalk, and our first PA Wilds Conservation Shop.

I found the fake front page my newsroom made me when I left the paper and laughed that some of the fake news actually came true. "Where will the future find (Ta)?" It asks in one story, later suggesting: "Homemaker. Three kids. Two-year winner at county fair in the jam and preserve competition."

Leonard would probably laugh at the homemaker suggestion given the regularly messy state of our house, and it was pigs, not jam, that the kids took to the fair, but there was a curious congruence that made me smile.

CHAPTER 28

SEE US

At the national level, the outdoor recreation industry is starting to get more organized and vocal about its role as an economic force, including for rural areas, and our work has been mentioned in several studies. But most state and federal economic development programs have yet to respond. Funding opportunities are still scarce.

By 2018, we are trying to crack the code of getting our stuff through the US Economic Development Administration for the first time. The federal agency played a critical role, making investments in economically distressed communities across the nation to stimulate industrial and commercial growth. We are pitching an investment to help us build ShopThePAWilds.com, the online marketplace we've envisioned that would allow rural vendors to sell directly to consumers but with the added marketing power of the region's brand, and to get a second brick-and-mortar shop opened, among other things.

Headquartered in Washington, D.C., EDA is comprised of several regional offices including one in Philadelphia, only a few hours away from the PA Wilds. There are people at the agency who can see the lift we are doing and the multifaceted challenges we are up against. Our region's Comprehensive Economic Development Strategy, which was a community-led plan, updated every five years, that was a requirement to access EDA investments, underscored the importance of growing the region's tourism industry. But we are not an industrial park or other traditional economic development project; getting our first application through their system is harder than I thought.

One day, on my way to drop off Dash at the Warren YMCA, I worry about what would happen if the investment doesn't come through soon. For the first time, I would have to lay off members of my team.

YMCAs played an important role in rural communities, filling gaps in childcare, health and wellness, and youth programming, services that were important to attracting and retaining local workforce. I appreciated our local Y and was grateful for it again today as I headed for the gym and a treadmill.

I put my earbuds in and turned on my running playlist. Imagine Dragons sang about feeling like a zero.

I thought about how many times I felt like a zero growing up, how many times I felt like rural PA was treated like a zero. How I had taken personal responsibility to try to change that. How proud I was for doing that, and how angry I was that it took this much effort to convince others to invest.

I thought again about the region's population loss, how it had put whole industries on the line, and how regional economic development plans included phrases like "avoid manufacturing cluster collapse." It reminded me of what one CEO of a mid-size manufacturer told me, shortly after I'd founded the Center: "This work that you guys are doing, it's not cute. It's real. It's serious. Livelihoods are at stake. Fortunes are at stake. We have to keep it going."

I turned up the treadmill speed and my music and ran harder than I have in a long time. Saved by a seven-minute mile and a sign above me that reminded me, *Whatever is lovely, whatever is pure, think on these things*.

A few weeks later, EDA came back with the news: we got the investment.

***

One night not long after, I was wrapping up the first day of a two-day meeting with my board of directors at the Gateway Lodge in Cook Forest, when I checked my email and saw an email from Earl Gohl, a former co-chair of the Appalachian Regional Commission. He mentions that he's at an Aspen Institute event about Rural Development Hubs; apparently, we are one. I'd never heard the term.

I was a huge fan of the Appalachian Regional Commission. Of all the federal funders we worked with, they understood rural asset-based development, or communities "building on what they do have," as McMahon put it. They didn't fund everything we submitted, but they were a federal funder that was truly of the place they served, and it came through in how they operated, their strategic plans and investment priorities, the metrics they used to track success, their leadership structure and peer networks, everything. Earl knew our work from different investments ARC had made in it over the years, and after he'd retired, we'd brought him up as a keynote speaker. I appreciated that he'd kept in touch with me. I'd not interacted with the Aspen Institute before. Curious, I Googled "Rural Development Hubs."

A report came up, "Strengthening America's Rural Innovation Infrastructure,"[1] stating: "In the rural places where development is being done differently, a certain set of intermediaries—Rural Development Hubs—are typically leading the effort."

It goes on to identify at least twelve types of organizations that in its national research had served as such hubs, including nonprofit social enterprises and fast-growing "unicorn nonprofits." Some defining characteristics: Hubs think and work "regional," take the long view, help bridge issues and silos, and collaborate as an essential way of being and doing. They analyze at the systems level and intentionally address gaps in the systems. Hubs create structures, products, and tools that foster collaborative doing. They translate, span, and integrate action between local and national actors. They flex, innovate, and become what they need to become to get the job done. They take and tolerate risk and hold themselves accountable to the whole community.

I sit up in my bed. *Holy. Shit.* We might not do all those things well, yet, but we sure as hell were trying.

Even more stunning, were the list of challenges listed in the report:

- Working in rural regions costs more in time, money, wear, and tear.
- There is no business model or blueprint for Rural Development Hubs.
- Hubs pursue transformational work, but most funding available to them remains siloed and transactional.
- It's hard to fund capacity-building and participation.

---

1. Rural Development Hubs: Strengthening America's Rural Innovation Infrastructure, Community Strategies Group, The Aspen Institute, 2019.

- Trust-building and collaboration is hard to fund.
- Sustaining a hub is hard, creative work that requires constant attention.
- Hubs need entrepreneurial, cross-discipline, systems-savvy, innovative leaders committed to a rural region over the long term.
- Some rural communities resist change.
- The power dynamic is threatened.
- Political divides eclipse action.
- Funding for Hub organizations, leaders, and innovation is restricted and scarce.

Good god, I thought. *They see us.*

CHAPTER 29

COVID

In 2004, a 9.3 earthquake off the coast of Indonesia in the Indian Ocean caused tsunamis and devastation that killed more than 200,000 people. It was one of the deadliest natural disasters in recorded history, prompting a worldwide response.

A C-130 squadron from Alaska's Elmendorf Air Force Base was called up to help deliver humanitarian relief, and I got to shadow them as they transported water, food, and supplies from Indonesia's capital city of Jakarta to its northwestern city of Banda Aceh, one of the hardest hit areas.

When we arrived, there was no radar tower to help guide the plane into the chaotic Banda Aceh landing strip, so the entire flight crew, including the loadmaster, who usually rides in back, crowded into the cockpit and each person took a window and called out what they saw to make sure the plane didn't hit anything as it came in for a landing.

The crew had clearly trained for this. I was in awe of their discipline, focus, and dedication to their mission. There were many helicopters and planes in the sky that day, but the crew kept level heads and got us and our supplies down safely.

This scene comes back to me in 2020 when the coronavirus pandemic hits. Our mission at the PA Wilds Center is not life or death, but as the world starts to shut down, it feels like everything we've worked so hard to build is on the line. Like so many others, we are flying without instruments and have to pull together to continue our mission amid the uncertainty.

As a virtual operation, most of my staff already works from home offices, so we have that on our side.

Abbi shuts down our PA Wilds Conservation Shop at Kinzua Bridge State Park and reassigns Libby and her team the job of calling the hundreds of rural small businesses we work with that have been shuttered by mandates to check on them.

We are down a staff person, so LaKeshia steps into the role of communications director, canceling advertisements, pivoting PAWilds.com and its related social media channels to have all the appropriate travel advisories, and crafting a new campaign to keep our business network informed of developments that might affect them.

A funding pitch to a major foundation that we've been working on for several months is completely derailed. A key funding stream is cut, along with the hit to our store revenues.

My three boys have been sent home from school. I play teacher and fail miserably, while their real teachers call me what feels like on the hour, every hour, to check on us. The schools set up WIFI hotspots so families without Internet can come sit in cars in the parking lots and do homework.

Max, who has just turned eleven, tells me one day as we are driving and he's looking out the window that he realizes he's living through a historic moment, like the kind he's read about at school. I tell him he's right, that he will always remember when everyone had to put on masks.

"Or maybe I'll remember a time when no one had to wear masks," he says, and my heart breaks.

There is a collective sense of loss and grieving for what was or might have been that is soon replaced by a collective exhaustion. For a beat, I am paralyzed by the idea that everything the region has done to grow its outdoor recreation sector has been destroyed, literally, overnight. I read an article in *Harvard Business Review* about the world's collective grief, and it makes me feel better to know I'm not alone.

Piper is going through similar emotions. She grieves for a few days and then swings into action, going door to door downtown to figure out which small businesses are open and then using her platforms to help spread the word. She orders to-go lunches and dinners from local businesses and sends them to the local hospital for the nurses.

But in the midst of the collapse of culture and systems, an extraordinary thing occurred across the country: people flocked to the outdoors.

Some states around us close their parks. At DCNR, Secretary Cindy Dunn, one of the architects of the Conservation Landscape program and a longtime champion of our work, announces that while the department's buildings will be closed and events canceled amid the pandemic, Pennsylvania's 121 state parks and millions of acres of forests will stay open. At a time like this, people needed the positive physical and mental health benefits of being outdoors.

For now, COVID case numbers in rural PA are low. Still, some visitors act like the pandemic doesn't exist out here in the sticks, refusing to social distance or wear masks at essential businesses that are still open. Communities are increasingly worried about the visitors bringing COVID with them and what that means for a place like ours, with an aging population and very little hospital capacity.

Everywhere I look, people are just trying to survive the madness. I have never been so grateful to live among two million acres of public land.

There were more than 40,000 seasonal residences in the PA Wilds, many of them modest cabins that people here called "camps." Locals and visitors alike embraced the region's camp culture, a chance to get away from the rush of everyday life. Many camps had been passed down for generations. As Pittsburgh, Harrisburg, Philadelphia, and other major cities within a day's drive of us go into lockdown, camps in the region fill up. In check-in calls with the Planning Team, county planners are estimating occupancy at 80 percent, unheard of in the off-season.

"It's like the trout opener, every day," one of them says.

I tell myself and my team that all we can do is focus on the things within our control. To build community and share best practices among small businesses in our network, we set up a Facebook Live series for rural entrepreneurs to share stories of how they are pivoting their operations to stay alive.

"There were many days at the beginning of this where I just didn't know what to do because everything changed daily and I couldn't plan," Karl Fisher from Alabaster Coffee Roaster & Tea Company, a growing business in Williamsport, told us. "I'm very much a person who likes to plan. I want to plan for a plan, for a plan."

I loved Fisher's coffee shop and always stopped in when I was in Williamsport.[2] Fisher really seemed to live his company mantra, "cultivating community through the elevation of coffee culture," investing in his staff and local causes and even visiting the farms in other countries where his coffee beans were grown. His shop had an artful vibe, with brick walls, wood slab tables, and friendly servers.

The pandemic shut down Fisher's robust walk-in business. His wholesale business, which was largely dependent on institutional customers like colleges and hotels, also zeroed out overnight.

I knew from my own experience building the nonprofit, watching Piper build Allegheny Outfitters, and working with so many other rural entrepreneurs, how hard Fisher had worked to build his company. How devastating and frightening it must have been to watch it all seemingly disappear, through no fault of his own.

Fisher explains how he gathered his thirteen employees together for a last staff meeting and walked everyone through how to apply for unemployment.

"It was one of the hardest things I've done as a leader and an employer," he tells us in the interview.

A father of four and former pastor, Fisher says he leaned heavily on his faith to get him through those first weeks of the pandemic. He shares that he has a sign at home near his front door, where he hangs his hats, that reads "What good shall I do this day." During the darkest moments of the shutdowns, the sign was a reminder that even though things might feel hopeless, and he didn't know what was coming next, he personally could choose to do something good that day. "I'd just think of the Lord's Prayer. Give us today our daily bread. Give us the things that we need for today."

A step at a time, the company got through it, pivoting to deliveries and online sales. In normal times, fear can hold you back from trying bold new approaches, Fisher said.

---

2. Other favorite spots were Otto Bookstore, America's oldest independently-owned bookstore, where I have literally spent hours, and Bullfrog Brewery. Williamsport had some great public art displays, too, including a bronze statue display called "Bases Loaded" which depicts young ballplayers on each corner of an intersection as though it were a baseball diamond. The display celebrates the Little League World Series, which is held in Williamsport each year. Next to Bullfrog, stretched across several three-story buildings, was one of the world's largest portrait murals, "Inspiration Lycoming County," by muralist Michael Pilato, depicting the history of Lycoming County. Jerry Walls, the founder of the PA Wilds Planning Team, was included on it because of the positive impact he had on the county and its residents.

"Going through these last few weeks has forced us to just try new things and be willing to do that," he says, explaining that he's leaning into this new freedom. "This is a great time to just try something new because the disruption is already there."

The Facebook Live series is all hands-on deck, and other nonprofits and business owners help us host the show and do the interviews. I host a joint session with the CEO of Organic Climbing, a manufacturer that employs twenty-four people making gear for rock climbing and bouldering, and the owner of Goat Fort, a new bouldering rock gym that had just opened in Warren next door to Allegheny Outfitters.

I loved both businesses. I'd met with Goat Fort's owner, Dana, several times over the last seven years as his idea was percolating. He had written a guidebook about bouldering on the Allegheny National Forest and set up a climbing wall in his garage that over time grew in popularity. He was married, had three kids, and a day job. If he left the day job, who was to say the rock gym would pan out?

There had been talk for many years about creating a recreation hub in downtown Warren to leverage the town's role as a gateway to the National Wild & Scenic Allegheny River, the National Forest, and a new world-class mountain bike system that locals had spearheaded with the U.S. Forest Service, called the Trails at Jakes Rocks.

If the town had a craft brewery and outfitters clustered together it would help pull the thousands of outdoor recreation enthusiasts using the forest and river and trails into the downtown to support local businesses.

It was a great idea in theory but developing such a hub, especially in a rural area where capital is harder to come by, and there are fewer entrepreneurs to begin with, is difficult to pull off. A lot of different interests, timelines, funding, and personalities have to come together to make it happen.

Incredibly, in Warren, this nexus started to happen. Bent Run Brewing, a craft operation named after a waterfall near Kinzua Dam, had started out in the country near my house and was looking for a new home. Dana was getting closer to making the leap, and Piper was looking for a place along the river where she could combine her retail and livery operations.

The local chamber started courting Piper to move her livery into downtown, thinking her foot traffic would help attract other synergistic businesses and increase the odds that a rec hub could get lift-off.

Piper had found a building, a former industrial site that had sat empty for twenty years and needed more work than any small business would be capable of doing. It was big enough to house both a brewery operation and a rock gym and maybe even other businesses.

Major redevelopment projects were not my wheelhouse, but they were Scott's. We'd collaborated on other similar projects in the region, and I thought the Warren rec hub would pass his litmus test for a closer look. It was a core community with major employers that was trying to revitalize. The proposed project would build on the state's many investments to grow the region as an outdoor recreation destination. It had local leadership; the city and chamber were both involved. A specific site had been identified, and a cluster of talented entrepreneurs were willing to put skin in the game and take risks. I was certain the rents for all three businesses would be higher moving into downtown, but the reward on the other side of that risk was the idea that together they could create a unique destination that none of them could achieve alone—much like the rural counties of the PA Wilds region had done two decades before.

The project involved my sister, which always made me queasy because of the appearance of a conflict of interest, but I stood to gain nothing from the project financially, and my discomfort wasn't enough of a reason to do nothing. We had to at least try to get the project an audience like we'd do for any similar project in the Wilds.

I called Scott on the phone.

"You really need to get up here and see this," I said.

He did, and over the next three years, he worked with the city and a local developer to make the redevelopment happen. The Center helped each of the businesses connect to Small Business Development Centers for business planning services and to other organizations for financing options. I was really proud when one of Warren's major employers, a manufacturing company, remarked in the newspaper about the rec hub and the good it could do for the future of the community.

Two days before Dana was set to open, the pandemic started to shut the world down. Because of the timing, Goat Fort missed out on the forgivable loans and other kinds of aid made available to most businesses, but Dana didn't give up. By the time I interviewed him for our series, he was in weekly calls with rock gym experts around the country trying to figure out best practices for opening amid a global pandemic.

In the interview, Dana recounted how for a long time, he saw rock climbing as something that happened somewhere else, like out West. Then he realized Pennsylvania had all these huge boulders, and there was a community focused on climbing them.

"Over twenty years, it just became what I did," Dana said.

Josh Helke, who started climbing when he was four, said it had been cool to watch bouldering progress over the last thirty-six years. "When bouldering first started, kind of in the late 1990s in terms of gaining popularity, I think there were a lot of people like Dana and I, who were in high school at the time, and probably getting a little bit sick of the mainstream aspect of rock climbing and the cost of it and started to see the counterculture aspect of the bouldering. It was almost like skateboarding to our generation. . . . I've seen bouldering go from this counterculture to now a sport that's in the Olympics for the first time."

Helke got a history degree and planned to be a history teacher when the 2000 recession hit, and he couldn't find a job. He was living in a rural town in Wyoming and started working at a local machine shop that made rock-climbing gear and had a sponsorship on the side for bouldering. He began dabbling in product design within the rock-climbing industry. "My family's all artists, so I was always really attracted to manufacturing and the making of stuff," Helke explained.

As more of America's supply chain got shipped overseas, he said, he watched craftspeople close up their production shops and then it was like a race to the bottom, who could make it faster, cheaper. "Every product that I was designing for bouldering ended up going from like the classic outdoor durability aspect of it, and then it just got super cheap, and it became a price war," he said. "There was this culture of making stuff that got completely lost when it all got exported."

Helke's wife was a geologist, so they'd spend the summers out in Utah doing geology research, and in the evenings, they'd climb. "We would just trash the gear that we were designing for other companies," he said.

Fed up, Helke started Organic Climbing. Over sixteen years, he built a global following for the company's high-quality climbing gear. He moved the operation to Minnesota, where he grew up, setting up shop in Minneapolis, and finally to Phillipsburg, a small town off Interstate

80, in the Pennsylvania Wilds. His manufacturing facility is located on a reclaimed coal strip mine and is solar-powered.

The lower cost of doing business helped attract him to rural PA, he said, as did the accessibility of "being able to go out our back door and product test" and the potential to "attract people who want that same standard of living where you have a good job, you get to make stuff, but it's relaxed, and you're not hustling as hard just to pay your rent."

"We love being where we are," Helke said. He tells Dana and me that a lot of climbers traveling the interstate from Toronto, Philadelphia, Washington, DC, and other cities stop by his facility.

"Dana, it was really interesting. On Friday, we had a customer pick-up from New York City who came out, got their crash pad and their daughter had your book."

Dana and I both smile at this. Despite being a few hours apart, there was a symbiosis happening. Helke noted the role passionate outdoor recreation companies played helping build community and connect people to recreation assets. Helke predicts that the pandemic is going to make more people rethink where they are living.

"I'm seeing a trend of a lot of people, you know, our age that have young families that are coming, falling in love with these areas because they have fallen in love with a sport or it's become a part of their life," he says. "They've been through a lot in a short period of time financially," Helke says, "and are going to think more about what makes them happy and try to follow that. We're gonna see a lot more change. And people that grew up in these towns are not leaving as much. I think they're going to stay if there are cool things and cool places to work. So, I think we need to focus on that as leaders in the communities."

The pandemic deals a major blow to tourism globally, as travel grinds to a halt during mandated shutdowns. Traveler spending in Pennsylvania declined by a whopping 37 percent in 2020. In the Pennsylvania Wilds, it drops by $530 million, to its lowest level since 2009.

We publish a white paper about how the pandemic is affecting the small family-run businesses we work with and shortly after that, we help get the entire PA Wilds region qualified as a priority investment area for statewide COVID grants for Main Street type businesses so applications coming from the region have a better chance of competing with

Philadelphia and Pittsburgh. We set up a call center to help small businesses with questions as they apply.

Slowly, things start to reopen and get back to normal. It feels like we've been through a war. My team is exhausted, and so am I, but the pandemic brings a silver lining. It fundamentally changes the ways many Americans value the outdoors. Suddenly, there is increased attention toward equity and access to the outdoors, and across the board, there is a growing recognition for outdoor recreation as an economic driver, especially for rural areas, like ours, which are so plentiful in public lands and other recreation assets.

These national shifts validate the work we've been collectively advancing for twenty years in rural PA. The PA Wilds region had seen tremendous results from these investments, including record-breaking growth in visitor spending in the years leading up to the pandemic, many small business startups and expansions, inspiring stewardship efforts, increased pride of place, and resiliency among them. Even the stark 2020 tourism report notes that our region's positioning as an outdoor recreation destination resulted "in a less severe decline than experienced by some of the other PA tourism regions."

My team and I, Meredith, and members of my board highlight these shifts in update presentations we do for the region's thirteen sets of county commissioners. We invite state legislators to join the conversations.

Beth Pellegrino, a board member who at the time led the human resources department at Whirley-DrinkWorks!, one of the largest employers in Warren and a repeat donor to our mission, tells our county commissioners that the company is about to go into "the most challenging climate for staffing positions ever."

"It is so important to us to support things like the Pennsylvania Wilds," she offers in the Zoom meeting. "To have something like the Pennsylvania Wilds to not only attract new people into the community but also to retain those that are already here. It is going to be a very key piece in our businesses recovering."

State Sen. Scott Hutchinson, a Republican that serves counties on the western side of the region, attends one of the virtual meetings. "This started as a top-down initiative and it has truly, truly become a local, grassroots partnerships thing happening at the local level," he said. "To hold cooperation together across such a huge geographic area, it's a model. It's amazing you've been able to do that. The brand 'Pennsylvania Wilds' is certainly a dynamic thing that can only continue to grow for our region."

Nick Hoffman, a board member who worked for a local foundation in Jefferson County, said in the past, when it came to tourism, communities in his county would often compare themselves to Punxsutawney, home of the world-famous prognosticating groundhog.

"I think that's where groups get in trouble in a lot of places because there is that comparison, that friction and competition that works against them, ultimately," Hoffman said.

The PA Wilds, he said, was helping communities get away from that with the message that each place can hold up its own unique attributes, and they can use the regional brand and platforms to help them do that. "We're part of a bigger whole rather than the individual parts," Hoffman said.

One of the Jefferson County commissioners tells us that sometimes it is hard to appreciate progress when you live in a place your whole life. But zoom out and consider things over time, and it shows a different picture. "Just look at our Main Streets," he says. "Brockway is full. Brookville is full. Punxsy is filling up. Kane is revitalized. St. Marys is filling up. Emporium. You go back thirty years, and all these main streets looked terrible. They really did. They are really rebounding."

When the calls are over, my staff and I are buoyed by the comments, and I feel like maybe this will be a watershed moment.

CHAPTER 30

DOING IT ON PURPOSE

Before the pandemic, before I had any staff and Abbi was still a contractor, she and I traveled to Utah for an arts conference and while there, locked ourselves in our hotel room for a day-long planning session. The room had a glass door to a small balcony, and we covered it with blue, pink, and yellow stickies, mapping out three years of work. For an under-resourced, grant-supported nonprofit trying to do big things, this was a giant jigsaw puzzle because certain funds could only be used in certain ways and only within specific timeframes, and then other buckets had to match up to them in particular ways and timeframes. Julie kept this all straight on the financial side of the nonprofit, and I had a similar job when it came to implementation.

Abbi was way more skilled and realistic than me at seeing all the steps of a given project, so we'd start with those stickies and then I'd reorganize all the projects and steps based on the realities of the funding we had. This could take a few minutes and I'd be up there whispering to myself and moving things around. Abbi and I were still getting to know each other back then, and she watched with interest as I twisted her fantastic project planning through the complex funding machinery holding it up.

"This is . . . all in your head?" Abbi asks, and I can tell she is both impressed and a little frightened. It probably doesn't help that the same day I informed her that I'd never, in six years, connected my laptop to the Internet because I didn't understand how to work the Wi-Fi (it had more than 300 updates when she showed me the toggle switch), which came on the heels of me stating I thought Amazon "just sold books." (In my defense, when I left journalism, I made that intentional decision to disconnect for a while, and I meant it!). If she'd been drinking something, it would have come out of her nose.

We each had our strengths, and by the time we finished that day in Utah, we had a rock-solid three-year plan. A month after we got back to rural PA, the Conservation Shop opportunity changed our whole course. Running a mission-driven retail operation was nowhere in our sticky notes, funding, or staff capacity. We'd been racing to keep up with our growth ever since.

Now here we were, five years later, sequestering ourselves again, this time in our audio-visual room at our new Media Lab, trying to take stock visually of where we were at.

We'd completed most of the projects in our strategic plan, and every internal and external indicator we had showed growth. We'd launched a second store, a mobile unit at Leonard Harrison State Park at the Pine Creek Gorge, while we waited for DCNR to finish construction on a new visitor center there, and were also about to launch our long-awaited online marketplace, ShopthePAWilds.com, that allowed rural small businesses to sell directly to consumers, controlling their own inventory and price points, but with the added marketing power of the Pennsylvania Wilds' brand.

An avalanche of state and federal aid, unlike anything I'd ever seen or could have imagined, had come down in the wake of the pandemic, and so the day was largely about trying to prioritize projects and figure out what wiggle room and available match dollars we had to try to leverage this incredible moment.

The nonprofit was at that difficult growth stage where it was trying to transition from a tiny nimble staff keeping a lot of information in their heads to getting all that knowledge into systems and manuals and policies so it could be shared, usefully, with a larger team. We were one hundred percent committed, but it was still a painful process for me, in part because it often involved learning new technology. Despite what my track record might suggest, I loved new technology that helped us operate more effectively and pushed Abbi to help us find such solutions. We were just moving at such a pace that I didn't always have the patience or brain space to learn it myself. Our sequestration today was a good case in point. Abbi was piloting a new project management system for us, but instead of pulling reports from that, I wanted to "see" things the old school way with stickies. So, we started writing on the colorful squares and placing them on a timeline on the wall.

"You know what happens when we plan things out with stickies," Abbi reminded me, and I smiled. By the end of the day, we found new leverage points and had a solid plan.

The next day, a partner forwarded me an email about a federal "Notice of Funding Opportunity" for a program called the Build Back Better Regional Challenge. This would be run by the Economic Development Administration, buoyed by a $3 billion influx in funding from Congress through the American Rescue Plan Act (ARPA).

"Build Back Better" was President Joe Biden's slogan for a lot of things, similar to how Trump wanted to "Make America Great Again," so it took a beat to understand this wasn't like everything else with the moniker but a once-in-a-lifetime opportunity for regions to self-identify what their strengths and opportunities were and compete for up to $100M in federal investment to help advance it. It was the president's marquee American Rescue Act program, the chance to do twenty years' worth of economic development in five years.

By then, we were at the tail end of the EDA investment that was helping us build the first iteration of ShopThePAWilds.com. But the Build Back Better Regional Challenge was a marked shift from the EDA I knew. Not only was the potential award larger than anything I'd ever seen available, the approach was regional and place-based. In webinars about it, program managers quoted Dolly Parton. "Find out who you are and do it on purpose," they said.

I was thrilled. We'd been doing place-based development on purpose for 20 years!

Outdoor recreation, as a sector, was in a different place now, and so were we. Historically, outdoor recreation interests had been somewhat disconnected from one another in the political process. Hikers came to talk about hiking trails, bikers about bike infrastructure, and skiers about ski resorts. Now, with increased recognition of the relationship between outdoor recreation and thriving economies and communities, and new data from the U.S. Bureau of Economic Analysis on the economic impact of outdoor recreation, the industry began to coalesce in new ways and make the case to policymakers for more support of the recreation economy and its benefits as a whole, including for rural places like the PA Wilds.

We'd watched the industry grow and get more organized at the national level over the last fifteen years and then supercharged during the pandemic as Americans flocked to public lands and recreation activities in record numbers. Across the country, manufacturers of bikes, kayaks, backpacks, fishing poles, bows, you name it, could not keep up. Government measurements showed an 18.9% growth in the outdoor recreation economy from 2020-2021, compared to 5.7% growth for the U.S. economy as a whole.

Its sheer economic and wellness power on full display, communities and funders now looked to harness it in new ways. Nearly 20 states had established offices of outdoor recreation to develop innovative collaborations between public, non-profit, and private sectors to help grow the sector and leverage its many multiplier effects.

People often thought of the Western United States when it came to outdoor recreation, but as I had learned in my journeys through the state, Pennsylvania was a bona fide heavy-weight, with one of the largest outdoor economies in the country, many outdoor recreation manufacturers and service sector companies, legions of outdoor enthusiasts (more hunters per capita than any other state, and that was just *one* activity), one of only a handful of states with environmental protections enshrined in its state constitution, and the home of innovative approaches, like the PA Wilds, which by that time had been included in at least five national studies as a rural model, including in the Outdoor Recreation Roundtable's (ORR) Rural Economic Development Toolkit. ORR was one of the organizations fighting for outdoor recreation's seat at the political table and began to incorporate the Wilds in its presentations to policymakers as an example of the ways outdoor recreation could benefit sustainable community development around the United States. The country's leading coalition of outdoor recreation trade associations, ORR represented more than 110,000 businesses. I especially appreciated their bipartisan approach to their work. As the country grew more and more politically divisive, outdoor recreation was still a place where people from both side of the aisle could find common ground.

My board, staff, and I were thrilled to see ORR seize the silver lining of the pandemic, building support to grow the sector in new ways, including for rural areas.

"It may seem simple for communities to build outdoor recreation economies but there are a ton of factors rural communities struggle with when attempting to broaden their communities' economies, from bandwidth and monetary resources to messaging and public perceptions," ORR said when it released its Toolkit.

Pennsylvania rode the wave too, with DCNR finally getting traction to hire a new state director of outdoor recreation, the precursor that would eventually turn into a full-fledged office of outdoor recreation with support from Gov. Josh Shapiro, who saw the value of the industry and made multiple trips to the PA Wilds region to showcase investments here. All told, outdoor recreation added $14 billion to Pennsylvania's gross domestic product in 2021, injecting more value into the commonwealth's gross domestic product "than all of Pennsylvania's farms, all of Pennsylvania's oil and gas wells, and even all of Pennsylvania's lawyers," the new director of Pennsylvania's office of Outdoor Recreation, Nathan Reigner, wrote in a blog post shortly after being hired.

I was ecstatic to finally have a statewide voice dedicated to beating the drum for outdoor recreation while working with dozens of partners, like us, to frame the role of the proposed new office. On one visit to hold a public outreach session in Warren, Dash, now six, joined Reigner, the DCNR team, and other outdoor recreation proponents for dinner at a restaurant downtown. Perhaps by osmosis, my only child carried entirely during the Center's founding years, Dash had a special interest in the PA Wilds work. He also liked being in charge of things and making his own rules. My staff called him Boss Baby. He sent them videos about the PA Wilds and made pictures and lists.[1]

Dash had recently stumbled upon the YouTube star Andymation and was in a flipbook phase. He made a flipbook about the PA Wilds and

---

1. And not just about the PA Wilds. For example, at the time, Cole played on a travel soccer league, a coalescence of an amazing group of kids and parents, led by an awesome coach, Jim Warner. The league was called "Kinzua Soccer Club," so of course that was neat for me, too. After one fall practice, the coach sent home a soccer drill sheet and on the back it had this list: "10 Things That Require Zero Talent: 1. Being on time (or early) 2. Making your best effort 3. Having high energy 4. Having a positive attitude 5. Being Passionate 6. Using good body language 7. Being coachable 8. Doing extra work on your own 9. Being prepared 10. Having a strong work ethic." Dash and I read the list together and then he reached for the paper. "This is good," he said, raising his 6-year-old eyebrows, "but it could use a few *slight* improvements." He added periods after each sentence and a #11. "Never quit."

brought it to the dinner to show the new outdoors director and "Ms. Hill, the Chocolate Lady," as he called Meredith, because she once took him to Hershey to give me time to prepare before a big presentation I had near the park. My kids didn't tag along often, but when they did, my colleagues always made time to make them feel welcome, and I appreciated it. After Dash's food arrived, we started talking work again.

"The success in the PA Wilds in many ways laid the foundation for the state office of outdoor recreation," Meredith told me, and the new director saw our work in rural PA as crucial, too. "We couldn't be doing this without you," he said.

The words meant a lot to me. So often in a rural place, you feel unseen and unheard. The Wilds work had given the region new visibility, and a stronger voice. How far we'd come.

The pandemic also laid bare many of the country's inequities, particularly along racial and socioeconomic lines, and a reckoning was happening across communities, institutions, businesses, brands, you name it. "Equity" moved up as a top investment priority for many funding agencies, and I was thrilled to find that EDA's definition included "underserved communities within geographies that have been systemically and/or systematically denied a full opportunity to participate in aspects of economic prosperity such as Tribal Lands, Persistent Poverty Counties, and rural areas with demonstrated, historical underservice."

It was a watershed moment for a lot of things, including the nexus of our work in outdoor recreation and rural development. When I read about the $100 million regional competition all I could think was, we have a shot. An actual shot.

I thought about how the PA Wilds started with the development of the brand, an initial wave of recreation infrastructure, and locally informed community and business development programs alongside those major state investments. No matter what way you cut it, the results from those investments, and that approach, had been tremendous. We had the data. As Scott liked to say, "It worked better than anyone ever imagined it would."

The success had sparked new community-driven recreation infrastructure projects, but progress was slow due to funding and capacity constraints. By completing a next wave of recreation infrastructure, scaling our marketing and commerce platforms, and improving entrepreneurial support around our efforts, we could accelerate our results and impact.

The Brady Tunnel in Clarion County in the PA Wilds was a great example of a project that might fit. It got shut down in 2002 by the state's Public Utility Commission because it needed repairs. At nearly a half-mile long, it would be one of the longest cycling tunnels in America. Part of the thirty-six-mile Armstrong Trails system, it would link the northern 4.5-mile portion of the Armstrong Trail to its southern thirty-one-mile portion and was also a critical link in the development of a longer Pittsburgh-to-Erie trail system, with a "PA Wilds Loop" through four counties, that was in development. Long trail systems could have enormous economic impact for communities because they bring visitors in for multiple days who then eat at local restaurants, sleep at local cabins or bed and breakfasts, and shop at local stores. They are also beneficial for residents, as locals had noted in the Pine Creek Valley. The Brady Tunnel project had great leadership and local support, and DCNR had already invested more than $1 million in it, calling it a top ten trail gap in the state to close. But it would take another $4 million to complete. The leaders behind it did what a lot of others in the region did. They held pig roasts or other fundraisers to try to raise enough "match" dollars to go after another state or federal grant to complete the next phase.

The people and organizations behind these projects were heroes to me, staying with them year after year. How incredible it would be to finish them in one fell swoop with this new federal funding opportunity. It made me think of the advice that Danny Twilley, a PhD colleague at West Virginia University's Brad and Alys Smith Outdoor Economic Development Collaborative, once shared at a conference: "Think big, start small, and scale fast." We had done step one and two in that list. This was the opportunity to scale for greater impact.

I called Meredith. If we couldn't get the state behind us, there was no way a regional application could come up with the match, and the whole idea would be moot. I went straight for the karate chop.

"We have to do this," I said and explained my thinking. She got it, right away. So did our partners at DCED, who were pushing all of the state's economic development regions to put forth proposals for the competition. "The place-based development strategies, the network of partners, our region has been working towards this for almost twenty years," I said.

Next, I had to make sure my staff was up for it. We'd learned a long time ago to be careful what we wish for, because it might just happen, and then you are on the hook to actually implement all the big dreams you outlined. To really compete, we were going to have to map out and visualize winning, in all its mind-numbing detail. We were going to have to own it. *Be* it.

I had a lunch meeting where I would see Abbi, but I hadn't yet figured out how to tell her. Maybe, *there's a once-in-a-generation opportunity in front of us, but it will take everything we've got to seriously compete. It will be a level of madness we've never experienced. And in the end, we may not get it.*

There were other people around, so I didn't say anything. I was quiet and tried to rush through the meeting and Abbi gave me these eyes, like what's up? When I finally came clean, a mini-volcano blasting out information, I saw her wheels immediately start to turn. At this stage, she fully understood, like me and Meredith, the opportunities and challenges of the regional work. A few seconds passed. She looked at me, smiled, smacked the table with her hand, and pointed at me.

"I told you," she said. "Never again with the sticky notes!"

We both laughed, and then we were speed walking and talking back to the Media Lab, like Piper and I did at her grand opening, only this time, I don't drop any change on the ground. Abbi peppered me with tactical questions.

"When is the deadline?"

"One month," I said. "It's two phases. Phase One is a five-page concept paper. From there they will choose sixty finalists. If we make Phase Two, we'll have three months to pull together a detailed proposal, budgets, all the things."

"Would all the money flow through the Center?" Julie, who I called next, asked the same question. It was one of my first concerns too. It is one thing to scale up our programs, another thing altogether for a small nonprofit to scale up an accounting department in a rural area with intense workforce issues to handle $100M in federal funds that will need to be spent down in record time and documented in a myriad of ways to meet compliance requirements.

"No," I said. "Just the funds to support our part of the proposal. Basically, all the connective tissue. The construction projects would be their own applications, and those monies would flow through the organizations spearheading the projects."

They both felt better knowing this. With those boxes checked, I took the idea to my board of directors, who agreed we should pursue it. EDA had several other buckets of relief funding it was rolling out, including, for the first time ever, one specifically to support travel, tourism, and outdoor recreation. If we didn't make it as a finalist, we'd have several projects vetted to submit to the other funding streams.

Time was of the essence. We only had a few weeks to assemble the Phase One application. DCNR had visibility on outdoor recreation infrastructure projects percolating because its grant programs helped fund many of them. We had additional lines of sight through the Planning Team and because many communities came to us for support letters as they pitched for investment. I knew our communities would want to know why we'd selected one project over another. Meredith and I spent a crazy week calling around, trying to figure out where different regionally significant projects were in their planning and implementation, if they could fit the grant program's definition of "shovel-ready," if there was the local political will and capacity to be part of the application, and if they could come up with the 20 percent match requirement. It wasn't a perfect process, but it was what we could do with the time we had.

Four regional economic development organizations, recognized by EDA and other state and federal funders, served the PA Wilds region and we pulled them into the conversation. They were important gatekeepers and capacity builders for state and federal applications from rural PA. The director of one, Jill Foys, had been a supporter of our first POWER grant, and as I unveiled our strategy for the Build Back Better Regional Challenge she said, "Oh my gosh, Ta, if they had hired anyone else . . ." and I was pretty sure she was talking about the ombudsman position, way back when. This made me smile. I admired Jill, and her counterparts in other parts of the region, Kim Wheeler, and North Central's Amy Kessler, as well as Cindy Nellis, who ran the Small Business Development

Center with the biggest footprint in the PA Wilds. All four had been advocates for the PA Wilds effort over the years and supported my leadership, and I was inspired to see women leading major economic development organizations and programs in rural Pennsylvania.[2]

With the support of a core group of partners, over the next few weeks, we framed out a concept paper that included six recreation infrastructure construction projects, a major scaling of our ecosystem and workforce efforts, and forward-looking plans around sustainability, resilience, and attracting private investment to support further growth of the region's outdoors sector.

A few days after we turned everything in, EDA announced it had received 529 applications from all fifty states and five territories. With robotics and artificial intelligence, advanced manufacturing, and clean energy as other possibilities, it was hard not to be intimidated. Pennsylvania alone had fourteen applications. It was October. They anticipated selecting sixty finalists by December.

***

In November, my mom called to let me know Uncle Charlie was near the end. He had a bed set up in the living room of his cabin, where Pugsa and I used to have our slumber parties. Everyone in the family took turns visiting. In many ways, it felt like any other time I'd been there, people sharing stories, being goofy and laughing, only now Uncle Charlie slept nearby. When he did wake up, he was lucid and upbeat. I reflected more than once that when my time was up, I hoped I could go like him, in my own home, surrounded by familiar sounds and smells and all the people I loved laughing and telling stories.

Charlie's son, my cousin Steven, a union welder who loved heavy metal and antiquing and looking for arrowheads, was staying at the cabin to help his dad in his final days when he died suddenly of a heart attack at age fifty. It was a devastating turn of events that Charlie, Carolyn, and Pugsa handled with stunning love, grace, and openness, allowing us all to be part of it.

At one point, after Steven had died, I went over and held Uncle Charlie's hand while he slept. Dash played on the floor, pretending

---

2. Pennsylvania is one of 18 states that has never had a female governor. It has also never had a woman in charge of its leading economic development agency.

to catch fish with one of those cat toys that looked like a fishing pole. When Charlie woke, he squeezed my hand. "Hey, kiddo!" he said. "How are you?"

Whitetail deer season had ended a few weeks prior, so he asked about hunting, and I told him about the ten-point I had harvested. "I'm so proud of this family," he said. "We've always just been a little different. You girls are incredible. You really are." He got quiet, and I thought he'd dozed off but then he turned his head and looked at me and rubbed my hand. "You spend your whole life trying to make sense of things and it's all right there," he said. "Take care of your family. That's all that really matters."

At his funeral, they played "Taps" and two Marines in full dress uniform folded the American flag and presented it to my aunt. A bunch of us wore his Zippo sponsor gear, and afterward, Pugsa let me keep mine, and I framed it in a shadow box and hung it on my wall.

There are still times when I am out on a run in the woods, alone among the hemlocks, that the weight of this loss hits me. I think of others dear to me, like the mom of the Alaska family who took me in, who died before she got to meet Leonard and my boys, and about people I'd worked with in rural PA who had died. Helen Nawrocki. Jan Hampton. Lisa Bainey. I could tell stories about each of their contributions but also about them as people. Such loss was part of the reality of doing partnership work in a landscape with an aging population. For many involved, the PA Wilds was legacy work, a highlight of their career, in part because of the lifelong friendships people built through it, which made each loss personal. Piper's wife Sue and Abbi both lost their moms suddenly in the time I'd been working on the Wilds. When it hits me, I cry, reminded how beautiful, fragile, and short life is and how thankful I am for all the good in my life. Leonard, our boys, our families, these woods, purposeful work.

"Things can always happen that are bad, but there is always a side that is good, and you have to look for that," Charlie told me before he died. "It's only one time around so you gotta make the most of everything you got."

I wipe away my tears and think, *Yes, we do, Uncle Charlie. Yes, we do.*

CHAPTER 31

ONE HUNDRED MILLION DOLLARS

Two days after my uncle passed, we got notification that the PA Wilds region was a finalist in the Build Back Better Regional Challenge competition.

One. Hundred. Million. Dollars.

I wasn't sure rural PA had ever had a shot at that kind of investment before. I had never spearheaded an investment anywhere close to it.

I was holding myself together pretty well until I got to my hairstylist, Erin, who had been cutting my hair since I'd moved home.

Erin knew about my uncle and cousin before I walked through the door. I cried when I told her about my last conversation with my uncle. Erin had watched me found and build the nonprofit, and we regularly shared stories of trying to face down our fears and deal with life's different seasons, including the one time when, juggling so many things and my mind racing, I almost left the YMCA locker room without my pants on.

Erin and I were roughly the same age, both married, both had three kids, both liked to exercise and spend time outdoors, and for several years, both had families involved in motor racing. Erin had watched me grow as a mom (I had my kids later than she did) and I watched her blossom as an entrepreneur, boldly breaking out during the pandemic to start her own salon, and then to pursue coaching and motivational speaking. She started a podcast which she sometimes recorded from the laundry room of her salon. I loved her grit and spirit, and that she had no problem looking at herself in a mirror a million times a day, being girly, fixing her hair and makeup, wearing giant earrings, being from the north and saying "y'all," all things I'd never do. I wore a pair of pearl stud earrings I rarely changed.

I told her about the competition and how self-doubts I thought I'd vanquished long ago had crept into my mind. "We are competing against major cities," I said as she brushed color on my roots. "Aerospace. Bio tech."

"And you're a finalist," she said, looking right at me through the mirror in front of both of us. "And for good reason. Do not listen to those negative thoughts. It's like whack-a-mole. You gotta get out your plastic hammer. Just whack them down. Stop comparing yourself to others. You have got to walk into a room thinking, everyone here likes and supports me."[1]

Julie told me something similar when I called her later. "We just do it like we've done everything else, Ta. One step at a time."

Whack-a-mole and step-by-step I totally knew how to do, so from then on out, I committed myself to completely shutting down any negative self-talk and putting all my energy into assembling the best outdoor recreation finalist application, one step at a time.

At the Center, we cleared the decks, pushing any project that did not have a hard deadline out by six months or a year to make way for the process. EDA provided finalists with a slug of funding to help assemble their Phase Two applications. It was a good thing because the process was unlike anything many applicants, including us, had ever been through. Months of workshops, meetings, conferences, pitch sessions, all while trying to get our regular work done and do all the research, planning, and assembly for the phase two application.

Deborah had just retired from the congressman's office, so we brought her on as a consultant to help coordinate with the dozens of partners involved in our application. We hired a consulting firm that had worked on innovative outdoor recreation investments across the country, to assist us in intense business and strategy planning.

We also invested in research, development, and a cost analysis for a mobile platform that would advance place-making efforts like ours through visitation, supply chain development, micro-lending, stewardship, volunteerism, and harnessing impact data. The private sector was not going to build what rural areas needed. The returns would never

---

[1]. No surprise, Erin went on to launch a successful coaching business focused on helping women find and channel their "inner abundant badass" and live unapologetically authentic lives. Find her at erinrenningercoaching.com.

be high enough. But we could. And there were a lot of other regions across Appalachia and beyond that were working on similar place-based revitalization efforts. If we could develop a transferrable model that other rural landscapes could use at a fraction of the cost, it would make our application that much more competitive and help achieve the economy of scale needed to make the platform really go.

The Regional Challenge was a painful process, and the opportunity cost as a rural region was incredibly high. Funding was everywhere, and we had to turn all of it down to try for the big prize. I found some solace that in our weekly virtual sessions, the people running the program looked just as haggard as the people competing in it. At one point, in a Zoom call with our consultants, Abbi mentioned that she had identified something that was going to help us through the next few months of the application process. I assumed, Abbi being Abbi, it was some kind of new system or technology, and then she pulled out this giant yellow button called the Thirty Second Dance Party and informed us that when things got too stressful, watch out because she would hit it and we would all be required to dance.[2]

There were other inspiring moments, too, thinking big with our partners in new ways, and being exposed to finalist's pitches from other parts of the country. At one point, Abbi and I were both at our home offices, an hour apart, listening in on the same pitch session where a coalition of economic developers, tribal entities, and finance and education partners wanted to leverage New Mexico's rich culture and heritage to become a global leader in the creative technology sector,[3] and by doing so, help address their state's staggering poverty rates and outmigration and equip Native American, Hispanic, and rural communities there with better access to economic opportunities. Native culture inspired so many things, from clothes to designs to furniture to movie backdrops. I could only guess that few systems existed to pay Native groups for any of it, or even to engage them in new opportunities for such designs. This group was trying to push back on the extraction.

"Did you hear New Mexico's presentation?" Abbi texted me.

"Yes, I see alignments, you?"

---

2. And chair dance we did!

3. Creative technology sector includes skills such as 3D design and printing; animation; artificial intelligence; digital storytelling; game design; projection light mapping; and visual effects.

"Totally. I've been taking notes on this one."

Another group, of female-led Native Community Development Financial Institutions, presented on creating a Native finance cluster. We'd long dreamt of having a CDFI based in the PA Wilds that could be an engine alongside us, like North Carolina-based Mountain Biz Works was to its partners in the western part of that state, funding outdoor recreation businesses, participating in the movement's stakeholder networks, and fully invested in and contributing to locally informed regional growth strategies.

"These groups are blowing me away," I texted Abbi.

"I was just thinking the same thing! This CDFI group is badass!"

At another point, in a group setting, the applicant from a major city said to me, yeah, they understood, "We all have capacity issues." I was so shocked by their lack of understanding about the difference in resources available to a place like theirs versus one like ours, and that most scoring criteria was also stacked in their favor, that I was left completely speechless.

Day after day we stayed at it, and it took a toll on everyone's health and home life, but we were excited, too, believing we had a real shot and knowing full well that just to be able to compete at this level as such a rural region was a statement unto itself.

A contact of mine at EDA told me and other finalists: look for a small part of the overall project to pivot into another application in case you don't win.

I put that idea in my back pocket. "Thank you," I said, "I really do appreciate that. But we are going to win this thing."

"You are a force of nature, Ta," my contact told me. "You are succeeding against all the odds. I love this project, and I'd love to see it funded. I am just saying, they are only funding twenty."

Our region's final proposal was $75 million. We stitched together an incredible patchwork of matching dollars, totaling $21 million. Six recreation infrastructure projects, ten sub-awards to other nonprofit partners, and a transformative buildout of our programs and capacity.

We received 151 pages of support letters from big and small businesses; local, state, and federal government; conservation and economic development; local and national philanthropic foundations and nonprofits; local artists and titans of industry. Working at the pace we had been working for so many years, there hadn't been much time to reflect on what had been collectively accomplished. The letters were stunning in their heartfelt support for the difference the Wilds' work made, how further investment was needed, and the good it could do. I was touched by the dozens of pages of testimonials from rural small businesses. As we'd grown, my role had changed, so I didn't get to work as closely with local entrepreneurs as I once did. It made me smile to read what they wrote and hear their voices.

"PA Wilds has been a tremendous help to me over the years to highlight our work as a PA-based producer and artisan; find and secure financial resources for business development; and opened many opportunities for us in the eco/outdoor recreation and commerce markets," Karl Fisher, from Alabaster, wrote. ". . . I look forward to their continued success and growth, and how that will continue to build a better Pennsylvania and quality of life for the thousands of people that will be impacted."

Tara Heckler, owner of Blackberry & Sage Market, just outside Punxsutawney in Jefferson County, shared in her letter how she ran a small, woman-owned business that incorporates homegrown herbs and flowers, as well as local honey and beeswax, into natural products. "We live on my husband's family land that has been in his family for 5 generations. I have a studio located on our 100- acre farm that my husband and I built ourselves with local materials," she wrote. "With the coal industry fading in the area, so has our population, employment rate, and income stability. Many have had to either move or be creative in how they make a living."

Heckler explained that when she joined our ecosystem six years prior and started selling on our platforms, her business took off. "Investments in our outdoor recreation assets and supporting infrastructure in or around our area—such as the proposed Brady Tunnel renovation project as part of the PA Wilds Loop—would not only improve the local economy, but also inspire others locally to make improvements," she wrote. She said the Center's programs opened doors for collaborations, opportunities, and friendships that she wouldn't have had access to otherwise. "It's more than just an organization, the staff and peer network serve as cheerleaders in your corner, helping you navigate through the trials and tribulations of being a small business owner in a rural area. . . . I know my business is just one of many in the region, but every little investment in rural PA trickles down to each and every one of us small guys. COVID really did hurt us all . . . I cannot express to you enough the importance of the proposed project and how many of us could truly benefit from the investments into the PA Wilds."

This is what an inclusive economy looks like, I thought as I read Heckler's letter. I smiled and felt proud. *We built this.*

I continued through the letters, stopping at one from The Wilds Sonshine Factory, a bold agricultural startup we'd worked with in Kane that had signed a long-term licensing contract with us. The owners were bringing an innovative new spirit to market, made exclusively from sunflowers grown in the PA Wilds region, making the product endemic to the area. A percentage of every bottle sold would come back to support our mission. Alongside this, the owners were building a stunning new visitor center and manufacturing facility that celebrated agriculture and the region's outdoors brand and lumber history, when the pandemic hit, and construction costs went soaring. They didn't give up, and I was grateful to see their letter today.[4]

I read Bill Brock's letter with interest. Before taking the helm at Straub, his family's legacy brewing business, and helping transition it during a dynamic period for the craft beer industry, Brock had a career in economic development, including in Pennsylvania and Alaska. I enjoyed talking to him about Alaska, and he intuitively got the PA Wilds strategy and was always there to write support letters when we asked. I was so moved by the first letter he wrote us that I shared it with Abbi and Julie and told them we should frame it.

This letter was just as good. Brock called out the dedication and vision of the Center's board and staff and its record of getting things done. The Center's accomplishments, he wrote, "include the ability to create a common vision and to execute the thousands of details necessary to first unify a region and then establish it as a destination. Regionalizing for any purpose is a daunting task. The PA Wilds' mission was to sell

---

[4]. The Wilds Sonshine Factory is another must-see when visiting the region. Family-friendly with an interpretive center, gift shop and a lineup of live music and other events, it is also home to what is believed to be the longest bar in the world made from a continuous piece of wood, a gigantic, beautiful slab of Eastern Hemlock (the PA state tree) that the owners and their logging friends felled themselves. Timber, conservation and tourism partners (and some of their kids!) joined the owners for a picture the day it was installed. It took several people and pieces of heavy equipment to set.

the idea of a commonality among the counties—which included both a stunning geography and the desire to responsibly leverage these geographic assets for the common good. Equally important, the PA Wilds had to convince the skeptics and demonstrate that managing these assets collectively and as a region would achieve far greater impacts than if they were managed individually, county by county. Despite the obstacles, the PA Wilds accomplished this insanely difficult and complex task and over time reached the goal of the PA Wilds of becoming a regional destination. The depth of what has been created goes far beyond a solid marketing campaign. It is my belief that the leadership of the PA Wilds board and staff have strategically leveraged their vision for the PA Wilds in such a way that allows for shared ownership by stakeholders from across the region. In short, the PA Wilds initiative continues to include the organization itself, serving as the epi-center—the organizer, convener, and connector. However, the initiative has now evolved to include dozens of interconnected public and private partnerships between government, NPOs, private businesses, and education, all using the platform and vision of the PA Wilds to transform a region. This is significant because it suggests a high return on the resources that have thus far been committed to the region. This return is about the ever-increasing sustainability of the initiative, where businesses like Straub and others are willing to invest their own resources because they believe in the region's potential."

A young LGBTQ+ woman-owned business, PA Made, a local clothing and arts company "inspired by nature, Pennsylvania, and all things outdoors," had joined our ecosystem shortly after being founded in 2017. The owner was very active, taking business workshops, competing for photography contracts, selling t-shirts and stickers with original designs through our commerce platform, and eventually, opening her own physical storefront. I had bought one of their t-shirts, "The Crick Is Calling" for Leonard.[5] "Our mission is deeply rooted in working in the community," owner Mickayla Poland wrote in her support letter. "The past five years have been paramount for PA Made and it wouldn't have been possible without our relationship with PA Wilds Center, the Wilds Cooperative of Pennsylvania, and the growing popularity of the outdoor recreation industry in the area."

---

5. A lot of people in Pennsylvania call creeks "cricks."

A few days after we hit submit, all the finalists were encouraged to cut their applications to $50 million. So, we started the process over.

The next few months passed in a blur as we tried to dig out. On September 1, after carpool, I started editing a video that was, at this point, more than a year overdue. I checked my email, knowing notifications were due out soon. After lunch, I got a form email from EDA.

We did not win.

While trying to process what I was reading, my phone rang. It was Abbi. We were both in shock and didn't say much. I pushed my feelings aside and tried to focus on notifications. I'd rather our partners heard the news from me. A few minutes after I hit send, a colleague involved in the application and in trails development statewide, emailed back.

"They have no vision!"

I wasn't sure I agreed—some really visionary stuff got funded—but his unbridled enthusiasm in defense of our application made me smile.

Silas Chamberlin, vice president of economic and community development for the York County Economic Alliance, reached out even though he wasn't part of our application. I had huge respect for Silas. He worked an hour south of Harrisburg and had almost as many people living in his one county as we did in all thirteen of ours. But he had spent a good deal of time in rural PA as a recreationalist and throughout his career, even facilitating the retreat we held to reorganize the Wilds work. A PhD, author, and a doer, he was that rare breed of economic developer that had gotten his start in conservation, which made him a great voice for outdoor recreation because as a strategy it lived at the intersection of those two worlds. To me, alongside Nathan Reigner at the Office of Outdoor Recreation, he was one of the best thinkers and communicators in Pennsylvania about how communities large and small could use outdoor recreation as an economic driver and to help address other social and environmental issues.[6]

"You and the PA Wilds Team are rockstars," Silas wrote, "your application and the thinking behind it are still incredibly important in paving the way for the outdoor economy and outdoor recreation clusters to be taken seriously by EDA and others."

The other Pennsylvania finalist, the Allegheny Conference in Pittsburgh, won $62 million to support its robotics and artificial intelligence

---

6. Silas is the author of *On the Trail: A History of American Hiking* (Yale University Press, 2016) and an upcoming book, *Wild Profits: Exploring America's $1 Trillion Outdoor Recreation Economy* (Island Press).

cluster. Governor Tom Wolf's Office put out a press release, congratulating them. I thought for sure that somewhere buried at the bottom, it would give a nod to the fact that the most rural quarter of the Commonwealth had put forth a valiant effort as a finalist for which they should be proud, but there was no mention at all.

Abbi texted me, #strongandproud.

I turned off my computer and cried.

It was almost Cole's tenth birthday, so I kept him home from school the following day, and we went on an "educational trip" to the Trails at Jakes Rocks, the new mountain biking system on the Allegheny National Forest. The course was about twenty-five minutes from my house and, embarrassingly, I had never been. It was one of the sad truths about founding a nonprofit dedicated to growing a rural outdoor rec movement. I spent a lot less time outside and a lot more time in front of a computer. I'd hunted or hiked very few days this year.

Warren County had come a long way as an outdoor recreation destination, and the trails were a shining example of it. The visitor bureau had energizing new leadership, and I was excited to see them plugging into our stuff and leveraging it. The local chamber continued to champion outdoor recreation projects, including the Trails at Jakes Rocks. Numerous local people, businesses, nonprofits, and public lands partners had come together to help make the trail system happen. We had written support letters for it over the years. It had been six years since the first ten miles opened, and now there were thirty-five.

A stacked loop course of varying difficulty, the Trails at Jakes Rocks wove around boulders that were as big as houses in some places, with overlooks offering stunning views of the Allegheny Reservoir and Kinzua Dam.[7]

I felt young again as Cole and I peddled through the national forest on the Tuttletown to Coal Knob section of the trail, an epic, "moderately challenging" ride that took us about an hour and a half. Tuttletown was another small village that had been destroyed by the building of the Kinzua Dam. I appreciated that the trail system gave a nod to that history.

---

7. Pennsylvania is sometimes called "Rocksylvania" for its many unique rock formations. The PA Trail Dogs, a volunteer group based out of Clinton County that puts on some of the most well-known trail races in the region, has a "Rocksylvania Trail Series." Many visitors also trek to "umbrella rock" in Elk County, and many more to designated rock viewing and climbing areas, like Bilger's Rocks in Clearfield County or Rim Rock near me.

"This is so amazing, Mom," Cole said, all smiles, as we stopped under the tree canopy in one area to catch our breath and grab a swig of water. "Can we come back next weekend?"

Few things made me happier than seeing my kids having fun outdoors. Especially these days, with so many screens and devices. As I sat there watching him, taking in the sun and the trees and the trail, I was reminded again that for all its potential as an economic driver, places like this also had an incredible ability to restore the spirit. I worked on a movement that inspired and enabled people to get outside and to support local businesses in the process. Even on the worst days, it was a privilege.

"You bet," I told Cole. "Next weekend. And we should bring Dad."

CHAPTER 32

PUTTING IT ALL BACK

In between the pandemic and the Build Back Better Regional Challenge, five program managers from the Richard King Mellon Foundation visited the PA Wilds on a three-day tour to learn more about our work and how it intersected with a new ten-year strategic plan the foundation had just released.

I'd shared an overview with some of the foundation's leaders in 2019. DCNR and DCED had relationships with the foundation, and Meredith and Scott helped us get a meeting. A group of us met in a private room at Straub Brewery. This trip was a follow-up, and my team and I were excited for the opportunity.

The PA Wilds region had a strong culture of giving. On almost any given day in a rural town, you could find a fundraiser for a family that had fallen on hard times or to advance a local cause or to support a social or emergency services organization. It wasn't unusual to see locals donate to national and global causes too. When Russia invaded Ukraine, Piper worked with a handful of local nonprofits to organize a giving and supplies campaign for Ukrainian families. People in Warren County and beyond came out in a big way. Piper and others made repeated trips to Poland to hand-deliver the aid, driving it across the border into Ukraine in passenger vans not unlike those she ran at her livery.

A handful of communities had established community foundations in the PA Wilds, but no large foundations were based here, and investments by them were rare.

The Richard King Mellon Foundation was helping change this reality. Based in Pittsburgh, it was one of the fifty largest foundations in the world and had a deep commitment to conserving and restoring critical habitats in Pennsylvania and beyond and to supporting sustainable community and economic development approaches around those investments. Since the start of the PA Wilds, it had made conservation investments in several of the region's counties (captured in a coffee table book, *From Sea to Shining Sea*). It had also supported the development of the Elk Country Visitor Center and other regionally significant recreation infrastructure, such as the seventy-four-mile Knox-Kane Rail Trail. It was now making investments in the regional commerce and marketing infrastructure we were building around assets like these to support rural small businesses, and in the Center's role as the hub and steward of these new regional systems.

I was cautious when I first started interacting with the foundation, as I am with any major potential investor that is not from this place. Big investors can help accomplish incredible things, but if it is not a good fit, the change that happens, I fear, will not be the one we've been entrusted to pursue.

My approach was not rocket science. I tried to understand what the investor was trying to accomplish, see if it aligned with what we were trying to accomplish, and if it did, I made a case for how investing in us would help them accomplish mutual goals. I wanted to stay open to new ideas and approaches and to the reality that while cash is still king (especially here, where there is so much less of it flowing), money is not the only value a big funder can bring to the table. Networks, expertise, and capacity, all can be pivotal in advancing rural development strategies. Starting with smaller projects helps partners get to know and trust each other. As with many things, throughout the process, I have people on my board, at the state, and in local communities, who helped me check my thinking. Most of all, I aimed to have them see the real us.

With the Richard King Mellon Foundation, there were many alignments. Part way into our first project, Richard P. Mellon, who served nearly half a century on the foundation's board, and a quarter century as its chair, passed away at age eighty-one. I'd never met him, but I read the testimonials people wrote about him. One said that in part through his leadership, the foundation had conserved 4.5 million acres of land in all fifty states. "These are some of the most environmentally precious lands in our nation," Sam Reiman, the foundation's director and also a trustee explained in one article. "But one would be unlikely to hear those simple facts from Richard P. Mellon. His goals were grand, but he pursued them with quiet modesty, rigor, and kindness."

"He really cared about conservation before it became a popular cause," said his brother, Seward Prosser Mellon. "He just loved the outdoors!"

It reminded me of the quiet conservation ethic I'd found in the PA Wilds and the steadfast commitment so many had shown to our collective regional work. I appreciated working with organizations that had people like that at the top.

The foundation's three-day trip to the region was a chance to build a deeper relationship. Our goal was to provide a glimpse of all of the work's moving parts—the recreation infrastructure investments, marketing and branding, small business and supply chain development, community character stewardship, and state and local partnerships.

We chose the Cobblestone in St. Marys as our hub and each day took trips from there. One day, we traveled north in a charter bus to Kane where our Board Treasurer welcomed the group to the PA Wilds Media Lab. The foundation was helping us set up the facility, and we gave them a tour of what would soon be our product photography booth, audio-visual room, and classroom space, and then took them next door for a tour of the passive house building. After lunch, we loaded back on the bus and headed to Kinzua Bridge State Park.

Abbi's mom was an incredible hostess who had operated a bed and breakfast in Ridgway until, in 2016, as Abbi was opening our first Conservation Shop, she died suddenly. Her welcoming spirit and thoughtfulness lived on in Abbi, on this occasion as on so many others. Abbi stocked the bus with locally made treats from across the region. There were bags of Triple Crunch Munch from King Crunch in Jefferson County and Tree Stumps from Highland Chocolates, a nonprofit factory in Tioga County that provides vocational training and employment for adults with disabilities. Abbi proudly shared each company's backstory and how they were part of our entrepreneurial ecosystem and rural supply chain.

On the way to the park, the director of Headwaters Charitable Trust, a nonprofit that had helped get the Knox-Kane Rail Trail established, and Farley Wright, who penned the ombudsman white paper nearly a decade prior and was now involved in trail work, pointed out different sections of the Rail Trail and shared background on where each section was in its development. At the state park, the group heard from DCNR about its investments in the PA Wilds, toured the visitor center and Skywalk, and then got to see our rural supply chain and commerce platform in action at the Conservation Shop, where Libby told a story about how one visitor loved the region so much, he'd gotten the PA Wilds logo tattooed on his leg. "I'm not sure it was a correct use of the logo, but we let it go," she joked.

We had dinner at Straub Brewery that night. The next day, Rawley Cogan, then CEO of the nonprofit Keystone Elk Country Alliance, welcomed the group to the Elk Country Visitor Center and shared background of how elk went extinct in Pennsylvania but were reintroduced in the early 1900s. He shared data on the growing number of visitors and school kids that now visited elk country and about the many investments that had been made in elk habitat. He echoed what he had told me years prior in a story I wrote for the *Keystone Edge*, "This is some of the most beautiful wilderness in the whole state—*country*—and thousands of people are coming here to experience it. They come to appreciate what we have and to help conserve it—that's pretty awesome."

After that, about two dozen organizations serving the region joined us for a facilitated discussion. Our Board Chair kicked off the conversation and Scott, now retired, helped facilitate.

After everyone left, we headed to Cogan's modest family camp nearby and ate dinner on picnic tables outside. Inside, on a mantle, I found a framed picture of Cogan, back in the 1990s when he was a state game biologist, riding horseback in elk country with Gov. Tom Ridge, and I was reminded again what a long journey this has been.

At dusk, we headed back to the Elk Country Visitor Center and Cogan's staff took us on horse-drawn wagon rides through elk habitat. It was mating season, called the rut, and the elk put on a stunning show, the bull elk sparring with each other, their huge racks locked in battle, as more than a dozen cows grazed nearby. At random intervals, the elk bugled, a haunting high pitch that gave way to a deeper throaty sound. Everyone on the wagon was quiet, holding up their phones to take pictures and videos. The scene reminded me of a story I read in the

Philadelphia Inquirer, about the early days of the Wilds effort, where DiBerardinis, the former DCNR Secretary who helped launch the Wilds work, recounted a trip he and his wife made to the Pennsylvania Wilds during the rut and saw a herd of about forty animals. "If you compare the Philadelphia sky at night and the sky there at night, you'd think you were on different planets," he told the paper. "The elk were bugling like mad. The stars were spectacular. That night was one of my most unforgettable outdoor experiences, ever."

The next day, we toured different conservation investments and two sustainable timber operations and did a walking tour of Ridgway. Jane Bryndel, a philanthropist whose family has lived in the area for generations, met us in a parking lot to give us a tour. Not wanting to be outdone by Cogan's cowboy hat, she wore her best fedora. She pointed out new businesses and told the group about different revitalization efforts the town was working on. Victorian homes that had been restored, an empty gas station that had been turned into a chamber and visitor center, and a crumbling historic hotel on the main street that had just been bought by a developer from New York City. Several of the sites were captured as case studies in the *PA Wilds Design Guide for Community Character Stewardship*.

We picked up Deborah Pontzer and Sam MacDonald, who both lived in Ridgway, and as we drove to other parts of town, they interpreted stories behind what we were seeing. At one point, Sam stood up at the front of the bus, pulled out an article from a popular national travel magazine, and read a few lines where the writer described the wilderness in one part of the region as "the pristine, never touched landscape." He lowered the paper, looked up, steadied himself on a bus seat as we go over a pothole, and smiled.

"That is complete bullshit," he said and laughs. "Seriously!"

And he was right, of course. Not far off, the picturesque National Wild and Scenic Clarion River flowed by. Ravaged at the turn of the century by the clear-cutting all around it and then chemical runoff from tanneries and coal mining, it was once the most polluted waterway in Pennsylvania. Sam told the group that when he was a kid the river was so disgusting no one wanted to touch it. Other locals on the bus nodded in agreement and joked that when you went swimming in it, it looked like you got a tan from the acid mine drainage that ran orange.

The Allegheny National Forest's regrowth helped the river tremendously, as did major cleanup efforts in the 1980s. That the region got from point A to point B, while growing a sustainable timber industry alongside it, was the real story of our wilderness, and I was proud that through the PA Wilds' work, we had more opportunities to share it.

Sam told the group that another thing the state and local partners got right was, "The PA Wilds wasn't here to shut anyone down." He continued, "They weren't like we want to get rid of manufacturing or timber or whatever." If anything, he said, the effort was strengthening the region's other industries because it was using locally informed approaches that were helping make communities more attractive and livable.

On our way back to the hotel, one of the foundation's program managers noted how the PA Wilds was a welcome break from the steady stream of negative headlines about people hurting the environment, killing their Main Streets, etc.

"The PA Wilds, it's like the story of putting it all back," he told me, and for the next few months, I reflected on this. The forest. The elk. The small businesses. The Main Streets. The pride of place. The young people. It was, indeed, the story of a bunch of us working together to try to put it all back. I smiled when, months later, he held up the PA Wilds' work as an example at a national forum for rural outdoor recreation development. "We used to see land conservation as the ceiling," he told the group. "Now we understand it is the floor and serves as a foundation on which we can build. It's the beginning of other possibilities."

Our region didn't invent the idea of outdoor recreation as an economic driver or as a way to leverage public lands to help revitalize rural communities. But we were helping to lead the way on *how* to do it in a rural area. Coming up with real, transferable approaches that actually worked.

It made me think of something Eubanks had told me after we brought him to the region to be the keynote at one of our dinners. His early studies for DCNR long since completed, it was the first trip he'd made to the region in many years.

"What surprised me the most," he told me, "was the direction it took. It's one thing to say this is what should happen. But the direction it goes is going to be up to the people involved." The PA Wilds had what he called "organic growth of its own inspiration."

"What the PA Wilds has done is help prove some of the theories," he said.

We aren't the only region doing this kind of revitalization work. Across Appalachia and the country, there are incredible efforts underway in rural landscapes to revitalize through place-based approaches. Work by the Outdoor Recreation Council of Appalachia around the Baileys Trail System in Southeast Ohio, and lifting up makers through Ohio's Winding Road initiative. The Mon Forest Towns and New River Gorge in West Virginia. Made by Mountains in Western North Carolina. The Tennessee RiverLine effort across Kentucky and Tennessee. The Friends of Southwest Virginia. The Okefenokee Swamp in Georgia. The Northern Forest region of Maine, Vermont, New Hampshire, and New York. The Blue Ridge Rising movement along the Blue Ridge Parkway. The list goes on.

"A lot here is about citizen engagement and communities coming to the conclusion that there is more they can do together than individually," Gohl, the former federal co-chair of the Appalachian Regional Commission told me. "It's not something that happens overnight. That's the challenge. People want things to be a success right away. Really, it takes being committed and committed long term."

I was a pioneer. I owned that now. Not the only one, by any stretch, but critical to the Wilds' transition from state-led to locally-led. To the local buy-in and long-term sustainability of something bigger than any one of us. As Erick Coolidge, a dairy farmer and Republican county commissioner from Tioga County, told me in front of a crowd at our annual awards dinner in 2023, upon receiving an award for his own contributions to the work, "These lands have always been here, but you and your team—you stood this all up. It is so important, and I know it has taken a lot of work and I thank you for it." I didn't expect the gesture, but instead of deflecting like I would have in the past, I smiled, patted my heart with my hand and mouthed the words from my seat, *Thank you*.

And I reflect sometimes that if I had ruled myself out of the ombudsman job because I didn't quite fit the part, or because I was a new mom, or because I'd listened to naysayers who said nature tourism could never work here, or not trusted my gut about Abbi and Julie, knowing at some weird bone-deep level they had the skills and temperament for the journey ahead, or if I had not learned to trust *myself* enough to step up and do what I thought needed to be done, the work would not be where it is today.

A few years after we founded the Center, we held our first holiday gathering as a staff. Abbi hosted it at her Georgian Schoolhouse. Meredith and Leonard were there. I was still in awe that we had found a way to build a team large enough to fill a dinner table. I toasted each person, and then Abbi raised her glass to me.

"I know there were a lot of times when you could have quit, but you didn't," she said. "I just want to say thank you for not quitting."

I've long been drawn to transformation stories, and for a few years, when my sons were little, I watched the television show *The Biggest Loser*, weight loss being one of the toughest transformations for a lot of people. I ordered a few workout videos by the show's trainer, Jillian Michaels, and in one of them in the middle of some muscle-burning set, she says, "Do something crazy. Don't quit."

I'd read dozens of self-help books by then, trying to form better habits and push through toward my own personal mental and physical transformation, but more than any, this quote stuck in my mind. It was short, which helped, but I also loved its accountability and its underlying promise of adventure. If you just start, and don't quit, who knows how far you can go? No one else can push through the hard parts for you. Will you give up? That decision is squarely yours.

People who are trying to make change happen are faced with this decision thousands of times over the course of their journey. It is often incredibly uncomfortable. As one rural entrepreneur told me after a particularly bruising encounter speaking up to their city council about how they treated their local entrepreneurs, "It keeps you up at night. It makes your guts turn and hurts you all the way down to your bones, but you can't give up because this is how change happens."

Refusing to give up was a critical skill in rural development, where so many things are stacked against you. It was in my own painful moments of gut churn and failure, that I discovered that the things I struggled with most in my life, my hardscrabble upbringing, moving all the time, often feeling like an unworthy outsider, and a lack of resources had prepared me better than anything else could, to make a difference in the rural landscape where I grew up. They had conditioned me to not give up. By committing, proudly, to this place and pushing through the discomfort of trying to stick up for it, I found out who I am and what I'm made of. I was proudly made in the Pennsylvania Wilds.

AFTERWORD

In our ongoing efforts to get more capital moving to support small businesses in rural PA, the PA Wilds Center at one point teamed up with Ben Franklin Technology Partners, a technology-based economic development program, to offer three $50,000-to-win "Big Idea" innovation contests for rural small businesses over three years. When we got to the final pitch events each year, I told the five or six finalists that while there can only be one or two winners, just being a finalist is something to celebrate and leverage. The visibility it brings, the networks and resources it expands and galvanizes around you, the putting things to paper in so much detail—there is incredible momentum and power in it that can be used to get your vision to the next step.

I was speaking from our own experience in the Build Back Better Regional Challenge. After learning we didn't win, we broke up our application and started pushing the projects through different funding streams one by one. Many of our partners did the same.

In 2024, we opened two new Conservation Shops, at Leonard Harrison State Park at the PA Grand Canyon and along the Knox-Kane Rail Trail in Forest County, the most distressed Appalachian county in PA, enriching the visitor experience while expanding market access for rural entrepreneurs. We secured funding to complete planning and market analysis for additional mission-driven stores across the region. We teamed up with the nonprofit Keystone Trails Association to develop a new PA Wilds branded hiking guidebook. We hired Purple Lizard, a premier outdoor recreation mapping company, to assess what it would take to map the entire region in their incredible maps. We teamed up with the PA Council on the Arts and the Richard King Mellon Foundation to launch a program to incentivize local manufacturers teaming up with local creatives to bring new PA Wilds branded products to market while helping the smaller businesses scale up alongside our commerce platforms. We made huge headway on our mobile platform project and secured an Economic Recovery Corps fellow, a mid-career economic developer, to help us evolve some of our key stakeholder structures, and explore new capital funds to help rural PA advance its tourism and outdoor recreation sectors. Parts of the Center's operation are still grant dependent, but we've begun building a fundraising arm and investigating what it would take to build an endowment that ensures that the nonprofit's work lives beyond its current leadership. As my Board chair at the time, Shane Oschman, put it, "The PA Wilds Center has in front of itself an almost insurmountable task of ensuring the sustainability of the hard work that is already making a difference."

Will legislators find a way to provide baseline support to Rural Development Hubs like ours? Will outdoor recreation infrastructure and strategies be more widely understood as economic development? Will economic development funders create more meaningful ways to judge rural applications instead of jobs and scale?

I am hopeful, but my gut tells me real change will be slow.

"Federal policy has historically played an important role in helping rural places contribute to American economic and social life, but it is no longer fit for purpose," Anthony Pipa, a Senior Fellow at the Brookings Institution, a nonprofit think tank whose mission is to conduct in-depth, nonpartisan research to improve local, national and global policy, wrote in an online commentary in 2023.[1] "This is leaving rural places starved for investment as they navigate 21st century shifts in the economy and seek to become more vibrant, inclusive, and sustainable."

I felt hopeful when I read this passage, but less so when I understood the reason Pipa felt compelled to write it. He was following up on a *New York Times* essay he'd published four months prior calling for a renaissance in federal rural policy. The essay included a call for a national rural policy to help "put local assets to creative use, unleash entrepreneurial activity, share the benefits widely, and retain the value locally."

Basically: evolving federal policy to support locally informed and designed approaches like the PA Wilds, across a variety of industries and landscapes. So smart!

---

1. Why US Rural Policy Matters, April 2023, Anthony Pipa. Find Pipa's "Reimagine Rural" podcast at: https://pod.link/1654532511

The result? Almost 1,700 comments showing distrust on both sides, but especially dismissive of rural America.

Here is my next moonshot. I invite you, dear reader, to be part of our virtuous cycle. Donate at PAWilds.com/give if you are able and moved to do so. Explore this beautiful region. Come hike a trail in our big woods and spend the night at a local bed and breakfast. Buy a locally made artisan ware from ShopThePAWilds.com or at one of our Conservation Shops or any of the locally owned retailers or galleries or artisan shops along the way. Ride the Trails at Jakes Rocks. Experience the Kinzua Skywalk. Visit the Sinnemahoning Wildlife Center and have lunch in the Emporium. Listen to the elk bugle in Benezette. Bring a blow-up mattress and lay it in the field at Cherry Springs State Park during a dark sky party and look at the stars. Visit the Pine Creek Gorge or the charming towns along the I-80 Frontier. Hike the North Country Trail. Paddle the Allegheny or the Clarion or the West Branch of the Susquehanna. Spend a weekend among the ancient trees in Cook Forest. Book a cabin in God's Country. Apply to the lottery to see our synchronous fireflies. Do the art walk in Williamsport. Visit the Eternal Tap. Eat at our family-run restaurants. Donate to our charity checkout campaign for conservation or pitch in to help with trail maintenance. Buy our *Outdoor Discovery Atlas* and a state park passport book and commit to adventuring with your kids to get stamps for all twenty-nine state parks in the PA Wilds. Motorcycle Scenic Route 6. Do the Lumber Heritage Trail. Go bouldering in the Allegheny National Forest. Unwind around a campfire. Above all, while you are here, be a good steward of the local culture and the natural landscape.

To local businesses that are just learning about the PA Wilds Center, join the nonprofit's free network!

To all the potential boomerangs out there, people who grew up here or in rural places similar to it, your place needs you. Whatever that looks like, however it makes sense for your life. Invest. As a visitor. As a resident. As a volunteer. As a financial backer of a good idea. As a donor. As an entrepreneur or public servant. As a steward.

All of it matters.

ACKNOWLEDGMENTS

This book would not have been possible without the support of my husband, the inspiration of my sons, and the input of my sisters, mom, stepmom, and extended family that includes aunts, uncles, cousins, in-laws, nieces, and nephews. Thanks also goes to my father-in-law, who has done so much for Leonard and me and our boys in the eight long years it took me to finish this book, to my mom, for always assisting when I need it, and to Sandoz and Piper for helping to keep me brave. Thanks also goes to Sherri for watching my boys when they were young, and to E-O and Mia for helping lighten my parenting load at incredibly busy junctures.

I owe a huge debt of gratitude to the entire staff and Board of Directors at the PA Wilds Center for Entrepreneurship. I especially want to call out founding staff members Julie Iaquinto, Abbi Peters, LaKeshia Knarr, Libby Bloomquist, and Carol Syzmanik for their early and unwavering commitment, sacrifice, and contributions to the nonprofit's mission and to their willingness to go all-in with an unconventional leader like me, and then to support my writing about it. I also want to call out Board members John Beard and Bob Veilleux for helping me found the nonprofit, and directors Shane Oschman, Beth Pellegrino, Jason Fink, Kate Brock, and Sam MacDonald, who each stepped up in volunteer officer roles to help steward the Center through a time of immense growth and uncertainty.

So many individuals have helped get the PA Wilds work where it is today and influenced my thinking as I crafted this story. Due to space constraints, I cannot name them all. The list is too long, and it grows every day. I do want to underscore how much I appreciate everyone who has contributed. I say that as Ta the nonprofit CEO and Ta the writer, but mostly as someone who grew up here and is raising a family here. This group, hailing from so many different sectors and walks of life, is full of pride for this place. Through good times and bad, that has shone through, teaching, inspiring, and fueling me. The list of organizations that have helped is also incredibly long, but I especially want to call out nonprofit, philanthropic, and government partners that helped launch the work or have been repeat collaborators on it: state partners PA Department of Conservation and Natural Resources, PA Department of Community and Economic Development, the PA Tourism Office, PA Office of Outdoor Recreation, and PA Council on the Arts; the PA Wilds Planning Team and the region's county governments; the region's designated visitor bureaus (or earlier iterations of them), currently Warren County Visitors Bureau, Allegheny National Forest Visitors Bureau, Great Outdoors Visitors Bureau, Visit Potter-Tioga, Lycoming County Visitors Bureau, Clinton County Economic Partnership and Visitors Bureau, Visit Clearfield County, Visit Jefferson County, Happy Valley Adventures Bureau, and Discover Clarion County; the region's designated Heritage Areas or greenways, the PA Route 6 Alliance, Lumber Heritage Region and Susquehanna Greenway Partnership; the region's four Local Development Districts, North Central PA Regional Planning and Development Commission, Northwest Commission, SEDA-COG, and Northern Tier Regional & Planning Development Commission; and other longstanding partners, the US Forest Service, the Western Pennsylvania Conservancy, Northcentral PA Conservancy, the PA Fish & Boat Commission, PA Game Commission, the PA Historical & Museum Commission, many local Conservation Districts, watershed groups, trail clubs, economic development, workforce and Main Street organizations and chamber groups, as well as the Potter County Education Council, the Community Education Center of Elk and Cameron Counties, Headwaters Charitable Trust, the Cameron County Chamber & Artisan Center, the Elk County Council on the Arts, Keystone Elk Country Alliance, the West Penn Energy Fund, Keystone Elk Country Alliance, the West Penn Energy Fund, Grow Rural PA, Ben Franklin Technology Partners, PennTAP, the PA Small Business Development Centers and Industrial Resource Centers serving the region, the Allegheny Hardwoods Utilization Group, the US Endowment for Forestry and Communities, the

Pennsylvania Environmental Council, Keystone Trails Association, the PA Parks and Forests Foundation, Pennsylvania's seven other designated Conservation Landscapes and their lead nonprofit organizations, The Conservation Fund, Outdoor Recreation Roundtable, the Center for Rural Pennsylvania, many state legislators, and U.S. Congressman Glenn Thompson's Office and other federal legislators, and numerous local, state and national funders, including state partners listed above as well as the Stackpole-Hall Foundation, The Collins Companies Foundation, First Community Foundation Partnership of Pennsylvania, Richard King Mellon Foundation, Just Transition Fund, Pennsylvania Industrial Development Authority, Appalachian Regional Commission, the US Economic Development Administration, and USDA. It takes a village!

I'd like to thank all the people who participated in interviews for this book or provided me with supporting documents, helped me check my own recollection of events, or agreed to let me include things they said in private conversations to help tell this story.

I want to thank Meredith Hill and Scott Dunkelberger for mentoring me in the early years of the Wilds work as I found my footing; breaking trail around me as I founded the nonprofit (and then serving that nonprofit as volunteers); and finally for their friendship and for providing feedback on this manuscript.

Dozens of journalism and author colleagues, family members and friends, and PA Wilds partners at local, state and national organizations provided constructive feedback on early versions of this manuscript, helping me correct errors of fact or omission, address gaps, fix grammar, and sand rough edges, which I am eternally grateful for. These include many people already named, as well as Jodi Brennan, Jim Weaver, John Schlimm, Deborah Pontzer, Shane Oschman, Kate Brock, Matt Marusiak, Coralee Wenzel, Holly Komonczi, Pat Evans, Jim Decker, Nathan Reigner, Cheryl Hargrove, Ed McMahon, Ted Eubanks, Chris Perkins, Tony Pipa, Sara Arno, Glen Klinkhart, Katie Pesznecker and Marc Lester.

I also want to call out author Kristine Gasberre, who was incredibly generous with her time, coaching me through the many ups and downs of the insanity that is book writing and publishing as a first-time author; as well as thank the Robert Wood Johnson Foundation for providing me with a professional development award through the Future Good program that allowed me to hire my first editor, Ellie Davis, and get the manuscript in shape to pitch.

I want to thank Andrea Lanich and the Laughing Owl Press Company for dedicating many hours, pro bono, to the book's cover design. My vision had always been to keep as much of the creative associated with the project as local as possible, but I had no budget for it. Andrea was not deterred. "If I can play a very small part in raising up the Wilds, then that is enough for me," she said. I also want to thank my sister, Piper, who made many creative contributions, large and small, including the cover photo, to this project and its launch, but mostly for letting me share some of the ups and downs she went through trying to grow Allegheny Outfitters and for being one of this book's biggest cheerleaders, even when parts of our shared history were hard to revisit. If you are in need of beautiful handcrafted letterpress invites, or inspired outdoor gear or outfitting services, these two businesses are worthy of your consideration!

Finally, I want to thank my colleague and fellow writer Brook Lenker for connecting me to Sunbury Press founder and CEO Lawrence Knorr, who took a chance on this first time author; and thank Sunbury's skilled team, including publishing assistant Katie Cressman and my editor, Gabrielle Kirk, for their skillful, cheerful support helping me get the manuscript the final mile.

ABOUT THE AUTHOR

Tataboline Enos has more than 15 years of experience building regional systems to advance outdoor recreation as a sustainable economic driver for rural communities. A former journalist, Ta has been recognized as a practitioner on the cutting edge of rural development. Ta has a bachelor's degree in journalism and public communications from the University of Alaska Anchorage. Prior moving home to rural PA and founding the nonprofit PA Wilds Center, Ta spent a decade as a reporter and editor, working for the *Anchorage Daily News*, *Anchorage Press*, *Dutch Harbor Fisherman*, *Bristol Bay Times* and other publications. She and her husband are raising three boys on 65 acres in the Pennsylvania Wilds. Find Ta on LinkedIn or Facebook or at Ta-Enos.com.

www.ingramcontent.com/pod-product-compliance
Lightning Source LLC
Chambersburg PA
CBHW010929180426
43194CB00045B/2843